RELIGION: NORTH AMERICAN STYLE

RELIGION: NORTH AMERICAN STYLE
third edition

edited by

THOMAS E. DOWDY
PATRICK H. McNAMARA

rutgers university press • *new brunswick, new jersey*

Library of Congress Cataloging-in-Publication Data

Religion : North American style / edited by Thomas E. Dowdy and
  Patrick H. McNamara.—3rd ed.
    p.   cm.
  Includes bibliographical references and index.
  ISBN 0-8135-2343-5 (hard : alk. paper).—ISBN 0-8135-2344-3 (pbk. : alk. paper)
    1. Religion and sociology.   2. United States—Religion.   I. Dowdy, Thomas E.,
  1955– .   II. McNamara, Patrick H.
  BL60.R35   1996
  200'.973—dc20   *96-18514*
                                                                                                             CIP

British Cataloging-in-Publication information available

soli Deo gloria

CONTENTS

ACKNOWLEDGMENTS

I thank those who have given direction, assistance, and encouragement throughout the production of this volume. First, I am grateful to Pat McNamara, who as my coeditor has been a voice of encouragement along the way, and whose cogent suggestions have helped me impose some order on the project. I thank him for letting me use parts of the second edition of *Religion: North American Style;* revisions are much easier when you begin with an excellent book. I extend special thanks to Roger Finke, whose cogent suggestions played a great part in the revisions. Larry Iannaccone and Jim Spickard also made excellent suggestions regarding some of the sections. As much as all these terrific people have helped, any criticism of the book must be directed at me.

Finally, I thank my wife Beverly, who has loaded the manuscript, edited my editing, and seen to the thousand small details that producing an edited volume entails. Without her input, this volume would not have been possible.

Thomas E. Dowdy

INTRODUCTION

Once thirteen colonies emerged victorious from their revolutionary struggle with the mother country, the leadership of the new United States of America was determined to disallow any overarching national church. No Anglican or Congregational establishment would serve as America's "official church," a declaration subsequently to be expressed in the First Amendment to the Constitution. By the time Count Alexis de Tocqueville visited the country in the early 1800s, he could note the vitality of American religion, with its pluralism of denominations and well-attended church services. No European country could match this scene. The voluntary principle was working well: an open marketplace assured a variety of beliefs, practices, and organizations reflective of a growing and diverse population.

Capturing that diversity in a variety of readings is a formidable challenge. Today's United States displays a kaleidoscope of religious groupings that goes much beyond the Catholic-Protestant-Jewish cultural predominance simply assumed by author Will Herberg in the 1950s. Yet these three church traditions still embrace by far the majority of American churchgoers. They are well represented in the readings selected for this volume.

No sociologist or student of sociology, however, is content with simply analyzing denominational differences. The past few decades have seen great shifts and switching of membership in favor of so-called stricter churches and at the expense of those pillars of American society, the mainline churches—Episcopalian, Presbyterian, and Congregational, to name a few. Why is strictness of doctrine and practice attractive? To whom? Younger Americans? Baby boomers? Senior citizens? Even that most centralized of large churches, Roman Catholic, has undergone changes, revealing a membership fragmented in many respects but also showing great vitality as women, the young, and ethnic minorities ask to be heard and included. In fact, women's voices cut across nearly all denominational lines, aided by a phenomenal growth in the number of women scholars who frame the issues both historically and contemporaneously.

Not the least visible and controversial phenomenon is church-member involvement in the political arena. The Christian Right represents those convinced that America is losing its moral and spiritual heritage to "secular trends" in family life, the media, and practices such as abortion and exclusion of prayer in schools.

These are but some of the issues and trends represented in the pages to follow. Your instructor may introduce still other themes. The interplay of religion and social change is a fascinating arena of study that extends world-wide. There is no better place to begin this study, however, than in the United States, with its rich and vital legacy of religious "effervescence."

Patrick H. McNamara

part one

RELIGION AND SOCIETY

Exploring the Relationships

How do we define religion sociologically? This is a complex question given the myriad forms religion takes in the contemporary world and has taken historically. One of the most common ways of defining religion has been according to *function*, that is, religion is defined by what it *does*. Durkheim (1915:44) defines religion as "a unified system of beliefs and practices relative to sacred things, that is to say, things set apart and forbidden—beliefs and practices which unite into one single moral community called a Church, all those who adhere to them" (1915:44). One of the major premises of structural functionalism, from which these sorts of definitions spring, is what Talcott Parsons called "system imperatives," that is, the needs that must be met for the system to survive. In Durkheim's analysis, religion satisfies the need of the individual to find a sense of identity and provides at least partial answers to some of the ultimate questions. Sociologically, religion also serves at the macro level by fulfilling the need to integrate the various elements of society.

In *The Elementary Forms of the Religious Life*,[1] Durkheim, unlike most rationalists of his time, considers religion one of the most universal and important categories of human social thought. He presents a theory of religion that links belief (faith, dogma, and thought) with action (ritual, rite, and ceremony). In this analysis, religious belief generates collective ritual, and collective ritual reinforces and supports belief. Durkheim sought to find the "real" source of these collective rituals, which were nearly universal in world religions. The motivation behind his study of aboriginal religion in Australia was that these more "primitive" forms were ostensibly less contaminated by modern forces and were closer to the common source of human religion. As a rationalist, Durkheim was not so much interested in the proclaimed intention of the ritual or the claims of the believers as in the "real reality" behind the ritual. For him

> the god of the clan, the totemic principle, can be none other than the clan itself, but the clan transfigured and imagined in the physical form of the plant or animal that serves as totem. (1915:208)

As W. S. F. Pickering (1984) puts it, "If the symbol of the group is sacred, is this not because the sentiments inspired by the group relate to the sign which is an expression and a reminder of it?" The collectivity then inspires sentiments in its members that are "religious" in the sense that the collectivity makes demands on the individual, requires sacrifice, and provides comfort and a sense of psychic rootedness. For Durkheim, religion unites all who adhere to it into a single moral community. It is the glue of society, the source of social solidarity. Religion represents society to its members in the form of sacred symbols that support a moral code and a sense of tribal unity.

In his analysis, the religious world is split into the *sacred* (that which is extraordinary, mysterious, and powerful) and the *profane*[2] (that which is part of the everyday normal world). How do normal objects such as cups or animals become sacred? Sacredness for Durkheim is not something that resides in a particular object, but sacredness is *created* in the ritual and interaction of humans. Contact with the sacred, through what Durkheim termed rituals of collective effervescence, is what radically affects the individual and gives the individual the sense of being "transformed." Because of this contact with the sacred, the individual "transforms his surroundings." In his study of aboriginal religions, Durkheim describes two types of rites: negative rites and positive rites, which separate the sacred from the profane through elaborate taboos and guarantee that the sacred will not be contaminated. Examples would be the elaborate taboos and safeguards against contact with a corpse[3] and against contact with blood. Positive rites bridge the gap between the sacred and the profane (i.e., between the worshipper and the object of his or her cult). Examples would be sacrificial rites and imitative rites. Because the sacred is so powerful, rites have elaborate trappings and safeguards that often require the worshipper to undergo purgation to be able to approach the sacred. Ritual, then, is located in what Durkheim referred to as *la vie serieuse* (the serious side of life).

Needs also lie at the heart of the reading for Clifford Geertz's "Religion as a Cultural System." Geertz suggests that ritual is particularly important as a symbolic reminder and reassurance to a society's members. Three critical and recurring human experiences (or needs) threaten to "break in" and create doubt, confusion, or even chaos and despair. These three episodes are bafflement, death and suffering, and the inability to make sound moral judgments. Geertz explains what he means by each of these conditions and shows how a religious system attempts to cope with them by defining a symbolic world that appears intellectually and emotionally whole and satisfying for a group of people—a tribe, a clan, a congregation, a nation. Here is Geertz's definition of religion:

> (1) a system of symbols which acts to (2) establish powerful, pervasive, and long-lasting moods and motivations in men by (3) formulating conceptions of a general order of existence and (4) clothing these conceptions with such an aura of factuality that (5) the moods and motivations seem uniquely realistic. (1973:90)

Geertz acknowledges the roles of other meaning systems as well. Religion is not the only one that people may use. Common sense, science, art—all confer meaning in their own right. He contrasts the functions of these meaning systems with the unique function of the religious symbol system.

Geertz reinforces Durkheim's conviction of the importance of ritual. Turning to the Navaho curing rites of "sings," he points out that these ceremonies give participants and observers a way of expressing suffering, therefore helping them understand and endure it. Such rites also reidentify the Navaho as a "Holy People" and symbolize their place in the larger cosmic order. World-as-lived-in and world-as-imagined are fused together so that they "turn out to be the same world." In this way, religion can truly give shape to the daily world in which people live out their lives.

In *The Sacred Canopy*, Peter Berger (1969) writes of religion as a "nomizing" (from the Greek *nomos:* law or rule) activity in the sense that religion is an attempt to make the cosmos meaningful to humans. In his analysis, the opposite of religion is not irreligion or atheism but chaos and meaninglessness. In his classic study *Suicide*, Durkheim (1894) argued that "anomie" or normlessness was one of the factors contributing to increased rates of suicide in the modern world. Berger has the same tenor when he argues that the same lack of psychic rootedness, which is one of the characteristics of modernity, is detrimental to the human psyche. Humans do not function well in a psychic vacuum. According to Berger, "Whenever the socially established nomos attains the quality of being taken for granted, there occurs a merging of its meanings with what are considered to be fundamental meanings inherent in the universe. Nomos and cosmos appear to be co-extensive. . . . Religion is the human enterprise by which a sacred cosmos is established. Put differently, religion is cosmization in a sacred mode" (1969:25–26). Much as Durkheim described the way that aborigines were somehow "taken out of themselves" by contact with the supernatural, Berger states that even in the modern world, contact with the supernatural is a "transcendent" experience that utterly changes those experiencing it. However, these experiences are ephemeral and must be constantly reinforced and supported by the testimony of like-minded believers; hence Berger's notion of "plausibility structures." In later works such as *The Heretical Imperative*, Berger (1981) sketches a world grown colder to spiritual life. In a world chilled by secularization, one must make a choice or *haresis* (the word from which we derive *heretic*) to believe something so contrary to "common sense." This is where structures of plausibility, such as those described here, come into play.

The last article in this section returns to the Durkheimian question of societal integration and societal legitimation. Nearly thirty years ago, Robert Bellah published an article entitled "Civil Religion in America." The article is fairly short and the arguments simple, yet it has been one of the most analyzed, empirically tested (Wimberly et al. 1976; Christenson and Wimberly 1978), and criticized[4] articles in American sociology.[5] The concept of "civil religion," although modified since Bellah's initial offering, is still being used as an analytical construct.[6]

What is in this thesis that has been so controversial? Bellah, beginning with an analysis of the rhetoric of presidential inaugurations, posited that alongside denominational religion in America there exists a civil religion. The two are so intertwined that the average person cannot tell where one stops and the other starts. By definition, a religion usually contains beliefs, some notion of the transcendent, and rituals and practices. Some of these beliefs include the idea of American particularism (Bellah found this especially in the rhetorical tropes of America as "God's New Israel" and the founding of the American republic as the new Exodus) and a belief in the special destiny of America. Transcendence was found in the rhetoric that linked the nation and all in it to a higher purpose and calling. In public rituals such as Memorial Day, the nation became the vessel of a type of corporate salvation and the president its high priest. In addition to this priestly role,[7] the rhetoric of inaugurations and presidential addresses (such as Lincoln's Gettysburg Address) also sketched a *prophetic* role for civil religion, in which the nation was held corporately responsible for its sins and challenged by a call to a higher moral purpose.[8]

ADDITIONAL READINGS

PICKERING, W. S. F. 1984. *Durkheim's Sociology of Religion: Themes and Theories.* London: Routledge and Kegan Paul.

This volume provides an analytical framework for understanding Durkheim's work in *Elementary Forms* and ties this work into his larger sociology of religion.

BERGER, PETER L. 1980. *The Heretical Imperative: Contemporary Possibilities of Religious Affirmation.* Garden City, New York: Doubleday.

Berger makes an elegant and compelling argument that an individual must make a conscious choice or haresis with regard to individual religious belief in a world grown ostensibly colder to religion. Plausibility cannot be maintained solely by reliance on religious tradition nor can one yield automatically to the blandishments of secularity.

BELLAH, ROBERT N., RICHARD MADSEN, WILLIAM M. SULLIVAN, ANN SWIDLER, AND STEVEN M. TIPTON. 1985. *Habits of The Heart: Individualism and Commitment in American Life.* Berkeley: University of California Press.

Bellah and his collaborators, using individual interviews and cultural analysis, search for integrative forces that bind Americans together in an era characterized by individualism and religious privatization.

emile durkheim

CONCLUSION FROM
THE ELEMENTARY FORMS OF
THE RELIGIOUS LIFE

Most often, the theorists who have set out to express religion in rational terms have regarded it as being, first and foremost, a system of ideas that correspond to a definite object. That object has been conceived in different ways—nature, the infinite, the unknowable, the ideal, and so forth—but these differences are of little importance. In every case, the representations—that is, the beliefs— were considered the essential element of religion. For their part, rites appeared from this standpoint to be no more than an external contingent and physical translation of those inward states that alone were deemed to have intrinsic value. This notion is so widespread that most of the time debates on the topic of religion turn around and about on the question of whether there is room alongside scientific knowledge for another form of thought held to be specifically religious.

But the believers—the men who, living a religious life, have a direct sense of what constitutes religion—object that, in terms of their day-to-day experience, this way of seeing does not ring true. Indeed, they sense that the true function of religion is not to make us think, enrich our knowledge, or add representations of a different sort and source to those we owe to science. Its true function is to make us act and to help us live. The believer who has communed with his god is not simply a man who sees new truths that the unbeliever knows not; he is a man who is *stronger*. Within himself, he feels more strength to endure the trials of existence or to overcome them. He is as though lifted above the human miseries, because he is lifted above his human condition. He believes he is delivered from evil—whatever the form in which he conceives of evil. The first article of any faith is belief in salvation by faith.

But it is hard to see how a mere idea could have that power. In fact, an idea is but one element of ourselves. How could it confer on us powers that are superior to those given us in our natural makeup? As rich in emotive power as an ideal may be, it cannot add anything to our natural vitality; it can only release emotive forces that are already within us, neither creating them nor increasing them. From the fact that we imagine an object as worthy of being loved and sought after, it does not follow that we should feel stronger. Energies greater

Reprinted with the permission of The Free Press, an imprint of Simon & Schuster, from The Elementary Forms of the Religious Life *by Emile Durkheim, a new translation by Karen E. Fields. Copyright © 1995 by Karen E. Fields.*

than those at our disposal must come from the object, and, more than that, we must have some means of making them enter into us and blend into our inner life. To achieve this, it is not enough that we think about them; it is indispensable that we place ourselves under their influence, that we turn ourselves in the direction from which we can best feel that influence. In short, we must act; and so we must repeat the necessary acts as often as is necessary to renew their effects. From this standpoint, it becomes apparent that the set of regularly repeated actions that make up the cult regains all its importance. In fact, anyone who has truly practiced a religion knows very well that it is the cult that stimulates the feelings of joy, inner peace, serenity, and enthusiasm that, for the faithful, stand as experimental proof of their beliefs. The cult is not merely a system of signs by which the faith is outwardly expressed; it is the sum total of means by which that faith is created and recreated periodically. Whether the cult consists of physical operations or mental ones, it is always the cult that is efficacious.

This entire study rests on the postulate that the unanimous feeling of believers down the ages cannot be mere illusion. Therefore, like a recent apologist of faith (James 1902), I accept that religious belief rests on a definite experience, whose demonstrative value is, in a sense, not inferior to that of scientific experiments, though it is different. I too think "that a tree is known by its fruits," and that its fertility is the best proof of what its roots are worth. But merely because there exists a "religious experience," if you will, that is grounded in some manner (is there, by the way, any experience that is not?), it by no means follows that the reality which grounds it should conform objectively with the idea the believers have of it. The very fact that the way in which this reality has been conceived has varied infinitely in different times is enough to prove that none of these conceptions expresses it adequately. If the scientist sets it down as axiomatic that the sensations of heat and light that men have correspond to some objective cause, he does not thereby conclude that this cause is the same as it appears to the senses. Likewise, even if the feelings the faithful have are not imaginary, they still do not constitute privileged intuitions; there is no reason whatever to think that they inform us better about the nature of their object than ordinary sensations do about the nature of bodies and their properties. To discover what that object consists of, then, we must apply to those sensations an analysis similar to the one that has replaced the senses' representation of the world with a scientific and conceptual one.

This is precisely what I have tried to do. We have seen that this reality—which mythologies have represented in so many different forms, but which is the objective, universal, and eternal cause of those sui generis sensations of which religious experience is made—is society. I have shown what moral forces it develops and how it awakens that feeling of support, safety, and protective guidance which binds the man of faith to his cult. It is this reality that makes him rise above himself. Indeed, this is the reality that makes him, for what makes man is that set of intellectual goods which is civilization, and civilization is the work of society. In this way is explained the preeminent role of the cult in all religions, whatever they are. This is so because society cannot make its influence felt unless it is in action, and it is in action only if the individuals who comprise it are assembled and acting in common. It is through common action that society becomes conscious of and affirms itself; society is above all an active cooperation. As I have shown, even collective ideas and feelings are possible only through the overt movements that symbolize them. Thus it is action that dominates religious life, for the very reason that society is its source.

To all the reasons adduced to justify this conception, a final one can be added that emerges from this book as a whole. Along the way, I have established that the fundamental categories of thought, and thus science itself, have religious origins. The same has been shown to be true of magic, and thus of the various techniques derived from magic. Besides, it has long been known that, until a relatively advanced moment in evolution, the rules of morality and law were not distinct from ritual prescriptions. In short, then, we can say that nearly all the great social institutions were born in religion. For the principal features of collective life to have begun as none other than various features of religious life, it is evident that religious life must necessarily have been the eminent form and, as it were, the epitome of collective life. If religion gave birth to all that is essential in society, that is so because the idea of society is the soul of religion.

Thus religious forces are human forces, moral forces. . . .

Only by seeing religions in this way does it become possible to detect their real meaning. If we rely on appearances, the rites often seem to be purely manual operations—anointings, purifications, meals. . . . But these physical operations are but the outer envelope in which mental operations lie hidden. In the end, the point is not to exert a kind of physical constraint upon blind and, more than that, imaginary forces but to reach, fortify, and discipline consciousnesses. The lower religions have sometimes been called materialistic. That term is incorrect. All religions, even the crudest, are in a sense spiritualistic. The powers they bring into play are, above all, spiritual, and their primary function is to act upon moral life. . . .

What defines the sacred is that the sacred is added to the real. And since the ideal is defined in the same way, we cannot explain the one without explaining the other. We have seen, in fact, that if collective life awakens religious thought when it rises to a certain intensity, that is so because it brings about a state of effervescence that alters the conditions of psychic activity. The vital energies become hyperexcited, the passions more intense, the sensations more powerful; there are indeed some that are produced only at this moment. Man does not recognize himself; he feels somehow transformed and in consequence transforms his surroundings. To account for the very particular impressions he receives, he imputes to the things with which he is most directly in contact properties that they do not have, exceptional powers and virtues that the objects of ordinary experience do not possess. In short, upon the real world profane life is lived, he superimposes another that, in a sense, exists only in his thought, but one to which he ascribes a higher kind of dignity than he ascribes to the real world of profane life. In two respects, then, this other world is an ideal one.

Thus the formation of an ideal is by no means an irreducible datum that eludes science. It rests on conditions that can be uncovered through observation. It is a natural product of social life. . . . A society can neither create nor recreate itself without creating some kind of ideal by the same stroke. This creation is not a sort of optional extra step by which society, being already made, merely adds finishing touches; it is the act by which society makes itself, and remakes itself, periodically. . . . A society is not constituted simply by the mass of individuals who comprise it, the ground they occupy, the things they use, or the movements they make, but above all by the idea it has of itself. . . .

Therefore the collective ideal that religion expresses is far from being due to some vague capacity innate to the individual; rather, it is in the school of collective life that the individual has learned to form ideals. It is by assimilating the ideals worked out by society that the individual is able to conceive of the ideal. It is society that, by drawing him into its sphere of action, has given him the need to raise himself above the world of experience, while at the same time furnishing him the means of imagining another. It is society that built this new world while building itself, because it is society that the new world expresses. There is nothing mysterious about the faculty of idealization, then, whether in the individual or in the group. This faculty is not a sort of luxury, which man could do without, but a condition of his existence. If he had not acquired it, he would not be a social being, which is to say that he would not be man. To be sure, collective ideals tend to become individualized as they become incarnate in individuals. Each person understands them in his own way and gives them an individual imprint, some elements being taken out and others being added. As the individual personality develops and becomes an autonomous source of action, the personal ideal diverges from the social one. But if we want to understand that aptitude for living outside the real, which is seemingly so remarkable, all we need to do is relate it to the social conditions on which it rests.

clifford geertz

RELIGION AS A CULTURAL SYSTEM

There are at least three points where chaos—a tumult of events which lack not just interpretations but *interpretability*—threatens to break in upon man: at the limits of his analytic capacities, at the limits of his powers of endurance, and at the limits of his moral insight. Bafflement, suffering, and a sense of intractable ethical paradox are all, if they become intense enough or are sustained long enough, radical challenges to the proposition that life is comprehensible and that we can, taking thought, orient ourselves effectively within it—challenges with which any religion, however "primitive," which hopes to persist must attempt somehow to cope.

Of the three issues, it is the first which has been least investigated by modern social anthropologists (though Evans-Pritchard's classic discussion of why granaries fall on some Azande and not on others, is a notable exception) (1937). Even to consider people's religious beliefs as attempts to bring anomalous events or experiences—death, dreams, mental fugues, volcanic eruptions, or marital infidelity—within the circle of the at least potentially explicable seems to smack of Tyloreanism or worse. But it does appear to be a fact that at least some men—in all probability, most men—are unable to leave unclarified problems of analysis merely unclarified, just to look at the stranger features of the world's landscape in dumb astonishment or bland apathy without trying to develop, however fantastic, inconsistent, or simple-minded, some notions as to how such features might be reconciled with the more ordinary deliverances of experience. Any chronic failure of one's explanatory apparatus, the complex of received culture patterns (common sense, science, philosophical speculation, myth) one has for mapping the empirical world, to explain things which cry out for explanation tends to lead to a deep disquiet—a tendency rather more widespread and a disquiet rather deeper than we have sometimes supposed since the pseudoscience view of religious belief was, quite rightfully, deposed. After all, even that high priest of heroic atheism, Lord Russell, once remarked that although the problem of the existence of God had never bothered him, the ambiguity of certain mathematical axioms had threatened to unhinge his mind. And Einstein's profound dissatisfaction with quantum

Reprinted with permission from Michael Banton, ed., Anthropological Approaches to the Study of Religion. *Copyright © 1966 Tavistock Publications, Ltd., London.*

mechanics was based on a—surely religious—inability to believe that, as he put it, God plays dice with the universe.

But this quest for lucidity and the rush of metaphysical anxiety that occurs when empirical phenomena threaten to remain intransigently opaque is found on much humbler intellectual levels. Certainly, I was struck in my own work, much more than I had at all expected to be, by the degree to which my more animistically inclined informants behaved like true Tyloreans. They seemed to be constantly using their beliefs to "explain" phenomena: or, more accurately, to convince themselves that the phenomena were explainable within the accepted scheme of things, for they commonly had only a minimal attachment to the particular soul possession, emotional disequilibrium, taboo infringement, or bewitchment hypothesis they advanced and were all too ready to abandon it for some other, in the same genre, which struck them as more plausible given the facts of the case. What they were *not* ready to do was abandon it for no other hypothesis at all; to leave events to themselves.

And what is more, they adopted this nervous cognitive stance with respect to phenomena which had no immediate practical bearing on their own lives, or for that matter on anyone's. When a peculiarly shaped, rather large toadstool grew up in a carpenter's house in the short space of a few days (or, some said, a few hours), people came from miles around to see it, and everyone had some sort of explanation—some animist, some animatist, some not quite either—for it. Yet it would be hard to argue that the toadstool had any social value in Radcliffe-Brown's sense or was connected in any way with anything which did and for which it could have been standing proxy, like the Andaman cicada (1952). Toadstools play about the same role in Javanese life as they do in ours, and in the ordinary course of things Javanese have about as much interest in them as we do. It was just that this one was "odd," "strange," "uncanny"—*aneh*. And the odd, strange, and uncanny simply must be accounted for—or, again, the conviction that it *could be accounted for* sustained. One does not shrug off a toadstool which grows five times as fast as a toadstool has any right to grow. In the broadest sense the "strange" toadstool did have implications, and critical ones, for those who heard about it. It threatened their most general ability to understand the world, raised the uncomfortable question of whether the beliefs which they held about nature were workable, the standards of truth they used valid. . . .

As a religious problem, the problem of suffering is, paradoxically, not how to avoid suffering but how to suffer, how to make of physical pain, personal loss, worldly defeat, or the helpless contemplation of others' agony something bearable, supportable—something, as we say, sufferable. It was in this effort that the Ba-Ila woman—perhaps necessarily, perhaps not—failed and, literally not knowing how to feel about what had happened to her, how to suffer, perished in confusion and despair. Where the more intellective aspects of what Weber called the Problem of Meaning are a matter affirming the ultimate explicability of experience, the more affective aspects are a matter of affirming its ultimate sufferableness. As religion on one side anchors the power of our symbolic resources for formulating analytic ideas in an authoritative conception of the overall shape of reality, so on another side it anchors the power of our, also symbolic, resources for expressing emotions—moods, sentiments, passions, affections, feelings—in a similar conception of its pervasive tenor, its inherent tone and temper. For those able to embrace them, and for so long as they are able to embrace them, religious symbols provide a cosmic guarantee not only for their ability to comprehend the world, but also, comprehending it, to give a precision to their feeling, a definition to their emotions which enables them, morosely or joyfully, grimly or cavalierly, to endure it.

Consider in this light the well-known Navaho curing rites usually referred to as "sings" (Kluckhohn and Leighton 1946; Reichard 1950). A sing—the Navaho have about sixty different ones for different purposes, but virtually all of them are dedicated to removing some sort of physical or mental illness—is a kind of religious psychodrama in which there are three main actors: the "singer" or curer, the patient, and, as a kind of antiphonal chorus, the patient's family and friends. The structure of all the sings, the drama's plot, is quite similar. There are three main acts: a purification of the patient and audience; a statement, by means of repetitive chants and ritual manipulations, of the wish to restore well-being ("harmony") in the patient; an identification of the patient with the Holy People and his consequent "cure." The purification rites involve forced sweating, induced vomiting, and so on, to expel the sickness from the patient physically. The chants, which are numberless, consist mainly of simple optative phrases ("may the patient be well," "I am getting better all over," etc.). And, finally, the identification of the patient with the Holy People, and thus with cosmic order generally, is accomplished through the agency of a sand painting depicting the Holy People in one or another appropriate mythic setting. The singer places the patient on the painting, touching the feet, hands, knees, shoulders, breast, back, and head of the divine figures and then the corresponding parts of the patient, performing thus what is essentially a bodily identification of the human and the divine (Reichard 1950). This is the climax of the sing: the whole curing process may be likened, Reichard says, to a spiritual osmosis in which the illness in man and the power of the deity penetrate the ceremonial membrane in both directions, the former being neutralized by the latter. Sickness seeps out in the sweat, vomit, and other purification rites; health seeps in as the Navaho patient touches, through he medium of the singer, the sacred sand painting. Clearly, the symbolism of the sing focuses upon the problem of human suffering and attempts to cope with it by placing it in a meaningful context, providing a mode of action through which it can be expressed, being expressed understood, and being understood, endured. The sustaining effect of the sing (and since the commonest disease is tuberculosis, it can in most cases be only sustaining), rests ultimately on its ability to give the stricken person a vocabulary in terms of which to grasp the nature of his distress and relate it to the wider world. Like a calvary, a recitation of Buddha's emergence from his father's palace, or a performance of *Oedipus Tyrannos* in other religious traditions, a sing is mainly concerned with the presentation of a specific and concrete image of truly human, and so endurable, suffering powerful enough to resist the challenge of emotional meaninglessness raised by the existence of intense and un-removable brute pain.

The problem of suffering passes easily into the problem of evil, for if suffering is severe enough it usually, though not always, seems morally un-deserved as well, at least to the sufferer. But they are not, however, exactly the same thing—a fact I think Weber, too influenced by the biases of a mono-theistic tradition in which, as the various aspects of human experience must be conceived to proceed from a single, voluntaristic source, man's pain reflects directly on God's goodness, did not fully recognize in his generalization of the dilemmas of Christian theodicy eastward. For where the problem of suffering is concerned with threats to our ability to put our "undisciplined squads of emotion" into some sort of soldierly order, the problem of evil is concerned with threats to our ability to make sound moral judgments. What is involved in the problem of evil is not the adequacy of our symbolic resources to govern our affective life, but the adequacy of those resources to provide a workable set of ethical criteria, normative guides to govern our action. The vexation here is the gap between things as they are and as they ought to be if our conceptions of right and wrong make sense, the gap between what we deem various individuals deserve and what we see that they get—a phenomenon summed up in that profound quatrain:

> *The rain falls on the just*
> *And on the unjust fella;*
> *But mainly upon the just,*
> *Because the unjust has the just's umbrella.*

Or if this seems too flippant an expression of an issue that, in somewhat different form, animates the Book of Job and the *Baghavad Gita,* the following classical Javanese poem, known, sung, and repeatedly quoted in Java by virtually everyone over the age of six, puts the point—the discrepancy between moral prescriptions and material rewards, the seeming inconsistency of "is" and "ought"— rather more elegantly:

> *We have lived to see a time without order*
> *In which everyone is confused in his mind,*
> *One cannot bear to join in the madness,*
> *But if he does not do so*
> *He will not share in the spoils,*
> *And will starve as a result.*
> *Yes, God; wrong is wrong:*
> *Happy are those who forget,*
> *Happier yet those who remember and have deep insight. . . .*

Thus the problem of evil, or perhaps one should say the problem *about* evil, is in essence the same sort of problem of or about bafflement and the problem of or about suffering. The strange opacity of certain empirical events, the dumb senselessness of intense or inexorable pain, and the enigmatic unaccountability of gross iniquity all raise the uncomfortable suspicion that perhaps the world, and hence man's life in the world, has no genuine order at all—no empirical regularity, no emotional form, no moral coherence. And the religious response to this suspicion is in each case the same: the formulation, by means of symbols, of an image of such a genuine order of the world which will account for, and even celebrate, the perceived ambiguities, puzzles, and paradoxes in human experience. The effort is not to deny the undeniable—that there are un-explained events, that life hurts, or that rain falls upon the just—but to deny that there are inexplicable events, that life is unendurable, and that justice is a mirage. The principles which constitute the moral order may indeed often elude men, as Lienhardt puts it, in the same way as fully satisfactory explana-tions or anomalous events or effective forms for the expression of feeling often elude them. What is important, to a religious man at least, is that this elusive-ness be accounted for, that it be not the result of the fact that there are no such principles, explanations, or forms, that life is absurd and the attempt to make moral, intellectual, or emotional sense out of experience is bootless. The Dinka can admit, in fact insist upon, the moral ambiguities and contradictions of life as they live it because these ambiguities and contradictions are seen not as ultimate, but as "rational," "natural," "logical" (one may choose one's own adjective here, for none of them is truly adequate) outcome of the moral structure of reality which the myth of the withdrawn "Divinity" depicts, or as Lienhardt says, "images.". . .

It seems to me that it is best to begin any approach to this issue with frank recognition that religious belief involves not a Baconian induction from everyday experience—for then we should all be agnostics—but rather a prior acceptance of authority which transforms that experience. The exis-tence of bafflement, pain, and moral paradox—of The Problem of Mean-ing—is one of the things that drives men toward belief in gods, devils, spirits, totemic principles, or the spiritual efficacy of cannibalism (an en-folding sense of beauty of a dazzling perception of power are others), but it is not the basis upon which those beliefs rest, but rather their most important field of application. . . .

But to speak of "the religious perspective" is, by implication, to speak of one perspective among others. A perspective is a mode of seeing, in that extended sense of "see" in which it means "discern," "apprehend," "understand," or "grasp." It is a particular way of looking at life, a particular manner of construing the world. . . .

If we place the religious perspective against the background of three of the other major perspectives in terms of which men construe the world—the common-sensical, the scientific, and the aesthetic—its special character emerges more sharply. What distinguishes common sense as a mode of "see-ing" is, as Schutz has pointed out, a simple acceptance of the world, its objects,and its processes as being just what they seem to be—what is some-times called naive realism—and the pragmatic motive, the wish to act upon that world so as to bend it to one's practical purposes, to master it, or so far as that proves impossible, to adjust to it (1962). The world of everyday life, itself, of course, a cultural product, for it is framed in terms of the symbolic conceptions of "stubborn fact" handed down from generation to generation, is the established scene and given object of our actions. Like Mt. Everest it is just there, and the thing to do with it, if one feels the need to do anything with it at all, is to climb it. In the scientific perspective it is precisely this givenness which disappears (Schutz 1962). Deliberate doubt and systematic inquiry, the suspension of the pragmatic motive in favor of disinterested observation, the attempt to analyze the world in terms of formal concepts whose relationship to the informal conceptions of common sense become increasingly problematic—there are the hallmarks of the attempt to grasp the world scientifically. And as for the aesthetic perspective, which under the rubric of "the aesthetic attitude" has been perhaps most exquisitely examined, it involves a different sort of suspension of naive realism and practical interest, in that instead of questioning the credentials of everyday experience, one merely ignores that experience in favor of an eager dwelling upon appearances, an engrossment in surfaces, an absorption in things, as we say, "in themselves": "The function of artistic illusion is not 'make-believe'. . . but the very opposite, disengagement from belief—the contemplation of sensory qualities without their usual meanings of 'here's that chair,' 'that's my telephone,'. . . , etc. The knowledge that what is before us has no practical significance in the world is what enables us to give attention to its appearance as such" (Langer 1953:49). And like the common sensical and the scientific (or the historical, the philosophical, and the artistic), this perspective, this "way of seeing" is not the product of some mysterious Cartesian chemistry, but is induced, mediated, and in fact created by means of curious quasi objects—poems, dramas, sculptures, symphonies—which, dissociating themselves from the solid world of common sense, take on the special sort of eloquence only sheer appearances can achieve.

The religious perspective differs from the common-sensical in that, as already pointed out, it moves beyond the realities of everyday life to wider ones which correct and complete them, and its defining concern is not action upon those wider realities but acceptance of them, faith in them. It differs from the scientific perspective in that it questions the realities of everyday life not out of an institutionalized scepticism which dissolves the world's givenness into a swirl of probabilistic hypotheses, but in terms of what it takes to be wider, nonhypothetical truths. Rather than detachment, its watchword is commitment; rather than analysis, encounter. And it differs from art in that instead of effecting a disengagement from the whole question of factuality, deliberately manufacturing an air of semblance and illusion, it deepens the concern with fact and seeks to create an aura of utter actuality. It is this sense of the "really real" upon which the religious perspective rests and which the symbolic activities of religion as a cultural system are devoted to producing, intensifying, and so far as possible, rendering inviolable by the discordant revelations of secular experience. It is, again, the imbuing of a certain specific complex of symbols—of the metaphysic they formulate and the style of life they recommend—with a persuasive authority which, from an analytic point of view, is the essence of religious action.

Which brings us, at length, to ritual. For it is in ritual—that is, consecrated behavior—that this conviction that religious conceptions are veridical and that religious directives are sound is somehow generated. It is some sort of ceremonial form—even if that form be hardly more than the recitation of a myth, the consultation of an oracle, or the decoration of a grave—that the moods and motivations which sacred symbols induce in men and the general conceptions of the order of existence which they formulate for men meet and reinforce one another. In a ritual, the world as lived and the world as imagined, fused under the agency of a single set of symbolic forms, turn out to be the same world, producing thus that idiosyncratic transformation in one's sense of reality to which Santayana refers in my epigraph. Whatever role divine intervention may or may not play in the creation of faith—and it is not the business of the scientist to pronounce upon such matters one way or the other—it is, primarily at least, out of the context of concrete acts of religious observance that religious conviction emerges on the human plane.

However, though any religious ritual, no matter how apparently automatic or conventional (if it is truly automatic or merely conventional it is not religious), involves this symbolic fusion of ethos and world view, it is mainly certain more elaborate and usually more public ones, ones in which a broad range of moods and motivations on the one hand and of metaphysical conceptions on the other are caught up, which shape the spiritual consciousness of a people. Employing a useful term introduced by Singer, we may call these full-blown ceremonies "cultural performances" and note that they represent not only the point at which the dispositional and conceptual aspects of religious life converge for the believer, but also the point at which the interaction between them can be most readily examined by the detached observer:

> Whenever Madrasi Brahmans (and non-Brahmans, too, for that matter) wished to exhibit to me some feature of Hinduism, they always referred to, or invited me to see, a particular rite or ceremony in the life cycle, in a temple festival, or in the general sphere of religious and cultural performances. Reflecting on this in the course of my interviews and observations I found that the more abstract generalizations about Hinduism (my own as well as those I heard) could generally be checked, directly or indirectly, against these observable performances. (Singer 1955:23–26)

For an anthropologist, the importance of religion lies in its capacity to serve, for an individual or for a group, as a source of general, yet distinctive, conceptions of the world, the self, and the relations between them, on the one hand—its model *of* aspect—and of rooted, no less distinctive "mental" dispositions—its model *for* aspect—on the other. From these cultural functions flow, in turn, its social and psychological ones.

Religious concepts spread beyond their specifically metaphysical contexts to provide a framework of general ideas in terms of which a wide range of experience—intellectual, emotional, oral—can be given meaningful form. The Christian sees the Nazi movement against the background of the Fall which, though it does not, in a causal sense, explain it, places it in a moral, a cognitive, even an affective sense. An Azande sees the collapse of a granary upon a friend or relative against the background of a concrete and rather special notion of witchcraft and thus avoids the philosophical dilemmas as well as the psychological stress of indeterminism. A Javanese finds in the borrowed and reworked concept of *rasa* ("sense-taste-feeling-meaning") a means by which to "see" choreographic, gustatory, emotional, and political phenomena in a new light. A synopsis of cosmic order, a set of religious beliefs, is also a gloss upon the mundane world of social relationships and psychological events. It renders them graspable.

But more than gloss, such beliefs are also a template. They do not merely interpret social and psychological processes in cosmic terms—in which case they would be philosophical, not religious—but they shape them. In the doctrine of original sin is embedded also a recommended attitude toward life, a recurring mood, and a persisting set of motivations. The Azande learns from witchcraft conceptions not just to understand apparent "accidents" as not accidents at all, but to react to these spurious accidents with hatred for the agent who caused them and to proceed against him with appropriate resolution. *Rasa*, in addition to being a concept of truth, beauty, and goodness, is also a preferred mode of experiencing, a kind of affectless detachment, a variety of bland aloofness, an unshakable calm. The moods and motivations a religious orientation produces cast a derivative, lunar light over the solid features of a people's secular life.

The tracing of the social and psychological role of religion is thus not so much a matter of finding correlations between specific ritual acts and specific secular social ties—though these correlations do, of course, exist and are very worth continued investigation, especially if we can contrive something novel to say about them. More, it is a matter of understanding how it is that men's notions, however implicit, of the "really real" and the dispositions these notions induce in them, color their sense of the reasonable, the practical, the humane, and the moral. How far they do so (for in many societies religion's effects seem quite circumscribed, in others completely pervasive), how deeply they do so (for some men, and groups of men, seem to wear their religion lightly so far as the secular world goes, while others seem to apply their faith to each occasion, no matter how trivial), and how effectively they do so (for the width of the gap between what religion recommends and what people actually do is most variable cross-culturally)—all these are crucial issues in the comparative sociology and psychology of religion. Even the degree to which religious systems themselves are developed seems to vary extremely widely, and not merely on a simple evolutionary basis. In one society, the level of elaboration of symbolic formulations of ultimate actuality may reach extraordinary degrees of complexity and systematic articulation; in another, no less developed socially, such formulations may remain primitive in the true sense, hardly more than congeries of fragmentary by-beliefs and isolated images, of sacred reflexes and spiritual pictographs. One need only think of the Australians and the Bushmen, the Toradja and the Alorese, the Hope and the Apache, the Hindus and the Romans, or even the Italians and the Poles, to see that degree of religious articulateness is not a constant even as between societies of similar complexity.

The anthropological study of religion is therefore a two-stage operation: first, an analysis of the system of meanings embodied in the symbols which make up the religion proper, and, second, the relating of these systems to social-structural and psychological processes. My dissatisfaction with so much of contemporary social anthropological work in religion is not that it concerns itself with the second stage, but that it neglects the first, and in so doing takes for granted what most needs to be elucidated. To discuss the role of ancestry worship in regulating political succession, of sacrificial feasts in defining kinship obligations, of spirit worship in scheduling agricultural practices, of divination in reinforcing social control, or of initiation rites in propelling personality maturation, are in no sense unimportant endeavors, and I am not recommending they be abandoned for the kind of jejune cabalism into which symbolic analysis of exotic faiths can so easily fall. But to attempt them with but the most general, common-sense view of what ancestor worship, animal sacrifice, spirit worship, divination, or initiation rites are as religious patterns seems to me not particularly promising. Only when we have a theoretical analysis of symbolic action comparable in sophistication to that we now have for social and psychological action, will we be able to cope effectively with those aspects of social and psychological life in which religion (or art, or science, or ideology) plays a determinant role.

peter berger

PLAUSIBILITY STRUCTURES

One of the fundamental propositions of the sociology of knowledge is that the plausibility, in the sense of what people actually find credible, of views of reality depends upon the social support these receive. Put more simply, we obtain our notions about the world originally from other human beings, and these notions continue to be plausible to us in a very large measure because others continue to affirm them. There are some exceptions to this—notions that derive directly and instantaneously from our own sense experience—but even these can be integrated into meaningful views of reality only by virtue of social processes. It is, of course, possible to go against the social consensus that surrounds us, but there are powerful pressures (which manifest themselves as psychological pressures within our own consciousness) to conform to the views and beliefs of our fellow men. It is in conversation, in the grandest sense of the word, that we build up and keep going our view of the world. It follows that this view will depend upon the continuity and consistency of such conversation, and that it will change as we change conversation partners.

We all exist within a variety of social networks or conversational fabrics, which are related in often complex and sometimes contradictory ways with our various conceptions of the universe. When we get to the more sophisticated of these conceptions, there are likely to be organized practices designed to still doubts and prevent lapses of conviction. These practices are called therapies. There are also likely to be more or less systematized explanations, justifications, and theories in support of the conceptions in question. These sociologists have called legitimations. . . .

Thus each conception of the world of whatever character or content can be analyzed in terms of its plausibility structure, because it is only as the individual remains within this structure that the conception of the world in question will remain plausible to him. The strength of this plausibility, ranging from unquestioned certitude through firm probability to mere opinion, will be directly dependent upon the strength of the supporting structure. This dynamics pertains irrespective of whether, by some outside observer's criteria of validity, the notions thus made plausible are true or false. The dynamics most definitely pertains to any religious affirmations about the world because these affirmations are, by their very nature, incapable of being supported by our own sense experience and therefore heavily dependent upon social support.

Each plausibility structure can be further analyzed in terms of its constituent elements—the specific human beings that "inhabit" it, the conversational network by which these "inhabitants" keep the reality in question going, the therapeutic practices and rituals, and the legitimations that go with them. For example, the maintenance of the Catholic faith in the consciousness of the individual requires that he maintain his relationship to the plausibility structure of Catholicism. This is, above all, a community of Catholics in his social milieu who continually support his faith. It will be useful if those who are of the greatest emotional significance to the individual (the ones whom George Herbert Mead called significant others) belong to this supportive community—it does not matter much if, say, the individual's dentist is a non-Catholic, but his wife and his closest personal friends had better be. Within this supportive community there will then be an ongoing conversation that, explicitly and implicitly, keeps a Catholic world going. Explicitly, there is affirmation, confirmation, reiteration of Catholic notions about reality. But there is also an implicit Catholicism in such a community. After all, in everyday life it is just as important that some things can silently be taken for granted as that some things are reaffirmed in so many words. Indeed, the most fundamental assumptions about the world are commonly affirmed by implication—they are so "obvious" that there is no need to put them into words. Our individual, then, operates within what may be called a specifically Catholic conversational apparatus, which, in innumerable ways, each day confirms the Catholic world that he coinhabits with his significant others. . . . The details of all this vary in different circumstances, especially as between a situation in which the plausibility structure is more or less coextensive with the individual's overall social experience (that is, where Catholics constitute the majority) and a situation in which the plausibility structure exists as an deviant enclave within the individual's larger society (that is, where Catholics are a cognitive minority). But the essential point is that the plausibility of Catholicism hinges upon the availability of these social processes.

robert n. bellah

CIVIL RELIGION IN AMERICA

While some have argued that Christianity is the national faith, and others that church and synagogue celebrate only the generalized religion of "the American Way of Life," few have realized that there actually exists alongside of and rather clearly differentiated from the churches an elaborate and well-institutionalized civil religion in America. This article argues not only that there is such a thing, but also that this religion—or perhaps better, this religious dimension—has its own seriousness and integrity and requires the same care in understanding that any other religion does.

THE KENNEDY INAUGURAL

Kennedy's inaugural address of 20 January 1961 serves as an example and a clue with which to introduce this complex subject. That address began:

> We observe today not a victory of party but a celebration of freedom—symbolizing an end as well as a beginning—signifying renewal as well as change. For I have sworn before you and Almighty God the same solemn oath our forebears prescribed nearly a century and three quarters ago.
>
> The world is very different now. For man holds in his mortal hands the power to abolish all forms of human poverty and to abolish all forms of human life. And yet the same revolutionary beliefs for which our forebears fought are still at issue around the globe—the belief that the rights of man come not from the generosity of the state but from the hand of God.

And it concluded:

> Finally, whether you are citizens of America or of the world, ask of us the same high standards of strength and sacrifice that we shall ask of you. With a good conscience our only sure reward, with history the final judge of our deeds, let us go forth to lead the land we love, asking His blessing and His help, but knowing here on earth God's work must truly be our own.

These are the three places in this brief address in which Kennedy mentioned the name of God. If we could understand why he mentioned God, the way in

"Civil Religion in America" reprinted by permission of Daedalus, Journal of the American Academy of Arts and Sciences, *from the issue entitled "Religion in America," 96(1):1–21 (1967).*

which he did it, and what he meant to say in those three references, we would understand much about American civil religion. But this is not a simple or obvious task, and American students of religion would probably differ widely in their interpretation of these passages.

Let us consider first the placing of the three references. They occur in the two opening paragraphs and in the closing paragraph, thus providing a sort of frame for the more concrete remarks that form the middle part of the speech. Looking beyond this particular speech, we would find that similar references to God are almost invariably to be found in the pronouncements of American presidents on solemn occasions, though usually not in the working messages that the president sends to Congress on various concrete issues. How, then, are we to interpret this placing of references to God?

It might be argued that the passages quoted reveal the essentially irrelevant role of religion in the very secular society that is America. The placing of the references in this speech as well as in public life generally indicates that religion has "only a ceremonial significance"; it gets only a sentimental nod which serves largely to placate the more unenlightened members of the community, before a discussion of the really serious business with which religion has nothing whatever to do. A cynical observer might even say that an American president has to mention God or risk losing votes. A semblance of piety is merely one of the unwritten qualifications for the office, a bit more traditional than but not essentially different from the present-day requirement of a pleasing television personality.

But we know enough about the function of ceremonial and ritual in various societies to make us suspicious of dismissing something as unimportant because it is "only a ritual." What people say on solemn occasions need not be taken at face value, but it is often indicative of deep-seated values and commitments that are not made explicit in the course of everyday life. Following this line of argument, it is worth considering whether the very special placing of the references to God in Kennedy's address may not reveal something rather important and serious about religion in American life.

It might be countered that the very way in which Kennedy made his references reveals the essentially vestigial place of religion today. He did not refer to any religion in particular. He did not refer to Jesus Christ, or to Moses, or to the Christian church; certainly he did not refer to the Catholic church. In fact, his only reference was to the concept of God, a word which almost all Americans can accept but which means so many different things to so many different people that it is almost an empty sign. Is this not just another indication that in America religion is considered vaguely to be a good thing, but that people care so little about it that it has lost any content whatever? Isn't Eisenhower reported to have said, "Our government makes no sense unless it is founded in a deeply felt religious faith—and I don't care what it is" (Herberg 1955:97), and isn't that a complete negation of any real religion?

These questions are worth pursuing because they raise the issue of how civil religion relates to the political society, on the one hand, and to private religious organization, on the other. President Kennedy was a Christian, more specifically a Catholic Christian. Thus, his general references to God do not mean that he lacked a specific religious commitment. But why, then, did he not include some remark to the effect that Christ is the Lord of the world or some indications of respect for the Catholic church? He did not because these are matters of his own private religious belief and of his relation to his own particular church; they are not matters relevant in any direct way to the conduct of his public office. Others with different religious views and commitments to different churches or denominations are equally qualified participants in the political process. The principle of separation of church and state guarantees the freedom of religious belief and association, but at the same time clearly segregates the religious sphere, which is considered to be essentially private, from the political one.

Considering the separation of church and state, how is a president justified in using the word *God* at all? The answer is that the separation of church and state has not denied the political realm a religious dimension. Although matter of personal religious belief, worship, and association are considered to be strictly private affairs, there are, at the same time, certain common elements of religious orientation that the great majority of Americans share. These have played a crucial role in the development of American institutions and still provide a religious dimension for the whole fabric of American life, including the political sphere. This public religious dimension is expressed in a set of beliefs, symbols, and rituals that I am calling the American civil religion. The inauguration of a president is an important ceremonial event in this religion. It reaffirms, among other things, the religious legitimation of the highest political authority.

Let us look more closely at what Kennedy actually said. First he said, "I have sworn before you and Almighty God the same solemn oath our forebears prescribed nearly a century and three quarters ago." The oath is the oath of office, including the acceptance of the obligation to uphold the Constitution. He swears it before the people (you) and God. Beyond the Constitution, then, the president's obligation extends not only to the people but to God. In American political theory, sovereignty rests, of course, with the people, but implicitly, and often explicitly, the ultimate sovereignty has been attributed to God. This is the meaning of the motto, "In God we trust," as well as the inclusion of the phrase "under God" in the pledge to the flag. What difference does it make that sovereignty belongs to God? Though the will of the people as expressed in majority vote is carefully institutionalized as the operative source of political authority, it is deprived of an ultimate significance. The will of the people is not itself the criterion of right and wrong. There is a higher criterion in terms of which this will can be judged; it is possible that the people may be wrong. The president's obligation extends to the higher criterion.

When Kennedy says that "the rights of man come not from the generosity of the state but from the hand of God," he is stressing this point again. It does not matter whether the state is the expression of the will of an autocratic monarch or of the "people"; the rights of man are more basic than any political structure and provide a point of revolutionary leverage from which any state structure may be radically altered. That is the basis for his reassertion of the revolutionary significance of America.

But the religious dimension in political life as recognized by Kennedy not only provides a grounding for the rights of man which makes any form of political absolutism illegitimate, it also provides a transcendent goal for the political process. This is implied in his final words that "here on earth God's work must truly be our own." What he means here is, I think, more clearly spelled out in a previous paragraph, the working of which, incidentally, has a distinctly biblical ring:

> Now the trumpet summons us again—not as a call to bear arms, though arms we need—not as a call to battle, though embattled we are—but a call to bear the burden of a long twilight struggle, year in and year out, "rejoicing in hope, patient in tribulation"—a struggle against the common enemies of man: tyranny, poverty, disease and war itself.

The whole address can be understood as only the most recent statement of a theme that lies very deep in the American tradition, namely the obligation, both collective and individual, to carry out God's will on earth. This was the motivating spirit of those who founded America, and it has been present in every generation since. Just below the surface throughout Kennedy's inaugural address, it becomes explicit in the closing statement that God's work must be our own. That this very activist and noncontemplative conception of the fundamental religious obligation, which has been historically associated with the Protestant position, should be enunciated so clearly in the first major statement of the first Catholic president seems to underline how deeply established it is in the American outlook. Let us now consider the form and history of the civil religious tradition in which Kennedy was speaking.

THE IDEA OF CIVIL RELIGION

The phrase *civil religion* is, of course, Rousseau's. In Chapter Eight, Book Four, of *The Social Contract*, he outlines the simple dogmas of the civil religion: the existence of God, the life to come, the reward of virtue and the punishment of vice, and the exclusion of religious intolerance. All other religious opinions are outside the cognizance of the state and may be freely held by citizens. While the phrase *civil religion* was not used, to the best of my knowledge, by the founding fathers, and I am certainly not arguing for the particular influence of Rousseau, it is clear that similar ideas, as part of the cultural climate of the late eighteenth century, were to be found among the Americans. For example, Franklin writes in his autobiography:

> I never was without some religious principles. I never doubted, for instance, the existence of the Deity; that he made the world and govern'd it by his Providence; that the most acceptable service of God was the doing of good to men; that our souls are immortal; and that all crime will be punished, and virtue rewarded either here or hereafter. These I esteemed

the essentials of every religion; and, being to be found in all the religions we had in our country, I respected them all, tho' with different degrees of respect, as I found them more of less mix'd with other articles, which, without any tendency to inspire, promote or confirm morality, serv'd principally to divide us, and make us unfriendly to one another.

It is easy to dispose of this sort of position as essentially utilitarian in relation to religion. In Washington's farewell address (though the words may be Hamilton's) the utilitarian aspect is quite explicit:

Of all the dispositions and habits which lead to political prosperity, Religion and Morality are indispensable supports. In vain would that man claim the tribute of Patriotism, who should labour to subvert these great Pillars of human happiness, these firmest props of the duties of men and citizens. The mere politician, equally with the pious man ought to respect and cherish them. A volume could not trace all their connections with private and public felicity. Let it simply be asked where is the security for property, for reputation, for life, if the sense of religious obligation *desert* the oaths, which are the instruments of investigation in Courts of Justice? And let us with caution indulge the supposition, that morality can be maintained without religion. Whatever may be conceded to the influence of refined education on minds of peculiar structure, reason and experience both forbid us to expect that National morality can prevail in exclusion of religious principle.

But there is every reason to believe that religion, particularly the idea of God, played a constitutive role in the thought of the early American statesmen.

Kennedy's inaugural pointed to the religious aspect of the Declaration of Independence, and it might be well to look at that document a bit more closely. There are four references to God. The first speaks of the "Laws of Nature and Nature's God" which entitles any people to be independent. The second is the famous statement that all men "are endowed by their Creator with certain inalienable Rights." Here Jefferson is locating the fundamental legitimacy of the a new nation in a conception of "higher law" that is itself based on both classical natural law and biblical religion. The third is an appeal to "the Supreme Judge of the world for the rectitude of our intentions," and the last indicates "a firm reliance on the protection of divine Providence." In these last two references, a biblical God of history who stands in judgment over the world is indicated.

The intimate relation of these religious notions with the self-conception of the new republic is indicated by the frequency of their appearance in early official documents. For example, we find in Washington's first inaugural address of 30 April 1789:

It would be peculiarly improper to omit in this first official act my fervent supplications to that Almighty Being who rules over the universe, who presides in the councils of nations, and whose providential aids can supply every defect, that His benediction may consecrate to the liberties and happiness of the people of the United States a Government instituted by themselves for these essential purposes, and may enable every instrument employed in its administration to execute with success the functions allotted to this charge.

No people can be bound to acknowledge and adore the Invisible Hand which conducts the affairs of man more than those of the United States. Every step by which we have advanced to the character of an independent nation seems to have been distinguished by some token of providential agency. . . .

The propitious smiles of heaven can never be expected on a nation that disregards the eternal rules of order and right which Heaven itself has ordained. . . . The preservation of the sacred fire of liberty and the destiny of the republican model of government are justly considered, perhaps, as *deeply*, as *finally*, staked on the experiment intrusted to the hands of the American people.

Nor did these religious sentiments remain merely the personal expression of the president. At the request of both houses of Congress, Washington proclaimed on October 3 of that same first year as president that November 26 should be "a day of public thanksgiving and prayer," the first Thanksgiving Day under the Constitution.

The words and acts of the founding fathers, especially the first few presidents, shaped the form and tone of the civil religion as it has been maintained ever since. Though much is selectively derived from Christianity, this religion is clearly not itself Christianity. For one thing, neither Washington nor Adams nor Jefferson mentions Christ in his inaugural address; or do any of the subsequent presidents, although not one of them fails to mention God. The god of the civil religion is not only rather "unitarian," he is also on the austere side, much more related to order, law, and right than to salvation and love. Even though he is somewhat deist in cast, he is by no means simply a watchmaker god. He is actively interested and involved in history, with a special concern for America. Here the analogy has much less to do with natural law than with ancient Israel; the equation of America with Israel in the idea of the "American Israel" in not infrequent. What was implicit in the words of Washington already uttered becomes explicit in Jefferson's second inaugural when he said: "I shall need, too, the favor of that Being in whose hands we are, who led our fathers, as Israel of old, from their native land and planted them in a country flowing with the necessaries and comforts of life." Europe is Egypt; America, the promised land. God has led his people to establish a new sort of social order that shall be a light unto all the nations.

This theme, too, has been a continuous one in the civil religion. We have already alluded to it in the case of the Kennedy inaugural. We find it again in President Johnson's inaugural address:

They came here—the exile and the stranger, brave but frightened—to find a place where man could be his own man. They made a covenant with this land. Conceived in justice, written in liberty, bound in union, it was meant

one day to inspire the hopes of all mankind; and it binds us still. If we keep
its terms, we shall flourish.

What we have, then, from the earliest years of the republic is a collection of
beliefs, symbols, and rituals with respect to sacred things and institutionalized
in a collectivity. This religion—there seems no other word for it—while not
antithetical to and indeed sharing much in common with Christianity, was
neither sectarian nor in any specific sense Christian. At a time when the society
was overwhelmingly Christian, it seems unlikely that this lack of Christian
reference was meant to spare the feelings of the tiny non-Christian minority.
Rather, the civil religion expressed what those who set the precedents felt was
appropriate under the circumstances. It reflected their private as well as public
views. Nor was the civil religion simply "religion in general." While generality
was undoubtedly seen as a virtue by some, as in the quotation from Franklin
above, the civil religion was specific enough when it came to the topic of
America. Precisely because of this specificity, the civil religion was saved from
empty formalism and served as a genuine vehicle of national religious self-
understanding.

But the civil religion was not, in the minds of Franklin, Washington, Jefferson, or other leaders, with the exception of a few radicals like Tom Paine, ever
felt to be a substitute for Christianity. There was an implicit but quite clear
division of function between the civil religion and Christianity. Under the
doctrine of religious liberty, an exceptionally wide sphere of personal piety and
voluntary social action was left to the churches. But the churches were neither
to control the state nor to be controlled by it. The national magistrate, whatever
his private religious views, operates under the rubrics of the civil religion as
long as he is in his official capacity, as we have already seen in the case of
Kennedy. This accommodation was undoubtedly the product of a particular
historical moment and of a cultural background dominated by Protestantism
of several varieties and by the Enlightenment, but it has survived despite
subsequent changes in the cultural and religious climate.

CIVIL WAR AND CIVIL RELIGION

Until the Civil War, the American civil religion focused above all on the event
of the Revolution, which was seen as the final act of Exodus from the old lands
across the waters. The Declaration of Independence and the Constitution were
the sacred scriptures and Washington the divinely appointed Moses who led
his people out of the hands of tyranny. The Civil War, which Sidney Mead calls
"the center of American history" (1963:12), was the second great event that
involved the national self-understanding so deeply as to require expression in
the civil religion. In 1835, Tocqueville wrote that the American republic had
never really been tried, that victory in the Revolutionary War was more the
result of British preoccupation elsewhere and the presence of a powerful ally
than of any great military success of the Americans. But in 1861 the time of
testing had indeed come. Not only did the Civil War have the tragic intensity

of fratricidal strife, but it was one of the bloodiest wars of the nineteenth century; the loss of life was far greater than any previously by Americans.

The Civil War raised the deepest questions of national meaning. The man who not only formulated but in his own person embodied its meaning for Americans was Abraham Lincoln. For him the issue was not in the first instance slavery but "whether that nation, or any nation so conceived, and so dedicated, can long endure." He had said in Independence Hall in Philadelphia on 22 February 1861:

> All the political sentiments I entertain have been drawn, so far as I have been able to draw them, from the sentiments which originated in and were given to the world from this Hall. I have never had a feeling, politically, that did not spring from the sentiments embodied in the Declaration of Independence. (Nevins 1961:39)

The phrases of Jefferson constantly echo in Lincoln's speeches. His task was, first of all, to save the Union—not for America alone but for the meaning of America to the whole world so unforgettably etched in the last phrase of the Gettysburg Address.

But inevitably the issue of slavery as the deeper cause of the conflict had to be faced. In the second inaugural, Lincoln related slavery and the war in an ultimate perspective.

> If we shall suppose that American slavery is one of those offenses which, in the providence of God, must needs come, but which, having continued through His appointed time, He now wills to remove, and that He gives to both North and South this terrible war as the woe due to those by whom the offense came, shall we discern therein any departure for those divine attributes which the believers in a living God always ascribe to Him? Fondly do we hope, fervently do we pray, that this mighty scourge of war may speedily pass away. Yet, if God wills that it continue until all the wealth piled by the bondsman's two hundred and fifty years of unrequited toil shall be sunk, and until every drop of blood drawn with the lash shall by paid by another drawn with the sword, as was said three thousand years ago, so still it must be said "the judgements of the Lord are true and righteous altogether."

But he closes on a note if not of redemption then of reconciliation—"With malice toward none, with charity for all. . . ."

With the Civil War, a new theme of death, sacrifice, and rebirth enters the civil religion. It is symbolized in the life and death of Lincoln. Nowhere is it stated more vividly than the Gettysburg Address, itself part of the Lincolnian "New Testament" among the civil scriptures. Robert Lowell has recently pointed out the "insistent use of birth images" in this speech explicitly devoted to "these honored dead": "brought forth," "conceived," "created," "a new birth of freedom." He goes on to say:

The Gettysburg Address is a symbolic and sacramental act. Its verbal quality is resonance combined with a logical, matter of fact, prosaic brevity. . . . In his words, Lincoln symbolically died, just as the Union soldiers really died—and as he himself was soon really to die. By his words, he gave the field of battle a symbolic significance that it had lacked. For us and our country, he left Jefferson's ideal of freedom and equality joined to the Christian sacrificial act of death and rebirth. I believe this is a meaning that goes beyond sect or religion and beyond peace and war, and is now part of our lives as a challenge, obstacle and hope. (Nevins 1961:88–89)

Lowell is certainly right in pointing out the Christian quality of the symbolism here, but he is also right in quickly disavowing any sectarian implication. The earlier symbolism of the civil religion had been Hebraic without being in any specific sense Jewish. The Gettysburg symbolism ("those who here gave their lives, that that nation might live") is Christian without having anything to do with the Christian church.

The symbolic equation of Lincoln with Jesus was made relatively early. Herndon, who had been Lincoln's law partner, wrote:

For fifty years God rolled Abraham Lincoln through his fiery furnace. He did it to try Abraham and to purify him for his purposes. This made Mr. Lincoln humble, tender, forebearing, sympathetic to suffering, kind, sensitive, tolerant, broadening, deepening and widening his whole nature; making him the noblest and loveliest character since Jesus Christ. . . . I believe that Lincoln was God's chosen one. (Eddy 1941:162)

With the Christian archetype in the background, Lincoln, "our martyred president," was linked to the war dead, those who "gave the last full measure of devotion." The theme of sacrifice was indelibly written into the civil religion.

The new symbolism soon found both physical and ritualistic expression. The great number of the war dead required the establishment of a number of national cemeteries. Of these, the Gettysburg National Cemetery, which Lincoln's famous address served to dedicate, has been overshadowed only by the Arlington National Cemetery. Begun somewhat vindictively on the Lee estate across the river from Washington, partly with the end that the Lee family could never reclaim it (Decker and McSween 1892:60–67), it has subsequently become the most hallowed monument of the civil religion. Not only was a section set aside for the Confederate dead, but it has received the dead of each succeeding American war. It is the site of the one important new symbol to come out of World War I, the Tomb of the Unknown Soldier; more recently it has become the site of the tomb of another martyred president and its symbolic eternal flame.

Memorial Day, which grew out of the Civil War, gave ritual expression to the themes we have been discussing. As Lloyd Warner has so brilliantly analyzed it, the Memorial Day observance, especially in the towns and smaller cities of America, is a major event for the whole community involving a rededication to the martyred dead, to the spirit of sacrifice, and to the American vision. Just as Thanksgiving Day, which incidentally was securely institutionalized as an annual national holiday only under the presidency of Lincoln, serves to integrate the family into the civil religion, so Memorial Day has acted to integrate the local community into the national cult. Together with the less overtly religious Fourth of July and the more minor celebrations of Veterans Day and the birthdays of Washington and Lincoln, these two holidays provide an annual ritual calendar for the civil religion. The public school system serves as a particularly important context for the cultic celebration of the civil rituals.

In reifying and giving a name to something that, though pervasive enough when you look at it, has gone on only semiconsciously, there is risk of severely distorting the data. But the reification and the naming have already begun. The religious critics of "religion in general," or of the "religion of the 'American Way of Life,'" or of "American Shinto" have really been talking about the civil religion. As usual in religious polemic, they take as criteria the best in their own religious tradition and as typical the worst in the tradition of the civil religion. Against these critics, I would argue that the civil religion at its best is a genuine apprehension of universal and transcendent religious reality as seen in or, one could almost say, as revealed through the experience of the American people. Like all religions, it has suffered various deformations and demonic distortions. At its best, it has neither been so general that it has lacked incisive relevance to the American scene nor so particular that it has placed American society above universal human values. I am not at all convinced that the leaders of the churches have consistently represented a higher level of religious insight than the spokesmen of the civil religion. Reinhold Niebuhr has this to say of Lincoln, who never joined a church and who certainly represents civil religion at its best:

> An analysis of the religion of Abraham Lincoln in the context of the traditional religion of his time and place and of its polemical use on the slavery issue, which corrupted religious life in the days before and during the Civil War, must lead to the conclusion that Lincoln's religious convictions were superior in depth and purity to those, not only of the political leaders of his day, but of the religious leaders of the era. (Niebuhr 1961:72)

Perhaps the real animus of the religious critics has been not so much against the civil religion in itself but against its pervasive and dominating influence within the sphere of church religion. As S. M. Lipset has recently shown, American religion at least since the early nineteenth century has been predominantly activist, moralistic, and social rather than contemplative, theological, or innerly spiritual (Lipset 1964). Tocqueville spoke of American church religion as "a political institution which powerfully contributes to the maintenance of a democratic republic among the Americans" by supplying a strong moral consensus amidst continuous political change (Tocqueville 1954:310). Henry Bargy in 1902 spoke of American church religion as "la poésie du civisme" (Bargy 1902:31).

It is certainly true that the relation between religion and politics in America has been singularly smooth. This is in large part due to the dominant tradition. As Tocqueville wrote: "The greatest part of British America was peopled by men who, after having shaken off the authority of the Pope, acknowledge no other religious supremacy: they brought with them into the New World a form of Christianity which I cannot better describe than by styling it a democratic and republican religion" (Tocqueville 1954:311).

The churches opposed neither the Revolution nor the establishment of democratic institutions. Even when some of them opposed the full institution-alization of religious liberty, they accepted the final outcome with good grace and without nostalgia for an *ancien régime*. The American civil religion was never anticlerical or militantly secular. On the contrary, it borrowed selectively from the religious tradition in such a way that the average American saw no conflict between the two. In this way, the civil religion was able to build up without any bitter struggle with the church powerful symbols of national solidarity and to mobilize deep levels of personal motivation for the attainment of national goals.

Such an achievement is by no means to be taken for granted. It would seem that the problem of a civil religion is quite general in modern societies and that the way it is solved or not solved will have repercussions in many spheres. One needs only to think of France to see how differently things can go. The French Revolution was anticlerical to the core and attempted to set up an anti-Christian civil religion. Throughout modern French history, the chasm be-tween traditional Catholic symbols and the symbolism of 1789 has been immense.

American civil religion is still very much alive. [In 1963] we participated in a vivid reenactment of the sacrifice theme in connection with the funeral of our assassinated president. The American Israel theme is clearly behind both Kennedy's New Frontier and Johnson's Great Society. Let me give just one recent illustration of how the civil religion serves to mobilize support for the attainment of national goals. On 15 March 1965 President Johnson went before Congress to ask for a strong voting rights bill. Early in the speech he said:

> Rarely are we met with the challenge, not to our growth or abundance, or our welfare or our security—but rather to the values and the purposes and the meaning of our beloved nation.
>
> The issue of equal rights for American Negroes is such an issue. And should we defeat every enemy, and should we double our wealth and conquer the stars and still be unequal to this issue, then we will have failed as a people and as a nation.
>
> For with a country as with a person, "What is a man profited, if he shall gain the whole world, and lose his own soul?"

And in conclusion he said:

> Above the pyramid on the great seal of the United States it says in Latin, "God has favored our undertaking." God will not favor everything that we

do. It is rather our duty to divine his will. I cannot help but believe that
He truly understands and that He really favors the undertaking that we
begin here tonight. (U.S. Congress 1965:4924, 4926)

The civil religion has not always been invoked in favor of worthy causes. On
the domestic scene, an American Legion type of ideology that fuses God,
country, and flag has been used to attack nonconformist and liberal ideas and
groups of all kinds. Still, it has been difficult to use the words of Jefferson and
Lincoln to support special interests and undermine personal freedom. The
defenders of slavery before the Civil War came to reject the thinking of the
Declaration of Independence. Some of the most consistent of them turned
against not only Jeffersonian democracy but Reformation religion; they
dreamed of a South dominated by medieval chivalry and divine-right monarchy
(Hartz 1955). For all the overt religiosity of the radical right today, their relation
to the civil religious consensus is tenuous, as when the John Birch Society
attacks the central American symbol of Democracy itself.

With respect to America's role in the world, the dangers of distortion are
greater and the built-in safeguards of the tradition weaker. The theme of the
American Israel was used, almost from the beginning, as a justification for the
shameful treatment of the Indians so characteristic of our history. It can be
overtly or implicitly linked to the idea of manifest destiny which has been used
to legitimate several adventures in imperialism since the early nineteenth
century. Never has the danger been greater than today. The issue is not so much
one of imperial expansion, of which we are accused, as of the tendency to
assimilate all governments or parties in the world which support our immediate
policies or call upon our help by invoking the notion of free institutions and
democratic values. Those nations that are for the moment "on our side"
become "the free world." A repressive and unstable military dictatorship in
South Vietnam becomes "the free people of South Vietnam and their government." It is then part of the role of America as the New Jerusalem and "the
last best hope on earth" to defend such governments with treasure and
eventually with blood. When our soldiers are actually dying, it becomes
possible to consecrate the struggle further by involving the great theme of
sacrifice. For the majority of the American people who are unable to judge
whether the people in South Vietnam (or wherever) are "free like us," such
arguments are convincing. Fortunately President Johnson has been less ready
to assert that "God has favored our undertaking" in the case of Vietnam than
with respect to civil rights. But others are not so hesitant. The civil religion has
exercised long-term pressure for the humane solution of our greatest domestic
problems, the treatment of the Negro American. It remains to be seen how
relevant it can become for our role in the world at large, and whether we can
effectually stand for "the revolutionary beliefs for which our forebears fought,"
in John F. Kennedy's words.

The civil religion is obviously involved in the most pressing moral and
political issues of the day. But it is also caught in another kind of crisis, the
theoretical and theological, of which it is at the moment largely unaware. "God"

has clearly been a central symbol in the civil religion from the beginning and remains so today. This symbol is just as central to the civil religion as it is to Judaism or Christianity. In the late eighteenth century this posed no problem; even Tom Paine, contrary to his detractors, was not an atheist. From left to right and regardless of church or sect, all could accept the idea of God. But today, as even *Time* has recognized, the meaning of the word *God* is by no means so clear or so obvious. There is no formal creed in the civil religion. We have had a Catholic president; it is conceivable that we could have a Jewish one. But could we have an agnostic president? Could a man with conscientious scruples about using the word *God* the way Kennedy and Johnson have used it be elected chief magistrate of our country? If the whole God symbolism requires reformulation, there will be obvious consequences for the civil religion, consequences perhaps of liberal alienation and of fundamentalist ossification that have not so far been prominent in this realm. The civil religion has been a point of articulation between the profoundest commitments of the Western religious and philosophical tradition and the common beliefs of ordinary Americans. It is not too soon to consider how the deepening theological crisis may affect the future of this articulation.

THE THIRD TIME OF TRIAL

In conclusion it may be worthwhile to relate the civil religion to the most serious situation that we as Americans now face, what I call the third time of trial. The first time of trial had to do with the question of independence, whether we should or could run our own affairs in our own way. The second time of trial was over the issue of slavery, which in turn was only the most salient aspect of the more general problem of the full institutionalization of democracy within our country. This second problem we are still far from solving though we have some notable successes to our credit. But we have been overtaken by a third great problem which has led to a third great crisis, in the midst of which we stand. This is the problem of responsible action in a revolutionary world, a world seeking to attain many of the things, material and spiritual, that we have already attained. Americans have, from the beginning, been aware of the responsibility and the significance our republican experiment has for the whole world. The first internal political polarization in the new nation had to do with our attitude toward the French Revolution. But we were small and weak then, and "foreign entanglements" seemed to threaten our very survival. During the last century, our relevance for the world was not forgotten, but our role was seen as purely exemplary. Our democratic republic rebuked tyranny by merely existing. Just after World War I we were on the brink of taking a different role in the world, but once again we turned our back.

Since World War II the old pattern has become impossible. Every president since Roosevelt has been groping toward a new pattern of action in the world, one that would be consonant with our power and our responsibilities. For Truman and for the period dominated by John Foster Dulles that pattern was seen to be the great Manichaean confrontation of democracy and "the false philosophy of Communism" that provided the structure of Truman's inaugural address. But with the last year of Eisenhower and with the successive two presidents, the pattern began to shift. The great problems came to be seen as caused not solely by the evil intent of any one group of men, but as stemming from much more complex and multiple sources. For Kennedy, it was not so much a struggle against particular men as against "the common enemies of man: tyranny, poverty, disease and war itself."

But in the midst of this trend toward a less primitive conception of ourselves and our world, we have somehow, without anyone really intending it, stumbled into a military confrontation where we have come to feel that our honor is at stake. We have in a moment of uncertainty been tempted to rely on our overwhelming physical power rather than on our intelligence, and we have, in part, succumbed to this temptation. Bewildered and unnerved when our terrible power fails to bring immediate success, we are at the edge of a chasm the depth of which no man knows.

I cannot help but think of Robinson Jeffers, whose poetry seems more apt than when it was written, when he said:

> *Unhappy country, what wings you have! . . .*
> *Weep (it is frequent in human affairs), weep for the terrible magnificence of the means,*
> *The ridiculous incompetence of the reasons, the bloody and shabby*
> *Pathos of the result.*

But as so often before in similar times, we have a man of prophetic stature, without the bitterness or misanthropy of Jeffers, who, as Lincoln before him, calls this nation to its judgment:

> When a nation is very powerful but lacking in self-confidence, it is likely to behave in a manner that is dangerous both to itself and to others.
>
> Gradually but unmistakably, America is succumbing to that arrogance of power which has afflicted, weakened and in some cases destroyed great nations in the past.
>
> If the war goes on and expands, if that fatal process continues to accelerate until America becomes what it is not now and never has been, a seeker after unlimited power and empire, then Vietnam will have had a mighty and tragic fallout indeed.
>
> I do not believe that will happen. I am very apprehensive but I still remain hopeful, and even confident, that America, with its humane and democratic traditions, will find the wisdom to match its power. (*New York Times*, 29 April 1968)

Without an awareness that our nation stands under higher judgment, the tradition of the civil religion would be dangerous indeed. Fortunately, the prophetic voices have never been lacking. Our present situation brings to mind the Mexican-American War that Lincoln, among so many others, opposed. The spirit of civil disobedience that is alive today in the civil rights movement and the opposition to the Vietnam War was already clearly outlined by Henry David Thoreau when he wrote, "If the law is of such a nature that it require you to be an agent of injustice to another, then I say, break the law." Thoreau's words, "I would remind my countrymen that they are men first, and Americans at a late and convenient hour" (Arieli 1964:274), provide an essential standard for any adequate thought and action in our third time of trial. As Americans, we have been well favored in the world, but it is as men that we will be judged.

Out of the first and second times of trial have come, as we have seen, the major symbols of the American civil religion. There seems little doubt that a successful negotiation of this third time of trial—the attainment of some kind of viable and coherent world order—would precipitate a major new set of symbolic forms. So far the flickering flame of the United Nations burns too low to be the focus of a cult, but the emergence of a genuine transnational sovereignty would certainly change this. It would necessitate the incorporation of vital international symbolism into our civil religion, or, perhaps a better of putting it, it would result in American civil religion becoming simply one part of a new civil religion of the world. It is useless to speculate on the form such a civil religion might take, though it obviously would draw on religious traditions beyond the sphere of biblical religion alone. Fortunately, since the American civil religion is not the worship of the American nation but an understanding of the American experience in the light of ultimate and universal reality, the reorganization entailed by such a new situation need not disrupt the American civil religion continuity. A world civil religion could be accepted as a fulfillment and not a denial of American civil religion. Indeed, such an outcome has been the eschatological hope of American civil religion from the beginning. To deny such an outcome would be to deny the meaning of America itself.

Behind the civil religion at every point lie biblical archetypes: Exodus, Chosen People, Promised Land, New Jerusalem, Sacrificial Death, and Rebirth. But it is also genuinely American and genuinely new. It has its own prophets and its own martyrs, its own sacred events and sacred places, its own solemn rituals and symbols. It is concerned that America be a society as perfectly in accord with the will of God as men can make it, and a light to all the nations.

It has often been used and is being used today as a cloak of petty interests and ugly passions. It is in need—as is any living faith—of continual reformation, of being measured by universal standards. But it is not evident that it is incapable of growth and new insight.

It does not make any decision for us. It does not remove us from moral ambiguity, from being, in Lincoln's fine phrase, an "almost chosen people." But it is a heritage of moral and religious experience from which we still have much to learn as we formulate the decisions that lie ahead.

part two

MAINSTREAM PROTESTANTISM

In the view of many analysts, groups designated as the "mainline" or "mainstream" denominations began to lose ground in the latter half of the twentieth century. As Michaelson and Roof (1986) point out, liberal Protestant churches in the nineteenth century helped to shape and define the dominant American culture so that, by the twentieth century, they had become the religious mainline. As these groups became mainstream, they were identified with and supported the dominant culture of the United States. Consequently, cultural upheavals affected them before those less connected to the center of things. Strong identification with the dominant culture also meant that any criticisms launched at the culture would indict them as well.

In the latter twentieth century, some of the indicators illustrating these churches' loss of preeminence include loss of membership (Kelley 1972; Wuthnow 1988), declines in religious attendance (Michaelson and Roof 1986; Roof 1982), and a decline in religious giving. These trends also affected groups outside the mainline, but they had the greatest effect on the mainstream groups. Robert Wuthnow (1988a) points out that the early 1960s was a time of a general lessening of interest in religion nationwide. This was also described as a time of increasing interest and participation in more individually oriented Eastern religions (Wuthnow 1976a, 1978) and a genesis of new religious movements (Tipton 1982). Within the ranks of organized religion, especially the mainline denominations, there was a shift in moral order from the traditional collective forms to more individualized "privatized" forms (Berger 1982) in the search for self-actualization and self-understanding.

The causes of these shifts are not as generally agreed upon as are the effects on mainline denominations. Martin Marty (1976) stated that the greater the social disorganization within the culture, the greater the likelihood that radical changes would occur in the religious sphere, and Peter Berger (1982) saw these trends as part of a general secularization in the culture, partially distinguished by the rise of a "counterculture." In any case, by many estimates, denominations that had been preeminent were hard pressed by these and other trends and began to exhibit losses of membership and prestige. The "prophetic" role that the liberal churches exhibited in the 1950s and 1960s (through their advocacy of the civil rights movement and the opposition of some groups to the Vietnam conflict) began to be usurped by the newly politically active denominations of the Christian Right with their calls to change America and the world.

Roger Finke and Rodney Stark, in their provocative book *The Churching of America, 1776–1990: Winners and Losers in Our Religious Economy,* maintain that the problems confronting the mainline denominations began virtually with their inception before the beginnings of the American republic. These problems were inherent in the very design of the older, established denominations. Eventually, they were unable to cope with the challenges of the newer "upstart sects" such as Methodists and Baptists. Finke and Stark maintain that the decline of mainline denominations actually began in 1776 rather than 1960.

American religious history is seen as competition between religious groups for market share. The metaphor of the market is used to explain why certain religious groups have done well in the United States for the past two hundred years whereas others have faltered. In the authors' estimation, religious economies are similar to commercial economies. The former consist of "a market made up of a set of current and potential customers and a set of firms seeking to serve that market." In other words, the organization of their polity, the way they trained clergy, and they way they did (or failed to do) evangelism made the Congregationalists and Episcopalians and, later, the Presbyterians unable to "cope with the consequences of religious freedom and the rise of a free market religious economy" in the new American republic. Methodist and Baptist groups that were characterized by local, close-knit congregations and a democratic structure exploded in market share. They were more than a match for the older, established denominations in competing for souls. Finke and Stark maintain that the lack of marketability of the "established" groups vis-à-vis the "upstarts" during the expansion of the American republic is one of the factors that made their present decline virtually inevitable.

In 1972 Dean Kelley wrote *Why Conservative Churches Are Growing* to explain the rapid growth of sectarian groups and the decline of the older Protestant "mainline" bodies. His much-debated and much-tested thesis was that churches that made the most demands on their members experienced the greatest gains, whereas mainline denominations that did not "cost" anything to belong to (in terms of time and commitment) experienced the greatest declines.

Kelley's thesis is extended in Laurence Iannaccone's insightful article, "Why Strict Churches Are Strong." Iannaccone provides a conceptualization of the church-sect distinction that transcends some of the limitations of the original model. One of the standard criticisms of the model was that it was too influenced by Western theology and church history to be applicable to all groups. In Iannaccone's model, one of the problems that plagues religious groups is "free riding." This is defined as members receiving more benefits from the group than they give back. "Because each member benefits whether or not he contributes to the common cause, each has a strong incentive to minimize his own efforts and 'free ride' off those of others." The presence of free riders thus dilutes the efforts of the group by reducing the average level of participation for all group members. Strict churches who make more demands on their members reduce free riding. Strictness "screens out members who lack commitment and stimulates participation among those who remain." This encourages the growth of the group. Professor Iannaccone attempts to transcend some of the limitations of the traditional church-sect model by positing the numerous religious demands of various groups as functionally equivalent solutions to free riding. He concludes that religions (not simply Christian or Western ones) that demand similar levels of sacrifice display fundamental behavioral similarities despite the peculiarities of their individual histories and theologies. Thus by using strictness and demand rather than specific theological makeup, he broadens the church-sect distinction to have greater utility.

In the excerpt from *American Mainline Religion: Its Changing Shape and Future,* W. Clark Roof and William McKinney explain the changes in mainline bodies since the 1960s in terms of changing religious demographics and religious switching. As they put it, "demography has proven to be destiny" for American Protestantism. Growth or decline of religious groups is based on natural growth (fertility and loyalty to the group) and conversion or defection. A high birth rate and substantial conversions from other groups equals some growth because of the high number of children in the group, whereas a low birth rate coupled with a high death rate and high conversions to other groups equals decline. The higher fertility rates of groups such as the Jehovah's Witnesses and Nazarenes give them an advantage in the religious marketplace over groups with lower birth rates such as Methodists and Episcopalians.

Another place where demographics catch up with mainline groups is the increasing age structure of these groups. Roof and McKinney point out that by the 1980s, the average age of liberal Protestants was almost four years older than that of conservative Protestants. When this increasing age is coupled with a general outmigration of younger Americans from organized religion in the 1970s and 1980s, the average age of mainline groups is pushed significantly upward.

Roof and McKinney also explore the importance of religious switching between denominations. They point out that 40 percent of American Protestants are in a denomination different from that in which they began their religious lives. Persons leaving the established faith communities can move either to other faith communities or into the secular and nonreligious sector. In the decades after World War II, mainline denominations benefited from switching as people changed to them as a matter of upward mobility.

Thus, the pattern of net gains or losses for a particular group is based on stability (the number it retains) and attractiveness (the number who switch into the group). In one of their most interesting contributions, Roof and McKinney maintain that membership stability is not simply a matter of theology. Groups at both ends of the theological continuum have relatively high rates of religious switching, obviously for different reasons. Stability is defined as a function more of "communal belonging" than theology. More conservative groups have stronger "ethnic or quasi-ethnic loyalties" than more liberal groups. The "nonaffiliates" lack these loyalties and ties and thus are among the highest switchers.

Roof and McKinney also note that liberal churches still gain members from conservative churches at a higher rate than conservatives gain from liberals, but liberal groups lose more to nonaffiliates. The real challenge to liberal groups is not losing out to the conservatives but to the "growing secular constituency." In their analysis, all groups have lost ground owing to the general outmovement of young people from organized religion, which began in the 1960s. The liberals have lost members and part of their future because of unfavorable demographics and "the growing secular drift of many of their not-so-highly-committed members." A small portion of these losses may be offset by others switching into mainline denominations, but those who switch into these groups tend to be older, and this trend exacerbates the aging problem. Also, the problems of the liberal denominations have now begun to affect the rest of the religious mainline.

ADDITIONAL READINGS

HAMMOND, P. E. 1992. *Religion and Personal Autonomy: The Third Disestablishment in America.* Columbia: University of South Carolina Press.
The focus of this well-written book is an evaluation of the movement in American religion since the 1960s as being away from a matter of collective import to a matter of individual import.

NEITZ, M. J. 1987. *Charisma and Community: A Study of Religious Commitment within the Charismatic Renewal.* New Brunswick, NJ: Transaction Publishers.
Chapter 7, "Enthusiastic Religion in American Culture," provides an excellent overview of the history of charismatic religion in the United States.

WARNER, R. S. 1988. *New Wine in Old Wineskins: Evangelicals and Liberals in a Small-Town Church.* Berkeley: University of California Press.
This in-depth study centered in a local church fleshes out some of the theories of why churches grow and how they change.

roger finke and rodney stark

THE CHURCHING OF AMERICA

ON RELIGIOUS ECONOMIES

Some readers may shudder at the use of "market" terminology in discussions of religion. But we see nothing inappropriate in acknowledging that where religious affiliation is a matter of choice, religious organizations must compete for members and that the "invisible hand" of the marketplace is as unforgiving of ineffective religious firms as it is of their commercial counterparts.

We are not the first to use an explicit market model to explore the interplay among religious organizations. Indeed, . . . Adam Smith did so very persuasively back in 1776. Moreover, it was typical for European visitors to use economic language to explain the religious situation in America to their friends back home. For example, Francis Grund, an Austrian who eventually became an American citizen, wrote in 1837:

> In America, every clergyman may be said to do business on his own account, and under his own firm. He alone is responsible for any deficiency in the discharge of his office, as he alone is entitled to all the credit due to his exertions. He always acts as principal, and is therefore more anxious, and will make greater efforts to obtain popularity, than one who serves for wages. The actual stock in any of these firms is, of course, less than the immense capital of the Church of England; but the aggregate amount of business transacted by them jointly may nevertheless be greater in the United States. (Powell 1967:77)

We will use economic concepts such as markets, firms, market penetration, and segmented markets to analyze the success and failure of religious bodies. Religious economies are like commercial economies in that they consist of a market made up of a set of current and potential customers and a set of firms seeking to serve that market. The fate of these firms will depend upon (1) aspects of their organizational structures, (2) their sales representatives, (3) their product, and (4) their marketing techniques. Translated into more churchly language, the relative success of religious bodies (especially when confronted with an unregulated economy) will depend upon their polity, their clergy, their religious doctrines, and their evangelization techniques.

The use of economic tools in no way suggests that the content of religion is unimportant, that it is all a matter of clever marketing and energetic selling. To the contrary, we will argue that the primary market weakness that has caused the failure of many denominations, and the impending failure of many more, is precisely a matter of doctrinal content, or the lack of it. That is, we will repeatedly suggest that as denominations have modernized their doctrines and embraced temporal values, they have gone into decline.

The primary value of analyzing American religious history through a market-oriented lens is that in this way some well-established deductions from the principles of supply and demand can illuminate what might otherwise seem a very disorderly landscape (as it indeed often appears to be in standard histories of the subject). Consider the following examples.

First, as in the analysis of market economies, a major consideration in analyzing religious economies is their degree of regulation. Some are virtually unregulated; some are restricted to state-imposed monopolies. In keeping with supply and demand principles, to the degree that a religious economy is unregulated, pluralism will thrive. That is, the "natural" state of religious economies is one in which a variety of religious groups successfully caters to the special needs and interests of specific market segments. This variety arises because of the inherent inability of a single product to satisfy very divergent tastes. Or, to note the specific features of religious firms and products, pluralism arises because of the inability of a single religious organization to be at once worldly and otherworldly, strict and permissive, exclusive and inclusive, while the market will always contain distinct consumer segments with strong preferences on each of these aspects of faith. This occurs because of "normal" variations in the human condition such as social class, age, gender, health, life experiences, and socialization.

In fact, because of this underlying differentiation of consumer preferences, religious economies can never be successfully monopolized, even when a religious organization is backed by the state. At the height of its temporal power, the medieval church was surrounded by heresy and dissent. Of course, when repressive efforts are very great, religions in competition with the state-sponsored monopoly will be forced to operate underground. But whenever and wherever repression falters, lush pluralism will break through. . . .

THE UPSTART SECTS WIN AMERICA, 1776–1850

We argue that, perhaps ironically, the decline of the old mainline denominations was caused by their inability to cope with the consequences of religious freedom and the rise of a free market religious economy. But before taking up these matters, it will be helpful to examine the great shift in religious fortunes that occurred between 1776 and 1850.

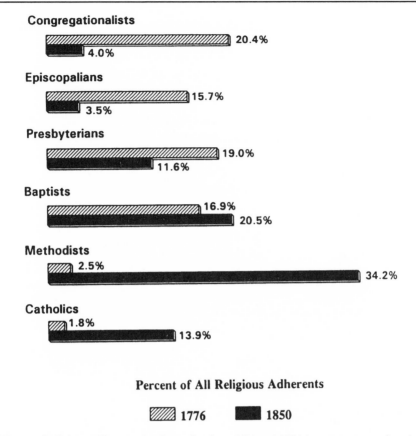

Percent of All Religious Adherents

▨ 1776   ■ 1850

Figure 1. Religious adherents by denomination, 1776 and 1850 (as percentage of total adherents).

If we compare the "market share" of major bodies in 1776 and 1850 (see Figure 1), we see that in 1776 Congregationalists, Episcopalians, and Presbyterians dominated—although their overall market penetration was very poor. Then, in just seventy-four years, the combined market total of these three bodies shrank to only 19.1 percent of religious adherents, even though the proportion belonging to churches had about doubled, to 34 percent.

For Congregationalism, the shift approached total collapse. The major denomination in 1776, it can only be described as a minor body less than eight decades later—falling from more than 20 percent of total adherents to but 4 percent. Despite this extraordinary shift in their fortunes, Congregationalist leaders during this era expressed surprisingly little concern, aside from complaints about a general decline in religion during the late eighteenth century. Perhaps they didn't think in terms of rates, and instead took pride in the fact that their number of members had more than tripled. It was not until the 1960s, when the failures of the Congregationalists first turned into losses in actual numbers rather than just in market share, that serious expressions of alarm were heard.

The Episcopalians also fared badly in terms of their share of the religious market, falling from a strong second to last place among leading denominations—from 15.7 percent to 3.5 percent of all church adherents.

The Presbyterians' share of the religious market also declined, from 19 percent to 11.6 percent. But the Presbyterians' growth in actual numbers, unlike that of the Congregationalists and the Episcopalians, did keep pace with the growth of the population. The Presbyterians fared better because they were able to achieve some growth on the new American frontiers. Their share declined, however, because their growth failed to match the expansion of the proportion who were churched.

During this same period, the Baptists achieved very substantial growth, primarily through conversion, and the Catholics grew rapidly, through immigration. But the major shift in the American religious market in this period was the meteoric rise of Methodism. In 1776 the Methodists were a tiny religious society with only sixty-five churches scattered through the colonies. Seven decades later they towered over the nation. In 1850 there were 13,302 Methodist congregations, enrolling more than 2.6 million members—the largest single denomination, accounting for more than a third of all American church members. For such growth to occur in eighty years seems nearly miraculous. But the general histories of American religion would make it even more of a miracle. Because all agree that religion fell into a state of sad neglect in the wake of the American Revolution, they would confine the rise of Methodism to less than fifty years. . . .

WHY THE UPSTARTS WON

Where there are winners there are losers. Much can be learned from a comparison of the two primary winners in the American religious economy between 1776 and 1850, the Methodists and Baptists, with the two primary losers, the Congregationalists and Episcopalians. There also is much to be gained from examination of the "also-ran" Presbyterians, whose growth kept pace with the population, but not with the increase in the proportions active in churches.

ORGANIZATIONAL STRUCTURES

Social scientists agree that the structure of an organization can have tremendous impact on its efficiency and success. This has been especially stressed in studies of religious organizations (Harrison 1959; Wood and Zald 1966; Szafran 1976). Nevertheless, it would appear at first glance that variations in denominational polity played little or no part in who grew and who did not.

The two most successful denominations, the Baptist and the Methodists, seem to be polar extremes in terms of polity. Historians have often cited the democratic structure of the Baptist church as an attractive feature to the people of the early frontier (Sweet 1952; Ahlstrom 1972; Hudson 1981), but the Methodist church was even more successful on the frontiers, and everyone knows the Methodists have a hierarchical structure with strong, centralized authority placing control firmly in the hands of the clergy. Similar variation would seem to exist among the losers. The Protestant Episcopal church and the Congregational church seem at opposite extremes, with the Presbyterians falling somewhere in between.

When we look more closely at these denominational organizations, however, we find that historians were correct to stress the way in which the democratic congregational life of the Baptists helped them church the frontiers. But with the exception of Hatch (1989), historians have failed to note that this applied to the Methodists as well. For in those days the Methodists were about as democratic locally as were the Baptists. The local congregations were divided into small, close-knit groups called classes. Each class met on a weekly basis and was composed of approximately a dozen members. Here is where the zeal of camp meetings was maintained, intimate fellowship was achieved, and the behavior of the faithful was monitored. But the class also helped to select potential leaders. Exhorters and local preachers were frequently recommended by their class, and each was subject to an "annual examination of character in the quarterly conference" (Gorrie 1852:295). And although class leaders, who were deemed responsible for the "moral and Christian conduct" of members, were appointed by the itinerant in newly established missions, the more common practice was for the local (unpaid) preacher to appoint and supervise their activities. As a result, the average Methodist congregation was a model of "Congregationalism," in the sense that control actually resided in the hands of the adult membership.

In this era, the actual pastoral functions were performed in most Methodist churches by unpaid, local "amateurs" just like those serving the Baptist congregations up the road. A professional clergy had not yet centralized control of the Methodist organization. True, the circuit riders were full-time professionals vested with substantial authority. But they only visited a congregation from time to time and played the role of visiting bishop and evangelist more than the role of pastor. It was only when the circuit riders dismounted and accepted "settled" pastorates that the "episcopal" structure of Methodism came to the fore. Indeed, it may well be that to the extent that the Methodists were able to create a national organization based on the circuit riders, they had the best of both worlds—centralized direction and local control (Miyakawa 1964). In any event, despite apparent differences in polity, both the Methodists and the Baptists were surprisingly democratic and thus able to respond to the actual desires of the market.

In contrast, the Congregationalists were not nearly so "congregational" as either of the upstart sects. That Congregationalism was dominated by a highly professional clergy was the result of two interrelated factors. First, . . . the Congregationalists had opted for a highly educated clergy. This led to a chronic shortage of clergy and maximized their bargaining power, both individually and collectively. A second factor was establishment. As the established church of most New England colonies, Congregational churches were organized at town meetings, were supported by the town's "religious taxes," and "the towns played the customary role in concurring in the choice of the minister"

(McLoughlin 1971:795). This system made the clergy influential in local governmental affairs. Moreover, establishment allowed the Congregationalists to depend on secular organizational structures to provide central coordination of their religious affairs within New England and left them with no alternative model for coordination among congregations. Whereas the Baptists would form regional associations whenever four or five Baptist churches were established, Congregational churches established outside of the New England region were often isolated units, lacking any regional support. In fact, to be united with churches beyond the local state line was contrary to the organizational plan of the early Congregational churches (Atkins and Fagley 1942).

The 1801 Plan of Union with the Presbyterians illustrates the organizational problems of the early Congregationalists. Although the plan, first supported by the Congregational General Assembly of Connecticut and later approved by the General Associations of Massachusetts, New Hampshire, Vermont, and Maine, was designed to unify the two denominations' frontier missionizing efforts, it resulted in the Congregationalists' being swallowed up by the Presbyterians. This was in large measure because the latter had established presbyteries, in addition to congregations, on the frontier. Because there was no alternative Congregational central structure, the Plan of Union led whatever individual Congregational churches that did arise to end up joining a presbytery and thus effectively to switch denominations (Sweet 1950). Although as Williston Walker (1894) claimed, the Plan of Union was a "wholly honorable arrangement, and designed to be fair to both sides," it inadvertently favored the Presbyterians because only they had a structure sufficient to sustain congregations in less settled areas. As "their presbyteries were rapidly spread over the missionary district," Walker continued, "the natural desire for fellowship . . . led Congregational ministers to accept the welcome offered therein" (1894:317–318). The Congregational associations in the individual New England states were simply not able, or not willing, to support the national expansion of their church. In the end, the plan slowed the decline of the Presbyterians and confined the Congregationalists to New England.

The Episcopalians and the Presbyterians did have national and regional organizations, but each was beset with organizational problems. The Revolution did great damage to the Episcopalians. Many members supported the Crown and fled at war's end. Sweet (1952) reported that the majority of Virginia's 100 Anglican parishes were defunct by the end of the war and that the number of active Anglican clergy had dropped from ninety-one to twenty-eight. Sweet also estimated that North Carolina, Georgia, and Pennsylvania each had only one active Anglican priest by the end of the Revolution. In addition to these disasters, the Episcopalians lost their formal connection with the Church of England, thus ending their supervision by the Bishop of London and the substantial flow of subsidies and mission clergy provided by the Society for the Propagation of the Gospel in Foreign Parts. Although the process of national reorganization began in 1783, effective new central authority was lacking for several more decades. Thus in a critical time, when rapid growth was shaping a new nation, the Episcopal church was struggling to support its remaining churches and to recover from the war. It lacked the resources to expand its share of the religious market.

In contrast, the Presbyterians were well organized and emerged from the Revolution with enhanced prestige. Sweet (1964:3) suggested that "no church in America, at the close of the War for Independence, was in a better position of immediate expansion than was the Presbyterian." The Presbyterians had established strong presbyteries throughout the nation, and, as we have seen, they fared much better than did the Congregationalists or the Episcopalians during this era. Their growth, however, was constantly plagued by divisions within their organization. Although the Plan of Union contributed to their increases, the new "presbygational" churches also contributed to doctrinal and polity controversies. Holding camp meetings similarly contributed to Presbyterian growth in rural and frontier areas, but this practice aroused disapproval "back East," leading to sharp regional and doctrinal controversy. The Presbyterians worked tirelessly for unity, which they understood to be rooted in uniformity. Through their efforts to enforce strict national standards on polity and doctrine, they frequently shattered the very unity they sought and prompted regional schisms.

It appears that the situation facing the churches in this period placed very stern demands on denominations to become competitive organizations prepared to seek souls to the ends of civilization and beyond. Polity alone would not achieve this, but organizational structures that prevented a *nationwide* effort were a fatal flaw.

laurence iannaccone

WHY STRICT CHURCHES ARE STRONG

In 1972 Dean Kelley published a remarkable book titled *Why Conservative Churches Are Growing* (Kelley 1972). In it he documented a striking shift in the fortunes of America's oldest and largest Protestant denominations. After two centuries of growth that culminated in the 1950s, virtually all mainline Protestant denominations had begun losing members. The losses, however, were far from uniform. Liberal denominations were declining much more rapidly than conservative denominations, and the most conservative were growing. The varying rates of growth and decline meant that the mainline denominations' misfortune could not be attributed to pervasive secularization. A valid explanation could only be rooted in traits or circumstances that differed from one denomination to the next. Kelley proposed such an explanation. He traced the success of conservative churches to their ability to attract and retain an active and committed membership, characteristics that he in turn attributed to their strict demands for complete loyalty, unwavering belief, and rigid adherence to a distinctive lifestyle. . . .

Twenty years have done nothing to weaken the force of Kelley's argument. The trends he identified continue unabated, so much so that "small sects" such as the Mormons and the Assemblies of God now outnumber "mainline" denominations such as the Episcopal church and the United Church of Christ. Statistical studies have confirmed that denominational growth rates correlate strongly with "strictness" and its concomitants (Hoge 1979), and new historical research has revealed that the mainline's *share* of the church-going population has been declining since the American Revolution (Finke and Stark 1992).

Even so, many researchers question the causal role of strictness. They look to other factors to account for commitment, participation, and membership. . . .

In this article, I argue that Kelley was correct. In showing how strictness overcomes free-rider problems I embed Kelley's thesis within a much broader rational choice approach to religion. I have previously claimed that rational choice theory provides an alternative paradigm in the sociology of religion, one that unifies many of the generalizations that currently compete for researchers'

This is a shortened version of Laurence R. Iannaccone, "Why Strict Churches Are Strong," American Journal of Sociology *99(5):1180–1211 (1994). Reprinted with permission of the* University of Chicago Press © *1994 and the author.*

attention (Iannaccone 1992; see also Warner 1993). Here I provide a unified approach to the study of Protestant denominations, Jewish denominations, cults, communes, and church-sect theory. . . .

I do not thereby assert that these benefits persist, no matter how strict a group becomes. To the contrary, both theory and data imply "optimal" levels of strictness, beyond which strictness discourages most people from joining or remaining within the group. . . .

RESTATING KELLEY'S THESIS

How do we define strictness? Kelley (1986:79–84) cataloged three traits of the ideal-typical strict church—absolutism, conformity, and fanaticism—and contrasted them to three traits of the more lenient church—relativism, diversity, and dialogue. Strict churches proclaim an exclusive truth—a closed, comprehensive, and eternal doctrine. They demand adherence to a distinctive faith, morality, and lifestyle. They condemn deviance, shun dissenters, and repudiate the outside world. They frequently embrace "eccentric traits," such as distinctive diet, dress, or speech, that invite ridicule, isolation, and persecution.

For the purpose of formal analysis, I shall narrow this catalog to a single attribute: the degree to which a group limits and thereby increases the *cost* of nongroup activities, such as socializing with members of other churches or pursuing "secular" pastimes. This radical simplification allows us to model and test Kelley's thesis. It also accords with Kelley's (1986:xxii) own belief that church strength depends largely on a single characteristic which he alternately called "seriousness," "strictness," "costliness," and "bindingness."

A cost-based definition of strictness highlights the paradox in Kelley's thesis. After all, it is the essence of rationality to seek benefits and avoid costs. If strictness increases costs, why should anyone join a strict church? The religious marketplace teems with less demanding alternatives. Why become a Mormon or a Seventh-Day Adventist, let alone a Krishna or a Moonie, when the Methodists and Presbyterians wait with open arms? Mormons abstain from caffeine and alcohol, Seventh-Day Adventists avoid eating meat, Krishnas shave their heads, wear robes, and chant in public, Moonies submit to arranged marriages, Jehovah's Witnesses refuse transfusions, Orthodox Jews wear side curls and yarmulkes, conduct no business on the Sabbath, and observe numerous dietary restrictions, and monks take vows of celibacy, poverty, and silence. These practices are problematic, not only because they deviate from "normal" behavior, but also because they appear completely counterproductive. Pleasures are sacrificed, opportunities foregone, and social stigma is risked, or even invited. The problem is epitomized by the burnt offering, a religious rite designed specifically to destroy valuable resources. How can burnt offerings and their equivalents survive in religious markets when self-interest and competitive pressures drive them out of most other markets? As Kelley pointed out, the question is not merely one of survival; religious groups that demand such sacrifices are more successful than those that do not.

I shall argue that strict demands "strengthen" a church in three ways: they raise overall levels of commitment, they increase average rates of participation, and they enhance the net benefits of memberships. These strengths arise because strictness mitigates free-rider problems that otherwise lead to low levels of member commitment and participation. Free riders threaten most collective activities, and religious activities are no exception. Church members may attend services, call upon the pastor for counsel, enjoy the fellowship of their peers, and so forth, without ever putting a dollar in the plate or bringing a dish to the potluck. Direct monitoring (of attendance, contributions, and other overt behaviors) fails to solve the problem because it tends to undermine critical group attributes such as commitment, enthusiasm, and solidarity. But seemingly unproductive costs provide an indirect solution. These costs screened people whose participation would otherwise be low, while at the same time they increase participation among those who do join. As a consequence, apparently unproductive sacrifices can increase the utility of group members. Efficient religions with perfectly rational members may thus embrace stigma, self-sacrifice, and bizarre behavioral standards. Strictness works.

HOW STRICTNESS LEADS TO STRENGTH

Religion is a social phenomenon, born and nurtured among groups of people. In principle, perhaps, religion can be purely private, but in practice it appears to be much more compelling and attractive when experienced in groups. In the austere but precise language of economics, religion is a "commodity" that people produce *collectively*. My religious satisfaction thus depends both on my "inputs" and on those of others. The pleasure and edification that I derive from a Sunday service does not depend solely on what I bring to the service (through my presence, attentiveness, public singing, etc.); it also depends on how many others attend, how warmly they greet me, how well they sing or recite (in English, Latin, Hebrew, Arabic, etc.), how enthusiastically they read and pray, and how deep their commitments are. The collective side of religion encompasses numerous group activities such as listening to sermons, scriptural studies, testimonial meetings, liturgies, worship, hymn singing, and sacramental acts. However, it also extends to religious belief and religious experiences—particularly the most dramatic experiences such as speaking in tongues, miraculous healings, prophetic utterances, and ecstatic trances—all of which are more sustainable and satisfying when experienced collectively.

FREE-RIDER PROBLEMS

Like other collective activities, religion is susceptible to "free riding," a problem first analyzed by Mancur Olson (1965) and the subsequent focus of much social-scientific research. The problem arises whenever the members of a group receive benefits in proportion to their collective, rather than individual, efforts. Because each member benefits whether or not he contributes to the common cause, each has a strong incentive to minimize his own efforts and "free ride" off those of others. If enough members yield to this temptation, the collective activity will surely fail. Free riding has wrecked many an enterprise, from small charities to global environmental initiatives. . . .

Two types of free-rider problems are particularly common in religion. The first arises in mixed populations where levels of religious commitment vary from person to person. In any such group, people with low levels of religious commitment tend to free ride off those with higher levels; they tend to take more than they give. They may do so unintentionally. Nevertheless, if only because their lower commitment inclines them to participate and contribute less than others, their mere presence dilutes a group's resources, reducing the average level of participation, enthusiasm, energy, and the like. Heterogeneity can thus undermine intense fellowships and major undertakings. Lacking a way to identify and exclude free riders, highly committed people end up saddled with anemic, resource-poor congregations. . . .

A second type of free-rider problem persists even when members share a common level of commitment.[1] Participation no longer varies from person to person, but the *average* level of participation remains suboptimal and hence inefficient. . . .

One need not look far to find an anemic congregation plagued by free-rider problems—a visit to the nearest liberal, mainline Protestant church usually will suffice. But case studies of cults and communes provide more striking examples. In such groups, which can only survive with high levels of commitment, the costs of free riding are laid bare. . . .

REDUCING FREE RIDING

Although it is theoretically possible for religious groups to overcome their free-rider problems through screening and monitoring, such schemes prove unworkable in practice. For example, one theoretically ideal solution is for groups to . . . pay people to participate fully. But this solution requires that individual behavior be accurately observed and appropriately rewarded. In reality, the aspects of religious participation that confer the greatest external benefits (effort, enthusiasm, solidarity, etc.) are intrinsically difficult to monitor and reward. The willingness to pay membership dues is a poor proxy for these qualities because income correlates weakly with most dimensions of religious commitment, and any attempt to directly subsidize the observable aspects of religious participation (such as church attendance) will almost certainly backfire. The Salvation Army will readily attest that the promise of free meals guarantees an audience of less than average commitment. How much greater would be the temptation to feign belief in the face of cash compensation? . . .

There remains, however, an indirect solution to the free-rider problem. Instead of subsidizing participation, churches can penalize or prohibit *alternative* activities that compete for members' resources. In mixed populations, such penalties and prohibitions tend to screen out the less committed members. They act like entry fees and thus discourage anyone not seriously interested in "buying" the product. Only those willing to pay the price remain. . . .

Penalties and prohibitions can also raise average levels of group participation and group utility in homogeneous populations (whether they began as homogeneous or became so after the prohibitions persuaded the less committed members to leave). To see why, note that prohibiting an activity effectively increases its price, since the activity's full cost now includes the penalties that may be meted out if it is discovered. Increasing the price of an activity reduces the demand for it, but increases the demand for its substitutes, that is, for competing activities. Hence, a religious group can indirectly increase its members' levels of participation by prohibiting or otherwise increasing the cost of alternative activities. Governments often employ similar strategies. For example, many countries encourage the use of public transportation both directly, through subsidized fares, and indirectly, through special taxes and constraints on automobile usage. . . .

It might at first seem that any group unable to monitor members' participation in its own activities will have an even harder time restricting their involvement in other activities, but this is not so. It is often much easier to observe and penalize mere involvement in competing groups than it is to accurately determine the level of involvement in one's own group. Alternatively, it may be possible to demand of members some distinctive, stigmatizing behavior that inhibits participation or reduces productivity in alternative contexts—having shaved heads, wearing pink robes, or being in an isolated location does the job quite effectively. Commenting on his religion's distinctive dress and grooming requirements, a Sikh put it thus: "The guru wanted to raise a body of men who would not be able to deny their faith when questioned, but whose external appearance would invite persecution and breed the courage to resist it" (Singh 1953:31). . . .

Costly strictures thus mitigate the externality problems faced by religious groups. Distinctive diet, dress, grooming, and social customs constrain and often stigmatize members, making participation in alternative activities more costly. Potential members are forced to choose whether to participate fully or not at all. The seductive middle ground is eliminated, and, paradoxically, those who remain find that their welfare has been increased. It follows that perfectly rational people can be drawn to decidedly unconventional groups. This conclusion sharply contrasts with the view, popular among psychiatrists, clinical psychologists, and the media, that conversion to deviant religious sects and cults is inherently pathological, the consequence of either psychological abnormality or coercive "brainwashing" (Robbins 1988:722–789).

EVIDENCE AND APPLICATIONS

The proposed model does not merely "rationalize" strange behaviors and deviant demands. It also predicts the empirical correlates of strictness, extends Kelley's thesis, and throws new light on the hoary theme of church versus sect.

MEASURING STRICTNESS

To address these issues, one must first assess the relative "strictness" of different religions. Objective measures are hard to obtain, both because religious demands take many forms and because most data sources ignore the issue of cost, but comparisons based on expert judgment and common sense will suffice here.

Consider, for example, the three major Jewish denominations. It goes without saying that Orthodox Judaism imposes the greatest costs on its members and that Reform Judaism imposes the least. Conservative Judaism falls between these extremes, though it is generally closer to Reform than to Orthodox. One may verify this ranking any number of ways—by employing expert judgment, conventional wisdom, official doctrine, or observable practices—the results never change.

Although Protestant denominations prove harder to classify, some generalizations again lie beyond dispute. Scholars, citizens, journalists, and church members all agree that "sectarian" groups, like the Jehovah's Witnesses, Mormons, and Seventh-Day Adventists, are stricter and more demanding than mainline denominations like the Episcopalians, Methodists, and the United Church of Christ. Indeed, the standard ranking begins with the "liberal," "mainline" denominations, and runs through "Evangelicals," "Fundamentalists," "Pentecostals," and finally "sects." A large body of empirical research confirms the general validity of this ranking (Stark and Glock 1968; Roof and McKinney 1987:72–147). The members of more conservative denominations do indeed adopt a more restrictive lifestyle than their mainline counterparts. They are, for example, less likely to drink (Cochran et al. 1988), engage in premarital sex (Beck et al. 1991), or experiment with alternative, "new age" religions (Tamney et al. 1991; Donahue 1991).

Expert judgments refine the standard Protestant ranking. Consider, for example, a study that surveyed twenty-one experts (church historians, sociologists of religion, denominational leaders, and seminary educators) nominated as "maximally knowledgeable and representative of the total spectrum of denominations" (Hoge and Roozen 1979:E-4).[2] The experts rated sixteen major Protestant denominations on a series of seven-point scales. One of these scales provides an excellent operational definition of strictness and cost. It asks the respondent to rate each denomination according to the following criteria: "Does the denomination emphasize maintaining a separate and distinctive lifestyle or morality in personal and family life, in such areas as dress, diet, drinking, entertainment, uses of time, marriage, sex, child rearing, and the like? Or does it affirm the current American mainline lifestyle in these respects?" The results are reassuring. Liberal mainline denominations (Episcopal, Methodist, Presbyterian, and the United Church of Christ) scored as the least distinctive, followed by moderate mainline denominations (Evangelical Lutheran, Reformed Church, Disciples of Christ, and American Baptist), conservatives and evangelicals (Missouri Synod Lutheran and Southern Baptist), and,

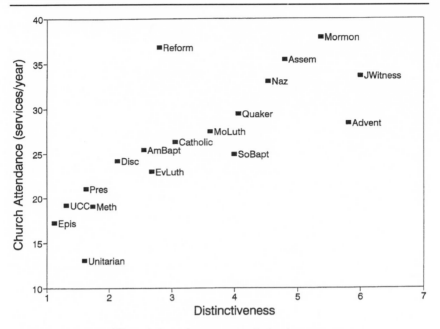

Figure 1. Attendance versus distinctiveness.

finally, Fundamentalists, Pentecostals, and sects (Nazarene, Assemblies of God, Seventh-Day Adventists, and Mormon).[3]

In order to assess this scale's reliability and to expand the set of denominations, I replicated the survey using sixteen new experts. Two findings stand out. First, the rankings remain unchanged across the two studies. Despite the passage of fifteen years and the use of different raters, the correlation between the new and old distinctiveness scales is an astonishing .99. Second, the level of agreement among the experts is extraordinarily high. The reliability of denominational scores (as measured by Cronbach's alpha) is over .98 and the mean correlation between each expert's ratings and the average standardized ratings of all other experts is .85. The experts' average score for each denomination can be read off the horizontal axis of Figure 1.

A THEORY OF CHURCH AND SECT

I have shown that cost-based scales are reliable. They are also useful, yielding a formal theory of church and sect more elegant, general, and empirically fruitful than its predecessors.

Traditional theories of church and sect have been justly criticized as not being theories at all, but rather complex, multiattribute typologies that offer static descriptions at the expense of testable implications (Stark and Bainbridge 1985:19–23).[4] The ideal-typical sect might be defined as a religious organization with a highly committed, voluntary, and converted membership, a separatist orientation, an exclusive social structure, a spirit of regeneration, and an attitude of ethical austerity and demanding asceticism. The ideal-typical church would have its own complex list of attributes: birth-based membership, inclusiveness and universalism, hierarchical structures, an adaptive, compromising stance vis-à-vis the larger society, and so forth. Not withstanding a certain "intuitive rightness," such lists fail to accommodate the majority of real-world religions, provide limited insight into nonideal, "mixed-type" cases, and lack predictions or causal arguments linking one attribute to another.

In contrast, the present scheme is simple, unidimensional, and powerfully predictive. It derives from a model that characterizes numerous religious demands as functionally equivalent solutions to free-rider problems. Religions that demand similar levels of sacrifice should therefore display fundamental behavioral similarities, despite the peculiarities of their individual histories, theologies and organizational structures.[5]

Similarities do in fact appear when we group religion according to the (rated) stringency of their demands. Consider, for example, the summary statistics in Table 1 obtained from the General Social Survey 1984–90. (The table's membership groupings reflect the respondents' self-described religious preferences.) Compared to members of other Protestant denominations, sect members are poorer and less educated, contribute more money and attend more services, hold stronger beliefs, belong to more church-related groups, and are less involved in secular organizations. The differences are strong, striking, and statistically significant. Moreover, for virtually every variable the pattern of variation is monotonic, increasing (or decreasing) steadily as one moves from liberal to moderate to conservative and, finally, to sect groups.[6] Figures 1–4 show that these relationships remain strong even when disaggregated to the level of individual denominations. In Figure 1, for example, the correlation between denominational distinctiveness and average rates of church attendance is .82.

The cost-based theory of church and sect rebuts the compliant that religious typologies are inherently ad hoc, rooted in the particulars of Christian theology and European church history and inapplicable to other religious traditions (Roberts 1984:225; Eister 1967). The theory grows from abstract considerations of collective production, rationality, and free riding and should therefore apply to other, collectively oriented religions, such as Judaism and Islam.

This proves, in fact, to be the case. Data from the 1990 National Jewish Population Survey reveal patterns of interdenominational variation virtually identical to those observed within Protestantism. (See Table 2, which arranges Jewish denominations using the same distinctiveness scale used in Table 1.) Compared to members of Reform Judaism, Orthodox Jews are poor and somewhat less educated, devote more time and money to religious activities, hold stronger religious beliefs, are more involved in their own religious community, and separate themselves more thoroughly from non-Jewish society. Here again, the differences are strong, significant, and consistent. One might even say that Jewish denominations fit the idealized church-sect continuum even more neatly than do the Christian denominations.[7]

Table 1
Protestant Denominational Differences

	Liberal	Moderate	Conservative	Sects	t Value
Household income	38.0	31.0	31.6	27.0	8.9
(in thousands/year)	(23.2)	(20.9)	(20.7)	(20.0)	
Respondent education	13.8	12.5	12.1	11.3	15.1
(in years)	(2.92)	(2.86)	(2.84)	(3.02)	
Sunday attendance	20.9	25.2	31.3	48.5	13.7
(services attended per year)	(25.4)	(29.2)	(33.4)	(42.7)	
Weekday attendance	2.7	6.3	11.5	32.3	14.4
(% attending weekday meetings)	(16.4)	(24.3)	(31.8)	(46.8)	
Church contributions	584	473	905	862	1.8
($ per year)	(1,388)	(937)	(1,843)	(1,818)	
Church contributions	1.94	1.94	2.81	3.16	2.3
(% of yearly income)	(6.49)	(3.80)	(4.65)	(4.81)	
Membership in church-	37.8	40.1	44.6	49.5	3.6
affiliated groups (%)	(48.5)	(49.0)	(49.7)	(50.1)	
Secular memberships	1.90	1.49	1.27	0.91	9.4
(no. of memberships)	(1.91)	(1.74)	(1.52)	(1.30)	
Strength of affiliation	32.6	38.7	45.5	56.0	8.5
(% claiming to be "strong" members)	(46.9)	(48.7)	(49.8)	(49.7)	
Biblical literalism	23.2	40.4	57.8	68.1	15.7
(% believing)	(42.3)	(49.1)	(49.4)	(46.6)	
Belief in afterlife	79.5	85.1	88.9	87.8	3.5
(% believing)	(40.4)	(35.6)	(31.4)	(32.6)	
No. of cases	763	1,802	941	575	

Source: NORC General Social Survey, 1984–90; sample consists of nonblack, non-Catholic Christians.

Note: In first four columns, numbers shown are means; nos. in parentheses are standard deviations. Definitions of denominational groups: liberal = Christian (Disciples of Chirst), Episcopalian, Methodist, and United Church of Christ; moderate = American Baptist, Evangelical Lutheran, Presbyterian, and Reformed churches; Conservative = Missouri Synod Lutheran and Southern Baptist; and sects = Assemblies of God, Church of Christ, Church of God, Jehovah's Witnesses, Nazarene, Seventh-Day Adventist, and other Fundamentalists and Pentecostals.

t Values are for two-tailed test comparing means for liberal and sect members.

PUTTING THE THEORY TO WORK

Unlike traditional typologies, the proposed theory of church and sect tells a causal story. It claims that a high-cost group maintains its strict norms of conduct precisely because they limit participation in competing activities and thereby raise levels of participation within the group.[8] The theory thus predicts that increased strictness (or distinctiveness, or costliness) leads to higher levels of church attendance and church contributions, closer ties to the group, and reduced involvement in competing groups.

Table 2
Jewish Denominational Differences

	Reform	*Conservative*	*Orthodox*
Individual practices:			
Attends synagogue regularly (%)	8.6	19.0	54.1
Lights candles each Friday (%)	5.4	15.3	56.8
Avoids money on Sabbath (%)	6.5	13.1	57.7
Household practices:			
Buys kosher meat (%)	3.5	20.7	68.5
Separates meat and dairy dishes (%)	3.4	18.9	66.7
Lights Hanukkah candles (%)	53.4	66.9	76.6
Has Christmas tree (%)	21.8	15.4	7.2
Networks:			
Closest friends are all Jews (%)	7.6	15.8	39.1
Lives in Jewish neighborhood (%)	6.6	11.5	36.0
Opposes marrying non-Jew (%)	1.9	9.6	47.7
Household contributions per year:			
Gives more than $1,000 to Jewish causes(%)	5.4	9.44	22.5
Gives more than $1,000 to non-Jewish causes (%)	6.53	4.31	0.0
Volunteer hours per week:			
Hours worked for Jewish organizations	1.08	2.34	5.62
	(4.45)	(7.40)	(14.54)
Hours worked for secular organizations	4.02	3.62	2.24
	(8.98)	(8.81)	(9.34)
Organizational memberships:			
Jewish (outside of synagogue)	0.55	0.85	1.46
	(1.45)	(1.49)	(3.24)
Non-Jewish	1.67	1.45	0.721
	(3.09)	(2.35)	(1.36)
Years of education	15.8	15.2	14.8
	(2.54)		(3.30)
Household income	64.7	55.5	41.7
(in thousands of $)	(46.7)	(42.8)	(35.7)
No. of cases	797	720	111

Source: 1990 National Jewish Population Survey.

Note: Numbers in parentheses are standard deviations; for each variable, the two-tailed *t* test comparing means for Reform and Orthodox is significant at the 5% level.

The observed patterns in Tables 1 and 2 support this prediction. Relative to their more mainstream counterparts, members of sectarian groups—both Christian and Jewish—attend more religious services, contribute more money, and (in the Jewish case, at least) choose more of their closest friends from within their religion. They are also less involved in competing activities. They hold fewer memberships in outside groups, contribute less to outside causes, and

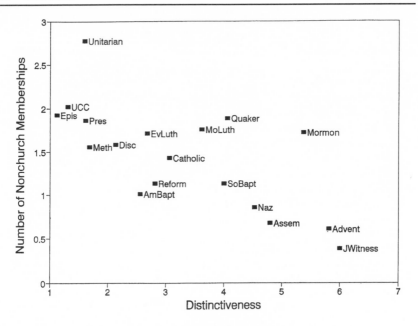

Figure 2. Nonchurch memberships.

have fewer outside friends. This last set of findings deserves special emphasis because it reverses a well-known individual-level pattern. Calculated at the level of the individual, correlations between church participation and outside participation are consistently positive and significant. People who regularly participate in church activities also tend to involve themselves in a wide range of organizations and activities outside of the church. So, for example, the zero-order, individual-level correlations between dollars contributed to non-Jewish causes are positive for all types of Jews (correlations are .56 for Reformed, .57 for Conservative, and .12 for Orthodox). The corresponding correlations between numbers of Jewish and non-Jewish organizational memberships are positive as well (.19, .33, and .32, for the three respective groups). For Christians the correlation between membership in church-affiliated groups and the number of nonreligious memberships is .26. But when they are calculated at the level of denominational averages, all these correlations are *negative*. Hence both theory and data underscore that the group-level patterns represent more than the mere aggregation of individual-level correlations.

Graphs provide another way to confirm the theory's predictions. Figures 1–3 show that the categorical patterns of Table 1 in no way depend on a few outlying denominations. Figure 2 plots the relationship between (expert-rated) distinctiveness and average attendance in all available denominations, including Catholic. Figure 2 confirms the prediction that distinctiveness functions to limit members' involvement in alternative activities and competing sources of satisfactions. Sect members do indeed forgo secular memberships. Figure 3 provides persuasive evidence that the members of costly groups free ride less.

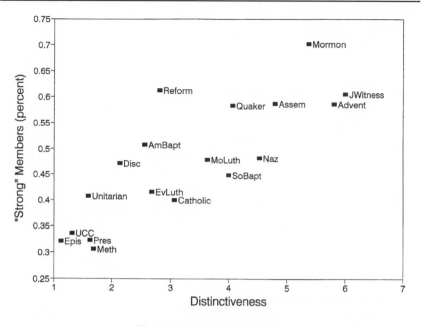

Figure 3. Strength of affiliation.

Even though mainline denominations demand relatively little of their members, far fewer of those members describe themselves as "strong" members of their religion.

A statistical analysis of these data shows that the group's impact persists even after controlling for demographic and socio-economic characteristics such as age, income, sex, education, race, and marital status. The analysis included multiple regressions which estimate how all these variables simultaneously affect individual rates of church attendance and contributions. In every equation, distinctiveness works in the predicted direction, is highly significant, and greatly enhances the model's predictive power. I also ran regressions that test whether this distinctiveness effect works through its correlation with (or impact on) individual beliefs and choice of spouse. These regressions show that although personal beliefs and choice of spouse are statistically significant, they in no way wash out the direct impact of denominational distinctiveness.[9] Indeed, I could not alter this fundamental result with any reasonable alternative subsample, estimation technique, time frame, or method of assessing denominational characteristics,[10] nor have I found contradictory results in regressions for other key dependent variables such as nonchurch memberships and contributions, church friends, and strength of membership. A corresponding regression analysis of the Jewish survey data, available upon request, yielded essentially the same results.

We thus arrive at a persistent and powerfully sociological finding. The character of the group—its distinctiveness, costliness, or strictness—does more to explain individual rate of religious participation than does any standard, individual-level characteristic, such as age, sex, race, region, income, education, or marital status. The impact appears across both Christian and Jewish denominations, and it remains strong even after controlling for personal beliefs.[11]

THE SOCIAL CORRELATES OF SECTARIANISM

A final set of predictions concerns the type of people most likely to affiliate with a group that limits one's involvement in alternative activities or constrains one's consumption of secular commodities. Simply put, those most likely to join are those with the least to lose. Losses grow in proportion to both the quantity and the quality of one's ties to the outside world. You are therefore less likely to join (or remain active in) an exclusive sect if you have an extensive set of social ties to friends and family outside the sect. You are more likely to join if you lack many such ties and are still more likely to join if you have friends or family in the sect. Stated in terms of cost and benefit, these predictions seem embarrassingly obvious. Yet it took years of research before scholars would accept that a potential member's social ties predict conversion far more accurately than his or her psychological profile.

Economic ties work in much the same manner as social ties. There is little chance that a successful business executive will forsake all for a strict sect, let alone a wilderness commune. The opportunity costs are simply too great. But the costs are substantially less, and hence the odds of joining substantially higher, for people with limited secular opportunities, such as those with low wage rates, limited education, or minimal job experience. This prediction is consistent with the patterns observed in Figure 4 and Tables 1 and 2—sect members average the lowest income and education; members of the most church-like denominations average the highest.

The prediction that sects tend to attract individuals with limited secular opportunities has two corollaries. First, classes of people experiencing relatively limited secular opportunities (such as minorities, women, and the young) are more likely than others to choose sect membership over mainline church membership. Second, a general decline in secular opportunities, such as that which occurs during recessions, will make sectarian groups more attractive relative to nonsectarian groups. Both corollaries are strongly supported by previous studies (reviewed in Iannoaccone 1988), and logistic regressions, available on request, show that being young, black, female, undereducated, or poor all significantly increase the odds of being a sect member.

LIMITS TO STRICTNESS

Kelley's argument would seem to imply that a church always benefits from increased strictness, no matter how strict it is already. The Presbyterians would grow faster if they became more like the Southern Baptists, who would, in turn, grow faster if they became more like the Mormons. In fact, Kelley himself has stated that "strong organizations are strict . . . the stricter the stronger" (Kelley 1986:95).[12] In contrast, the present model implies that organizational strictness

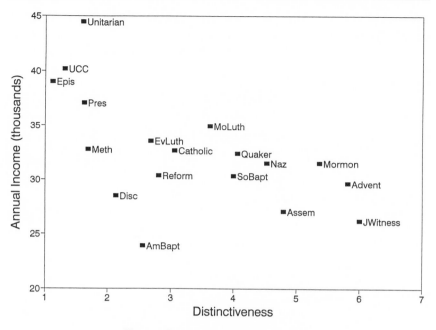

Figure 4. Income versus distinctiveness.

displays diminishing returns and that the optimal amount of strictness will depend on the socio-economic characteristics of the members.

To see this, recall that in the rational choice model, increased strictness adds to the attractiveness of a church only because its benefits outweigh its costs. The benefits take the form of greater group participation, commitment, or solidarity. These benefits can be quite large, since free riding is a serious problem. But they are not infinite. They must be set against the costs of strictness, costs that take the form of stigma, self-sacrifice, social isolation, and limited opportunities to earn "secular" rewards or to enjoy "worldly" pleasures. As a group becomes progressively more strict, it eventually reaches a point beyond which the additional benefits of increased strictness are outweighed by additional costs.

Consider, for example, a group that has already isolated itself geographically, thereby eliminating all part-time members (at the cost of secular social ties and occupations). It is not at all clear that people who join such a group would also wish to submit to ritual disfigurement, vows of silence, regular fasting, or the rejection of all modern conveniences. Rather, it is clear that beyond some point increased strictness/costliness *must* drive away virtually all current and potential members. Even though hundreds were willing to join the Bhagwan Rajneesh in Antelope, Oregon, few would have followed him to the Arctic Circle. For any target population of potential members, there will therefore exist an *optimal* level of strictness. Groups that exceed this level will tend to scare off many potential members with what are perceived as excessive demands. Groups that fall short of this level of strictness will suffer from free-rider problems and hence from a pervasive lack of commitment that leaves many potential members feeling that the group has little to offer.

Kelley's thesis and data thus address only one tail of a two-tailed phenomenon. Closer inspection should reveal the existence of another class of unsuccessful groups, those that are so strict and sectarian that they simply wither and die. Stark and Bainbridge's (1985) study of more than 400 American-born sects strongly confirms this prediction. Mormons, Jehovah's Witnesses, and Seventh-Day Adventists notwithstanding, only 6% of all identifiable American sects are growing rapidly. Moreover, "nearly a third of all sects (32 percent) reached their high-water mark on the day they began. Twenty-one percent of these sects began to decline in membership from their very first day. Another 11 percent have not grown since formation" (1985:133–134). Relating these growth rates to the sects' levels of tension with society, Stark and Bainbridge (1985:134) arrived at a conclusion that fits the rational choice model perfectly: "Many sects fail to grow (and are never transformed into churches) because their initial level of tension is so high as to cause their early social encapsulation. Once encapsulated, a sect may persist for centuries, depending on fertility and the ability to minimize defection, but it will rarely be able to recruit an outsider." . . .

CONCLUSION

The strength of strict churches is neither a historical coincidence nor a statistical artifact. Strictness reduces free riding. It screens out members who lack commitment and stimulates participation among those who remain. Rational choice theory thus explains the success of sects, cults, and conservative denominations without recourse to assumed abnormality, irrationality, or misinformation. The theory also predicts differences between strict and lenient groups, distinguishes between effective and counterproductive demands, and demonstrates the need to adapt strict demands in response to social change.

The rational choice theory of organizational strictness accounts for empirical regularities that have fascinated sociologists for most of a century. Mainstream churches and extremist sects emerge as analytically distinct modes of religious organization rather than as ad hoc descriptive categories. The empirical correlates of sectarianism are derived as formal consequences of a sectarian strategy aimed at enhancing group commitment.

Survey data strongly confirm the theory's key predictions. Members of stricter denominations devote more time and money to their religions and are more likely to describe themselves as strong members of the faith. They socialize more extensively with fellow members and are less involved in secular organizations. They have, on the average, lower incomes and less education. The patterns hold across the full spectrum of denominations, Christian and Jewish. . . .

Like Kelley's original study, this article has addressed the issue of church growth only indirectly. I have tended to assume that "strong churches— churches with high rates of commitment, participation, and contributions—

will find it much easier to achieve high rates of growth." This assumption certainly seems reasonable and is supported by empirical studies of church growth (Iannaccone et al. 1993). However, it blurs the distinction between necessary and sufficient. In commercial markets, the strongest firms are not always the fastest growing. Highly profitable businesses sometimes choose to maintain their current size and forgo an increased market share. The Amish have pursued an analogous strategy in the religious marketplace. The current, static version of the strict church model does not adequately address this distinction. A dynamic version is needed to clarify the relationship between the strength and growth.

Rational choice theories of religious behavior are new, provocative and relatively undeveloped. This article has explored one such theory and has thereby sought to show how costly, apparently unproductive demands can strengthen an organization and benefit its members. The relative ease with which it has integrated Kelley's strict church thesis, traditional church-sect topologies, and the basic feature of American denominationalism suggests that further work is well worth the effort.

wade clark roof and william mckinney

AMERICAN MAINLINE RELIGION

Its Changing Shape and Future

TWO BASIC DEMOGRAPHICS: AGE AND FAMILY PATTERNS

Of all the information now available, two basic demographics are the age structures and family patterns for the religious groups. By examining these we are able to determine, in the first instance, the "location" of a particular group in the larger American population and, in the second, the fundamental relations between religion and family. Far from being constants, or common features of the mainline groups, these two can vary in ways that are important for understanding how religion fits into the social structure. In both instances the demographics point to significant shifts since midcentury and changing institutional patterns for religion in America.

AGING CONSTITUENCIES

Normally religious involvement varies by age, which means that churches and synagogues have a disproportionate number of older people within them. This observation has long been made by commentators, indeed for as long as we have had reliable data on congregations. In the 1930s the Lynds, for example, commented on "the same preponderance of gray-haired persons" that they observed in Middletown's churches (Lynn and Lynn 1937:298). Returning to Middletown in the late seventies, Theodore Caplow and his research associates found much the same patterns; they concluded that "regular attendance and intermittent attendance increase for each increment of age" (Caplow et al. 1983:77).

Age differentials in religion have become even more pronounced since midcentury. The reason for this is simple: the American population is growing older. Low birth and death rates have pushed the average age upward. This finding might not be of much significance if all groups were affected uniformly, but such is hardly the case. Some religious groups, depending on their location relative to the mainstream culture, are far more influenced by general population trends than are others.

Mainline Protestants especially have aged. For some Protestant denominations there have been noticeable increases in the average age levels. The proportion of members fifty years of age or older within these churches has grown considerably in just the last twenty-five years:

	1957	1983
Episcopalians	36%	46%
Methodists	40	49
Lutherans	36	45
Presbyterians	42	49
Baptists	33	40

While this trend is most evident in the Protestant mainline churches (both old-line and moderate), the Catholic and Jewish communities have aged as well. Similar proportions of members fifty or older increased for Catholics during this period from 31 percent to 34 percent and for Jews from 33 percent to 39 percent. Religious constituencies generally have aged while just the opposite is true for those with no religious preference: nonaffiliates are considerably younger today than they were a quarter century ago. As the social composition of this secular constituency has undergone a metamorphosis, so too has its demographics. With large numbers of youth dropping out of the churches in the 1960s, and religious nonaffiliation becoming more acceptable, the average age within this sector declined significantly.

Among the religious communities there are disparities in age structures, some being more lopsided than others. This is apparent in Table 1, which looks at the percentage distribution of mainline religious group members by age. Affiliates of all faiths are older than nonaffiliates; Jews are older than both Protestants and Catholics; Protestants are older than Catholics. Within Protestantism there are some striking differences: white Protestants are older than black Protestants, and liberal Protestants are older than conservative Protestants.

More is involved here than simply the aging of the American population: in the seventies and eighties the greater voluntarism of young Americans took

Table 1
Percentage Distribution of Religious Families by Age

Family	18–34	35–54	55+
Liberal Protestants	27	34	39
Moderate Protestants	31	32	38
Black Protestants	37	31	32
Conservative Protestants	35	34	31
Catholics	40	34	27
Jews	31	31	38
No religious preference	59	26	15

many out of the churches and synagogues and in turn "pushed" the average age levels upward. Protestants, Catholics, and Jews all felt the impact of growing numbers of disaffected and "unchurched" members, the upshot of which was to shift the location of religious mainstream in the direction of a somewhat older age base. Age would thus join the list of social correlates, along with class, ethnicity, and region, as an aspect of fundamental change for these historic traditions. Perhaps no other feature is so apparent in observing many congregations today.

The age shift would have its most profound consequences for Protestantism. Within this community a growing age gap now exacerbates existing tensions and cleavages between liberals-moderates and conservatives. By the 1980s liberal Protestants were on the average almost four years older than conservative Protestants. United Church of Christ members have, along with Christian Scientists, the oldest constituencies, with mean ages greater than fifty years of age. Forty-three percent of the United Church of Christ, 41 percent of Methodists, and 42 percent of Disciples of Christ are age fifty-five or older. This stands in marked contrast to the lower mean ages of the conservative Protestant denominations, the lowest being 41.2 for Pentecostal/Holiness members. Not one of the conservative Protestant groups has as many as 40 percent of its members over fifty-five years of age; fewer than one-third of Jehovah's Witnesses, Pentecostals, and Assemblies of God members are this age or older.

Young adults under the age of thirty-five, on the other hand, account for only 26 percent of the members of the Reformed church, 21 percent of the United Church of Christ, and 28 percent of the Methodists. Proportionately these numbers are small, a fact that becomes clear when one considers that almost 40 percent of the nation's adult population belongs to the eighteen-to-thirty-four age category. Young adults are far better represented in the conservative churches: more than 50 percent of Jehovah's Witnesses belong to this younger category. Compared with moderate and liberal Protestants, the conservative churches are more successful in holding on to their young members.

The fact is that liberal, mainline Protestant denominations are aging more rapidly than the more Evangelical, Fundamentalist faiths. A lopsided age distribution obtains broadly within the liberal Protestant sector, resulting in death rates that are high and likely to become higher still unless the denominations are able to replenish their ranks with younger members in their child-rearing years. As it stands at present, the situation amounts to what Benton Johnson describes as a fundamental "demographic weakness" for liberal Protestantism, and one that does not augur well for its future (1985:39). For the other religious traditions the age shifts are not as critical, although they are discernible and creating institutional repercussions.

The youthful rebellion against the churches served also to broaden the age gap between the religious and secular cultures. Fifty-nine percent of non-affiliates are under thirty-five years of age, which is much higher than for any of the religious clusters; only 15 percent of nonaffiliates are age fifty-five or older. The age profile for this more secular constituency has shifted dramatically in the post-1960s period. Nonaffiliates have on the average become younger as they have become more educated and more affluent, all of this happening when the mainline churches were aging. The combination of trends now creates a widening cultural rift between the religious and nonreligious sectors.

FAMILY PATTERNS

Another set of demographic changes are underway in the relation between family life and religion. Both of these fundamental institutions have had to adjust to the dominant values of individualism, freedom, and equality in the modern world. Both also have had to accommodate the massive social and cultural upheavals of the post-1960s period. New lifestyles, changing roles for women, increased divorce rates, and new family forms all pose serious challenges to the traditional family—especially the Norman Rockwell portrait of the normative American family consisting of the husband who is the breadwinner, the wife who is the homemaker, and young children in the home.

Today almost one-fifth of all families are maintained by single parents, about two-fifths have dual wage earners, and one-tenth of the population lives in nonfamily arrangements (D'Antonio and Aldous 1983:81ff). Varying patterns of family and household types have become more and more common, and the highly sentimentalized view of the traditional family is now very much a minority family type. Consequently, a huge "gap" exists between the idealized image of the American family and the great diversity of family patterns that now exist. And increasingly, as the range of new family and household types has expanded, so too have ways in which religious institutions accommodate these changes.

Family patterns vary across religious traditions, more so than is often realized [Table 2]. Norman Rockwell's normative family is not commonly found among conservative Protestants and next among moderate Protestants. Seventy-one

Table 2
Percentage Distribution of Religious Families by Marital Status

Family	*Married*	*Widowed*	*Separated/divorced*	*Never married*
Liberal Protestants	66	12	10	12
Moderate Protestants	68	12	9	11
Black Protestants	46	14	21	19
Conservative Protestants	71	10	10	9
Catholics	65	9	9	18
Jews	65	12	7	16
No religious preference	48	4	14	34

percent of the conservatives and 68 percent of the moderates are married. For many Protestants of the center and right, the more Evangelical and Fundamentalist ones especially, the nuclear family is considered not only normative in American culture but God given. This pattern is viewed as in keeping with the "biblical concept of the family," which defines marriage as heterosexual and lifelong and the primary function of the family as that of home building and parenting. Roles in the family are traditional: the conservatives strongly prefer that women remain in the home or that, if they must work outside, it not interfere with child-rearing responsibilities. Theological conservatives encourage churches and synagogues to exercise social control and socialization functions that support the traditional family, though not without some difficulty in the face of secular pressures.

For Jews, Catholics, and liberal Protestants, there is a wider diversity of marital and family styles. All three have large numbers of singles, reflecting the growing number of Americans choosing not to marry, or more commonly, to postpone marriage until a later age, and sizable numbers of widowed. That the numbers of the widowed would be high for Jews and liberal Protestants is understandable given their above-average age structures. The proportion who are separated or divorced is not unusually high (except for Episcopalians); the proportion of Jews who are separated or divorced is actually the lowest, at 7 percent of all the major groupings. While the nuclear family is held up as a model, norms of pluralism and freedom of choice are deeply ingrained within these traditions. There is less emphasis upon maintaining a particular family style and more openness to diversity. Even within the Catholic community, where traditional family norms are deeply ingrained, there is awareness of diversity among the laity and among many parish priests and a growing effort to deal with changing family forms. Most mainline churches and synagogues recognize a variety of family patterns and lifestyles, and in official stands and statements religious authorities have moved toward a greater nurturance and support. Such emphasis does not mean abandoning values crucial for the survival of the family but rather, as William V. D'Antonio points out, helping people to "draw out the love and caring features of religious teachings" (D'Antonio and Aldous 1983:106).

Two of the religious constituencies differ significantly from the mainstream family norms. Black Protestants have the lowest proportion of married persons, the highest separated or divorced and widowed, and large numbers of singles, which is not surprising in view of the long history of strains on the black family. The growing number of single-parent families and serial marriages within this community suggests that it may become even more distinctive in its religious and family patterns. Also not surprising, the nonaffiliates have the highest number of singles and, next to blacks, the highest number of separated and divorced—34 percent and 14 percent, respectively. Considering that many of the nonaffiliates are young, many will likely marry in time, but it is also evident that this subculture will remain distinctive for its large number of "alternative" households. Neither of the two groups is likely to become an exemplar of, much less a strong advocate for, the traditional family.

FACTORS AFFECTING RELIGIOUS GROWTH

Both the aging of the mainline religious constituencies and their changing relations with the family bear upon the theme that has become of such paramount concern in recent years—whether the churches are growing or declining. This is a complex issue involving internal institutional as well as contextual factors, and one that has attracted much attention in both scholarly and popular circles. Here our concern is not so much to identify the various reasons why some churches grow and others do not as it is to describe specifically the demography of religious change.

The size of a group's membership over time is dependent upon two fundamental sets of factors: its natural growth and its net gains or losses from conversion. Most faiths are able to hold the loyalty of a majority of the children born to members, and thus the higher the fertility among members the greater the likelihood of numerical growth. Such growth is so obvious that it is usually taken for granted. In contrast, conversion involves the addition or subtraction of members by means of willful choice. Persons join or leave on their own accord—"religious switching" as sociologists describe such movement. A group with a sufficiently high birth rate can, within limits, lose substantial numbers to their faiths and still grow faster than its rivals. Provided it does not lose too many of its members, the group will grow simply because of the large numbers of children born to its members. By the same token, a group with a low birth rate and a high death rate can be a net gainer as a result of conversions and still show membership declines over time. Its losses due to deaths exceed its gains from membership transfer.

These two sets of actors are critically important in the demographic balance and thus determine whether a congregation, or church, grows or shrinks in its membership base. So important are they for understanding the changing American religious mainline that we give extended treatment to them in the pages that follow.

BIRTH RATES

Within the natural growth equation the most significant variable is the birth rate, which varies across traditions and over time as well. Factors of theological heritage as well as group experience combine to create differential fertilities, which once in place tend to be perpetuated. Norms of family size and birth control all vary from one religious subculture to another. Conformity to religious norms is itself a factor. Among Catholics, for example, John Scanzoni found that religious devoutness and traditional attitudes toward sex were mutually supportive: "Wives who have been more traditional have been more devout, which in turn reinforces and perhaps increases traditionalism, and so forth. Acting together, both elements have evidently resulted in larger families" (Scanzoni 1975:87).

Catholics' birth rates are higher than Protestants' or Jews', Protestants' are higher than Jews', and blacks' higher than whites'. Among white Protestants there are differences that, for the most part, reflect the wide span of class and educational levels found within this large religious family. Thus Methodists typically have had more children than Episcopalians, but fewer than Nazarenes, Jehovah's Witnesses, or many other conservative Protestants. In some instances where fertility levels are high, class may not be so important; for example, the Mormons, Hutterites, and Mennonites lay great emphasis upon the regeneration of the community of believers and have created close ties between kinship and religious roles. But these are minority faiths outside the mainstream, where, generally speaking, fertility varies in direct relation to a group's socio-economic standing. As with political party affiliation, personal and family styles, and social attitudes, fertility is a fairly sensitive index of status and class.

Those groups that have collectively moved upward in the social structure have typically experienced declining fertility. Churches originating as working-class movements a hundred years or more ago and evolving into middle-class constituencies in the early decades of this century have experienced this pattern. The number of children born to Methodists, for example, dropped as members moved from the farms and small towns to the cities and adopted more middle-class values and lifestyles. With the exception of Catholics, whose church prohibits artificial birth control, only small minorities in other religious communities have recognized any religious direction on matters of contraception—maybe as few as 20 percent of the most religious Protestants and 30 percent of the most devout Jews. Consequently, nonreligious factors have had a greater influence in shaping fertility patterns. Urbanization, the changing relations of work and family, women in the work force, and better methods of birth control have all contributed to a reduced fertility.

More generally, norms of family size vary from one period to another. The postwar baby boom of the 1950s is a good example. At midcentury, birth rates were at an all-time high for the modern period, and familial and child-centered themes (for example, The Family That Prays Together, Stays Together) figured prominently in the religious milieu of the period. Middle-class families with three or more children were not uncommon in those years, and more often than not, new parents followed their children to the Sunday schools and churches. "A Little Child Shall Lead Them" was the title of Dennison Nash's popular essay on the role of children in bringing about the so-called religious revival at the time (Nash 1968:238). The symbolism of religion, family, and country was pervasive; for the religious establishment, the market was bullish indeed.

In the late 1950s, however, birth rates began trending downward. The postwar baby boom peaked and was followed by an extended period of declining or stabilized low fertility. The declines affected virtually all sectors of the society. Among young Catholics, for example, the declines throughout this period were especially evident. In a Gallup poll conducted in 1971, 58 percent of Catholics interviewed agreed that one could ignore *Humanae Vitae*, the pope's encyclical proscribing birth control, and still be a good Catholic (Rosten 1975:393). Only 40 percent of the priests surveyed in 1969 agreed with

Table 3
Average Number of Births per Woman by Religious Family

Family	Total	Age 45+	Under age 45
Liberal Protestants	1.97	2.27	1.60
Moderate Protestants	2.27	2.67	1.80
Black Protestants	2.62	3.08	2.24
Conservative Protestants	2.54	3.12	2.01
Catholics	1.69	1.96	1.37
Jews	1.69	1.96	1.37
No religious preference	1.39	2.30	1.18
National	2.25	2.75	1.73

the encyclical, and opposition was almost unanimous among the younger priests (Wilson 1978:252). For a variety of reasons the gap in birth rates for Protestants and Catholics was narrowing. Even by the late fifties, overall birth rates for Protestants and Catholics under forty-five years of age were already coming together. Throughout the sixties and seventies, the gap continued to diminish. Broad changes in the society and within Catholicism led in the direction of greater convergence—in fertility as in many other cultural aspects.

Today Catholic and mainline Protestant birth rates are roughly similar, but differences remain among the Protestant communities. Table 3 shows the number of children born per woman, both the total figures and those broken down by age. With the exception of blacks, conservative Protestants have the highest birth rates of any of the religious families (for older women the rates are even higher than that of blacks). Despite declining birth rates and converging patterns generally in the United States, historic differentials within Protestantism are still readily apparent. At present, differences within Protestantism far transcend those between Protestants and Catholics.

The patterns are indeed striking. Among women under forty-five years of age, the child-to-woman ratio is 2.01 within the conservative Protestant family as compared to 1.60 for liberal Protestants. This translates into four-tenths of a child less for every liberal Protestant adult female under forty-five. If indeed liberal Protestant women had as many babies as do conservative Protestant women, the size of the liberal sector would increase by more than 2.2 million! Not only, however, do liberal Protestant women have fewer children, but there are fewer women in these churches in the child-bearing ages. Thus numbers and fertility work against a strong and sustained liberal mainline: the natural growth potential for the liberal denominations is fairly weak, while the opposite is true for conservative bodies.

Against conservative Protestantism's strong demographic base, the other white religious communities have far less potential for growth. None of the others are positioned as well in age structure and family patterns—the essential prerequisites for a strong fertility. Except for northern Baptists and Reformed members, birth rates for the under-forty-five females in the moderate Protestant family are relatively low, almost as low as for liberal Protestants. Catholics' birth rates are similar to those of moderate Protestants: both hover around the national average. Young Jewish women have the lowest fertility of any comparably aged, religiously affiliated Americans. The nonaffiliates have the lowest of all of the major groupings, especially for the under-forty-five category. The nonaffiliates, Unitarian-Universalists, and Christian Scientists have, in that order, the lowest birth rates among younger women. In contrast, black Protestants have exceedingly high birth rates, the very highest in fact among young women.

RELIGIOUS SWITCHING

Religious switching is another significant factor in the demographic equation of mainline religion. Inflow and outflow amount to migratory stream of religious movement—in and out of the established faith communities. Some churches benefit from what is described as the "circulation of the saints," that is, they pick up members from other churches; other churches pick up fewer members this way and must aggressively proselytize from among those who have no religious background. As with inflow, so with outflow. Churches and synagogues lose members either to another faith community or to the more secular, nonreligious sector. Losing members to the former does not mean that these members have lost faith, but rather that they are simply opting for a different religious style; losses to the ranks of the nonaffiliated are more serious and many suggest a general secular drift as a competitor to faith.

Movement from one church to another is common in the United States, especially among Protestants. The most common pattern is an "upward movement" of switching from low-status to high-status denominational affiliations. Long observed in Protestant church life, this type of switching has contributed to the making of a diverse and socially conscious denominational order. Much impressionistic evidence, throughout the nineteenth century and much of the twentieth, points to religious movement associated with upward social mobility. Closely linked symbolically with the prevailing mobility ethos, religious switching has often been celebrated as part of the American Way of Life. Abraham Lincoln's own celebrated life course was not all that atypical religiously: from a hard-shell Baptist background, through a "good" marriage and a successful law practice, to regular Presbyterian attendance (Ahlstrom 1972: 847). Americans can generally relate to the character type that Peter Berger describes as "the young Baptist salesman who becomes an Episcopalian sales executive" (Berger 1961:74). Education, hard work, success, good marriage, recognition—all are clues given expression in the upward religious movement, which Jay Demerath amusingly describes as "playing musical church to a status-striving tune" (Demerath 1965:71n). . . .

Especially in times of economic growth and middle-class expansion such as the post–World War II era, high-status Protestant churches likely benefited from above-average levels of religious switching. Old-line establishment churches such as the Episcopal and Presbyterian often received membership transfers from lower-status churches; so did Congregationalism, particularly in New England and the Midwest. A dynamic, achievement-oriented society generated a secular, accommodating religious stance favoring these churches. Higher-status churches have benefited up the line; upwardly mobile Nazarenes and Baptists often became Methodists, affluent Methodists joined the Presbyterians, and many out of diverse backgrounds, if successful, found a home with the Episcopalians. . . .

CURRENT PATTERNS OF SWITCHING

Many surveys and studies show that at least 40 percent of American Protestants have at one time or another switched denominational affiliations. Switching within this tradition remains much higher due to its size and diversity of churches. For Catholics and Jews there is less switching "in" or "out," but all indications are that it has increased in recent years. Not only has switching increased since the 1960s, but patterns of movement generally have changed. The new voluntarism, involving greater individual choice and preference, has produced more diverse types of switching and far more value-laden and symbolic movement into and out of the religious communities.

To grasp the full import of switching, we must look at both its quantitative and qualitative aspects. Even the quantitative switching, which in one sense is obvious, must be sorted out carefully. We begin with levels of stability of the religious groups. By stability we mean the extent to which those who grow up in a religious group stay with it throughout their lives. The more stable a group, the stronger most likely will be its institutional attachments and religious bonds and the more likely it will add the children of its members. . . .

Groups vary far more than might be expected in how well they hold on to their members. Jews and Catholics do much better than Protestants: 87 percent and 85 percent, respectively, remain in their faiths. Eighty percent of Mormons and 78 percent of Jehovah's Witnesses continue to maintain their original religious ties. Among more mainline Protestants, the range is wide—from 75 percent (Lutherans) to 37 percent (Evangelical and Fundamentalists). A ranking of Protestant denominations shows the following groups to be the most stable: Lutherans, 75 percent; black northern Baptist, 73 percent; white Southern Baptist, 73 percent; Pentecostal and Holiness, 70 percent; Adventists, 69 percent; and black Methodists, 69 percent. At the bottom of the rank order, or the least stable, are three disparate groups: Christian Scientists, 39 percent; Unitarian-Universalist, 39 percent; and Evangelicals and Fundamentalists, 37 percent.

Most of the large, Protestant mainline denominations fall in the middle, Episcopalians (65 percent), Methodists (63 percent), United Church of Christ (61 percent), Disciples (58 percent), and Presbyterians (60 percent) all have majorities that have remained stable, yet there are large numbers of switchers. This is not too surprising: to be in the mainline is to be in the middle, tending toward neither extreme. By virtue of their size and social location, they are the religious institutions most likely to experience tensions arising out of the larger society. The cross-pressures of switching versus nonswitching are felt most acutely within these structures.

One thing is clear—membership stability is not a matter simply of literal or conservative theology. Groups in the most stable category do not all share a strong conservative theology, nor are those least stable necessarily similar in this respect. Christian Scientists and Unitarian-Universalists are among the most liberal; many Evangelicals and Fundamentalists are known to switch to other churches. Stability appears to be more a reflection of communal belonging. Mormons, Lutherans, Jehovah's Witnesses, black Baptists and Methodists, and white Southern Baptists all have strong ethnic or quasi-ethnic loyalties, at least compared with more mainline groups. The role of communal attachments in creating stability becomes even more apparent in view of the fact that nonaffiliates are also among the least stable of all groupings. Only 45 percent of those reared as nonaffiliates have retained a nonreligious preference. Known to be highly individualistic and to have weak communal attachments, they are also unstable as a constituency of nonbelievers or, more correctly, nonbelongers. . . .

There is another aspect to switching: a group's capacity to attract new members. Net gains or losses for a particular group are a function of both its stability (or the number it retains) and its attractiveness (or the number who switch in). Thus very stable religious groups need not attract many persons in order to show a net gain, but denominations that lose many of their members must attract large numbers of new members if they are to avoid net losses through switching.

LIBERAL GAINS OFFSET BY LOSSES

Many mainline Protestant churches enjoy membership gains from other churches but lose equal numbers, if not more, to the ranks of the nonaffiliates [Table 4]. Liberal Protestants show a gain of 34.3 percent through transfers from other families, which is offset by a loss of 24.8 percent to other families, or a resulting net interfamily gain of 9.5 percent. This suggests that liberal Protestantism is attractive as a religious alternative and actually does better in interfamily switching than any other religious family. Liberal churches continue to pick up members out of the conservative churches. But with other types of membership flow they do not come out as well. Liberal churches show a gain of 2.2 percent from the nonaffiliates, which is offset by a loss of 8.0 percent to them, or a net loss of 5.8 percent. This leads to the observation, one which goes against popular wisdom, that the challenge to liberal Protestantism comes not so much from the conservative faiths as from the growing secular drift of many of their not-so-highly-committed members.

SECULAR DRIFT ACROSS THE RELIGIOUS SPECTRUM

The big "winner" in the switching game is the growing secular constituency. Of all seven groupings, nonaffiliates are the greatest beneficiary of switching; all the groups lose more persons to this category than they receive from it. In the exchange, Jews, liberal Protestants, and Catholics have the greatest losses, while

Table 4
Family Gains and Losses Due to Switching

Denominational family	Total number in sample	Percent	Under age 45		Age 45+	
			Number in sample	Percent	Number in sample	Percent
Liberal Protestants						
Base (age 16)	1,255	100.0	635	100.0	620	100.0
From other families	431	34.3	154	24.3	277	44.7
Fron nonaffiliation	27	2.2	18	2.8	9	1.5
To other families	(311)	−24.8	(159)	−25.0	(152)	−24.5
To nonaffiliation	(101)	−8.0	(73)	−11.5	(28)	−4.5
Net gain/loss	46	3.7	(60)	−9.4	106	17.1
Moderate Protestants						
Base (age 16)	3,896	100.0	1,862	100.0	2,034	100.0
From other families	708	18.2	353	19.0	355	17.5
From nonaffiliation	84	2.2	41	2.2	43	2.1
To other families	(796)	−20.4	(340)	−18.3	(456)	−22.4
To nonaffiliation	(225)	−5.8	(167)	−9.0	(58)	−2.9
Net gain/loss	(229)	−5.9	(113)	−6.1	(116)	−5.7
Black Protestants						
Base (age 16)	1,499	100.0	814	100.0	685	100.0
From other families	33	2.2	20	2.5	13	1.9
From nonaffiliation	3	0.2	3	0.4	0	0
To other families	(133)	−8.9	(62)	−7.6	(71)	−10.4
To nonaffiliation	(63)	−4.2	(55)	−6.8	(8)	−1.2
Net gain/loss	(160)	−10.7	(94)	−11.5	(66)	−9.6
Conservative Protestants						
Base (age 16)	2,307	100.0	1,278	100.0	1,029	100.0
From other families	550	23.8	272	21.3	278	27.0
From nonaffiliation	53	2.3	32	2.5	21	2.0
To other families	(448)	−19.4	(208)	−16.3	(240)	−23.3
To nonaffiliation	(90)	−3.9	(72)	−5.6	(18)	−1.7
Net gain/loss	65	2.8	24	1.9	41	4.0
Catholics						
Base (age 16)	4,012	100.0	2,438	100.0	1,574	100.0
From other families	331	8.3	178	7.3	153	9.7
From nonaffiliation	37	0.9	18	0.7	19	1.2
To other families	(287)	−7.2	(175)	−7.2	(112)	−7.1
To nonaffiliation	(294)	−7.3	(245)	−10.0	(49)	−3.1
Net gain/loss	(213)	−5.3	(224)	−9.2	11	0.7
Jews						
Base (age 16)	357	100.0	171	100.0	168	100.0
From other families	19	5.3	12	7.0	7	4.2
From nonaffiliation	3	0.8	3	1.8	0	0
To other families	(12)	−3.4	(7)	−4.1	(5)	−3.0
To nonaffiliation	(36)	−10.1	(23)	−13.5	(13)	−7.7
Net gain/loss	(26)	−7.3	(15)	−8.8	(11)	−6.5
No religious preference						
Base (age 16)	387	100.0	247	100.0	140	100.0
From other families	809	209.0	635	257.1	174	124.3
To other families	(207)	−53.5	(115)	−46.6	(92)	−65.7
Net gain/loss	602	155.6	520	210.5	82	58.6

conservative Protestants come closest to holding their own. The liberal religious traditions especially have a serious institutional problem of holding on their own.

Stark and Glock hypothesized some twenty years ago that the leftward trend of switching might not end with movement into the liberal churches, but that in time many liberals might simply drop out of the churches altogether. They surmised that should this happen, what had seemed like a favorable situation for liberals Protestantism could turn into a serious problem of membership collapse. To some extent, their predictions appear to have been borne out. Liberal Protestantism's greatest losses come from those dropping out of religion altogether. But Catholics and Jews, and to a lesser extent some conservative Protestants, also lose considerable numbers to the nonaffiliate ranks. What was once a liberal Protestant "problem" is now more generally one for the mainline faiths. . . .

OLDER SWITCHERS WITHIN THE RELIGIOUS COMMUNITIES

Many of the mainline Protestant and Catholic churches pick up more recruits from other religious communities than they lose, yet it is important to note who these persons are. The net switching gains for liberal Protestants are wholly accounted for by older switchers. Among older persons this community experiences a net gain of 17.1 percent, among younger persons a loss of 9.4 percent. Conservative Protestants and Catholics pick up older members and break even or lose the young. Both increasing numbers of switchers to nonaffiliation and a decline in the number of persons switching from other religious communities have contributed to this more pronounced age-related phenomenon. Generally, religion's "market share" of potential recruits has grown older.

LOSSES IN THE MIDDLE

The big "losers" are the moderate Protestants. The large, middle-American denominations—Methodists, Lutherans, Disciples, northern Baptist, Reformed—have disproportionately lost to other groups since the 1960s. Because of their size and close identity with mainstream culture, they have been unable to hold their own and have become the major suppliers of recruits to other faiths. As the nation's cultural and religious center has weakened, movement is greatest at the extremes—in the conservative religious and the secular, nonaffiliated directions. Such switching reflects the more fragmented and polarized culture that so rocked that religious establishment in the sixties and seventies. The strains run deep in the large moderate Protestant bodies, those truly mainline in faith and cultural experience. . . .

CONCLUSION

The demography of American religion offers many clues to how and why the religious establishment is changing. Age structures and family patterns are becoming more diversified in the religious mainline. These fundamental shifts in the social and demographic structure have implications for the social location and institutional characteristics of religion, now and for the future.

Generally demographers who study population dynamics concern themselves with three basic variables—births, deaths, and migrations. All three of these bear upon the changing religious scene. As we have seen, differential birth rates are important, death rates are crucial especially for those traditions with low birth rates, and religious switching, or the migration equivalent, has become more significant in the modern period. A particular church or tradition may enjoy added numbers as a result of a favorable birth rate or net gains from switching, or both; similarly it may suffer serious institutional losses depending upon how the numbers fall. Both natural growth and additions by switching are crucial elements that figure in the formula of institutional and group survival. It is difficult to imagine that either will become any less important as considerations in the future, and one or the other may well become even more critical. Switching as a factor especially is likely to take on greater significance.

Demography has proven to be destiny for American Protestantism. Since midcentury, demographic and switching trends have literally reshaped the Protestant establishment. Declining birth rates have diminished the chances that liberal Protestants will reproduce themselves. Liberal churches continue to attract upwardly mobile switchers but at a reduced rate, and those they attract tend not to be very active. The liberal churches at present suffer from severe demographic weakness: they have aging constituencies and have become, or are dangerously close to becoming, in Hadaway's phrase, "unstable destination denominations" (Hadaway 1983:262). Large numbers of members who are only nominally committed and many who now are leaving the churches altogether make the liberal churches vulnerable as continuing vital religious institutions. With their lopsided age distributions, death rates are high and likely to become higher still unless the churches are able to replenish their ranks with younger people. Of all the major traditions, liberal Protestantism is suffering the most from the secular drift of the post-1960s. Lack of strong group cohesion means that many individuals either disaffiliate or simply become nominal members having little to do with congregational life. The greater religious voluntarism of modern life produces "alumni associations," or collectives with vague ties to the churches. Even though many are attracted to a liberal stance of openness and pluralism, such traits tend not to generate strong institutional commitment.

Protestant conservatives, in contrast, fare better. Fewer of them are now switching to liberal denominations, and they hold on to more of their younger members. Their death rates are lower, and their birth rates higher—a winning combination in the game of religious growth. Compared with other Protestants, they gain the most committed converts, retain the most committed members, and lose those who are least likely to be regular participants and supporters. Loyalty to traditional doctrines runs deeper, and mechanisms of member commitment are stronger. Perhaps most important, conservative churches have stronger socioreligious groups attachments, which play an important role in undergirding them as communities of belief. More emphasis upon the gathered community of believers and a sense of responsibility and accountability to one another serve as a "buffer" protecting the conservative churches more from the privatizing forces of modern society. Secular forces are strong, of course, and are propelling these churches in the direction of greater religious voluntarism, but relatively speaking they still enjoy greater social cohesiveness.

part three

SECTARIAN GROUPS

The church-sect distinction has generated more discussion and more print than perhaps any conceptual framework in the sociology of religion. As "ideal types" in the tradition of Max Weber, church and sect possess polar characteristics. These are well summed up by sociologists Demerath and Hammond:

> The ideal-typical "church" and "sect" differ in both internal and external characteristics. Externally the church seeks to make its peace with the secular society surrounding it, whereas the sect is either aloof or hostile. Internally, the church has many of the earmarks of a bureaucracy with professionalized leadership, high valuation of ritual, and an impersonal evangelizing strategy that welcomes persons wherever and whatever they may be. The sect, on the other hand, is more of an amateurish social movement with lay, charismatic leadership, an emphasis upon perfervid spontaneity, and a sense of religious exclusiveness as reflected in high membership standards. (1969:157)

The distinction has also been used to devise ways of looking at the process by which religious groups grow and evolve. In this light, new religious movements begin as cults and proceed to succeeding stages of sect, denomination, and finally church, each stage reflecting more accommodation to, and "being comfortable with," the larger secular society.

A sect-like group, however, may retain many or most of its characteristics over time, even in the face of growing membership. Adaptation to the larger society is by no means inevitable. In fact, as Stark and Bainbridge point out, some sects—such as the Amish and Mennonites, the snake handlers, those Mormon groups still advocating polygamy, and some "urgently millenarian" assemblies (such as Jehovah's Witnesses)—stay in a state of high tension with the larger society. High-tension groups may "encapsulate" themselves, allowing little contact with outsiders and therefore rarely recruiting from the larger society.

Contemporary researchers William S. Bainbridge and Rodney Stark have written extensively on sects, focusing centrally on the concept of tension between sect members and the "outside world." In their words, tension is

> equivalent to broad subcultural deviance marked by (1) *difference* from the standards set by the majority or by powerful members of society; (2) *antagonism* between the sect and society manifested in mutual rejection; and (3) *separation* in terms of social relations between the group and outsiders. (1981:138–139)

Bainbridge and Stark, in their article "Sectarian Tension," attempt through survey research to *measure* the degree of tension. High tension is manifested in strong opinions, "different" behavior, and social relations that cut members off from alignment and contact with the larger society. On a continuum of tension, for example, the Protestant Episcopal church and the United Church of Christ would exhibit very low tension (or high accommodation) with their environment. The American Lutheran church would show moderate tension, Southern Baptists moderately high tension, and Pentecostal churches and Jehovah's Witnesses very high tension. The authors call on survey research to measure the other side of the equation as well: to what extent do members of the larger society (as shown in a California survey) accept or reject persons belonging to various churches, in terms of "feeling friendly and at ease" with them? The difference-antagonism-separation theme is thus empirically illustrated. Formulation of research methods by which to measure tension is important, not least because similar research can reveal whether the second (and later) generations of sect members continue to retain sect-like character-istics, or whether, instead, they show accommodative tendencies, making their peace with the surrounding environment.

The Assemblies of God is one of the fastest-growing groups in the United States and one of the fastest-growing Christian groups in the world. Margaret Poloma uses Weber's insights on the nature of charisma and charismatic leaders to analyze the recent history and possible future of the Assemblies of God. Professor Poloma characterizes this group as being at the crossroads in its development. This is a charismatic group from the Pentecostal tradition that has traditionally practiced all of the "sign gifts" such as speaking in tongues and Divine healing. These distinctive practices have set them apart from other Christian groups, yet they have moved (socially and to some extent psycholog-ically) along the continuum from being a sectarian group in high tension with the outside world to being a denomination, with the concomitant accommoda-tion and compromise that that status entails. Indeed, as can be seen from the excerpt presented, Assemblies of God members are not greatly different from (and in some categories exceed) the American public on such indicators of success in mainstream America as socio-economic status. In such a group, rejection of the world is not absolute but instead selective. Some parts are easily adapted and adopted. In the case of the Assemblies of God, Poloma points out that instrumental rationality, one of the key components of "modernity," does not displace the sacred worldview but rather is absorbed by it. Many modern charismatics are able "to incorporate their belief in and experience of a personal and active God with a decidedly modern worldview." Professor Poloma com-bines an insider's understanding of the lives of Assemblies of God members with a sociologist's rigor to provide insight into ways in which the members attempt to "keep alive the vitality of its charismatic traits" along with the costs of maintaining this distinctiveness. An individual might gain more in social acceptablity if he or she gives up some practices considered somewhat bizarre by the larger American culture. However, shedding those practices comes at the cost of the loss of group distinctiveness. For the future of groups such as the Assemblies of God, success and accommodation may present more of a threat than the world's severest opposition.

ADDITIONAL READING

AMMERMAN, N. T. 1987. *Bible Believers: Fundamentalists in the Modern World.* New Brunswick, NJ: Rutgers University Press.
An excellent in-depth study of how the members of one particular Fundamentalist church construct their religious realities in the face of the vicissitudes of modernity.

william s. bainbridge and
rodney stark

SECTARIAN TENSION

We are engaged in an effort to construct an integrated set of deductive theories of major religious phenomena. In a recent paper (Stark and Bainbridge 1979), we developed concepts necessary for a theory of religious movements. There we demonstrated why the long tradition of church-sect typologies failed to provide concepts useful for theorizing. Each of these typological schemes in the literature is constructed of a mass of loosely correlated features that result in a proliferation of mixed types which cannot be ordered. With no basis of ordering groups as more church-like or more sect-like, it is impossible to develop or test theories which attempt, for example, to account for the transformation of sects into churches. Many other social scientists also have pointed to the serious inadequacies in church-sect conceptualizations (Gustafson 1967; Goode 1967; Eister 1967; Dittes 1971; Knudsen et al. 1978).

We found no need, however, to develop our own conceptualizations of church and sect. Instead, we found that Benton Johnson (1963) has provided the needed conceptual clarity. By identifying a single axis of variation along which religious organizations may easily be ranked, Johnson achieved what is, in our judgment, the most important advance in this area since Niebuhr first proposed a church-sect theory in 1929. We are at a loss to know why others have continued to pursue obviously unsuitable typologies since Johnson's work appeared.

Johnson identified *tension with the surrounding sociocultural environment* as the *single* defining criterion of the church-sect dimension. Sects are in a state of high tension with their environment; churches are in a state of low tension, or even no tension at all. By excluding the multitude of loose correlates from the definitions of churches and sects, Johnson's conceptualization frees these other features for inclusion in theories about the origins and transformations of churches and sects. For example, since sects are no longer defined as having a converted rather than a socialized membership (and therefore no longer confront us with the need for mixed types when we observe sects such as the Amish with wholly socialized memberships), it now becomes possible to seek propo-

Reprinted from Review of Religious Research *22:105–124 (1980) with permission of the Association for the Sociology of Religion and Rodney Stark.*

sitions about why and how the arrival of a generation of socialized members transforms religious movements. And, indeed, since discovering such propositions is our primary concern, we gladly adopted Johnson's definition for use in our theories.

Nevertheless, since we are concerned to produce theories that are easily testable, the question arises whether the notion of "tension" is specific enough to be operationalized. When this question was first raised by reviewers for a paper in which we used Johnson's tension axis of sectarianism, we were satisfied to point out some obvious and dramatic symptoms of tension. That is, we suggested that public disputes in which sects attacked more worldly institutions or in which society inflicted punishment on sects demonstrated a way to identify high degrees of tension.

Thus, for example, the annihilation of a sect by fire and the sword would be a sure indicator of extreme tension. Less violent conflict would also count, such as the recent court battle between the Amish and the State of Wisconsin over compulsory secondary education (Keim 1975). Even in our tolerant society, acts of violence and repression against sects are common enough to serve as indicators in the most extreme cases. For example, members of many high-tension religious groups have recently suffered kidnapping and "deprogramming," including such groups as the Moonies, the Hare Krishnas, the Love Family, the Children of God, and the New Testament Missionary Fellowship (Patrick and Dulack 1976).

Upon further reflection, however, we recognized that this was not a wholly satisfactory way to measure tension. To operationalize our theories it must be possible to rank groups along *all* degrees of the tension axis, not just at its end points. More continuous and sensitive measures are necessary.

We then noted that Johnson himself (1963:543) had suggested that a church-sect scale developed by Russell Dynes (1955) might serve. Dynes had in fact come rather close to defining the church-sect dimension in terms of tension with the sociocultural environment:

> The construct of the church has generally signified a type of religious organization which accepts the social order and integrates existing cultural definitions into its religious ideology. The sect, as a contrasting type, rejects integration with the social order and develops a separate subculture, stressing rather rigid behavioral requirements for its members. (Dynes 1955:555)

However, Dyne's scale is not adequate. He did not follow his own definitions when he constructed it, but instead fell back on a list of putative correlates of the sect proposed by Liston Pope (1942). Thus Dynes created a scale rooted in the same tradition of typologies we seek to avoid. His scale is extremely culture-bound (consider the item "a congregation should encourage the minister during his sermon by saying *amen*" (Dynes 1955:556). This agree-disagree battery seeks to determine individuals' commitment to the particular trappings of *some* sects, primarily those of the rural South. Such a measure will not do what we need. Indeed, our concern is not to identify the religious preferences of *individuals*, but to find a way to characterize *groups* in terms of their degree of tension. For it is the origins and changes of groups that our theory about churches and sects seeks to explain.

Therefore, in this paper, we have turned aside from our theoretical pursuits in order to demonstrate the adequacy of the concept of tension. First, we discuss and specify the concept more fully. Then we examine data on several ways in which tension can be measured. Our first assessment of these data is to see whether they successfully differentiate among religious groups. The second is to see if they order groups in a way consistent with our qualitative sense of which groups are more and less sect-like. Finally, we assess whether these several different ways of measuring tension are consistent—do they rank the same groups in the same order. If we can demonstrate that the answer in each case is yes, then we can return to our theorizing with confidence that Johnson has provided us with an efficient and measurable way to define church and sect.

THE SAMPLE

All the tables reported in this paper are based on a sample of church members in four counties of northern California who were sent a lengthy questionnaire. Complete details are given in Glock and Stark (1966). The tables reported here are based on responses from 2326 members of sixteen different Protestant denominations and from 545 Catholics. We present the Catholic data primarily for comparison with the higher-tension Protestant groups and will discuss the pattern of Catholic responses only briefly at the end of this paper. Previous publications intuitively ranked the Protestant groups from the most church-like to the most sect-like (Glock and Stark 1965, 1966; Stark and Glock 1968), and we have followed the same ranking here. In all past usage a number of small denominations were collapsed into a single category and identified as "sects": the Church of God, the Church of Christ, Nazarenes, Assemblies of God, Seventh-Day Adventists, the Gospel Lighthouse, and the Foursquare Gospel Church. Here we have decomposed this generic category into its constituent denominations. Two of these groups, the Gospel Lighthouse and the Foursquare Gospel Church, did not provide a large enough number of respondents for stable statistical results. They have been excluded from the analysis except for computations based on the total "sects" category or on "total Protestants."

Since even fifteen denominations produce very large tables, we have collapsed some Protestant denominations into "low-tension" and "medium-tension" groups. The "low-tension" category included Congregationalists, Methodists, Episcopalians, and members of the Disciples of Christ. The "medium-tension" category consists of the Presbyterian, American Lutheran, and American Baptist denominations. Because Missouri Synod Lutherans and Southern Baptists stand at the borderline of sectarianism, we report data for these two "sect-like denominations" separately. The collapsing was done after careful examination of the data showed there was very little variation among the denominations making up the low- or the medium-tension categories. Economy is gained and no pertinent information is lost thereby.

THE CONCEPT OF TENSION

In his classic paper, Johnson only once uses the term *tension:* "a sect tends to be in a state of tension with its surroundings" (1963:544). In his primary definitions he speaks instead of sects rejecting their social environments. We, however, based our concepts on tension rather than on rejection, because rejection blurs a relationship that is a two-way street. The sect not only rejects society—it, in turn, is rejected by society. This two-way relationship is best captured by the inclusive concept of tension, as Johnson once says and often implies.

Tension with the sociocultural environment is equivalent to *subcultural deviance*, marked by *difference, antagonism,* and *separation.* The sect and the society disagree over proper beliefs, norms, and behavior. They judge each other harshly, each asserting its superiority over the other. The dispute is reflected in the social relations of sect members. Rejected by and rejecting the larger society, sects draw together in relatively closed and cohesive groups. In the case of extreme tension, sects will be socially encapsulated, and the members will have relatively little intimate contact with nonmembers (cf. Wallis 1977).

It might be objected that defining subcultural deviance in terms of difference, antagonism, and separation is to introduce yet another unideal collection of disparate variables that defies unambiguous measurement and confident use. But this triad of terms really describes a single concept, and the three are worth distinguishing primarily because they allow us to arrange the indicators of subcultural deviance in a meaningful pattern, thereby rendering them more intelligible and easier to survey. Traditional definitions of deviant behavior describe it not only as different from the standard set by dominant groups in the society, but also as punishable, drawing disapproval and negative sanctions of at least some level of severity. A deviant subculture provides a competing standard, setting deviant norms and thus asserting antagonism toward those of the larger society. Social relations across the border of a deviant subculture are strained, and therefore there is a strong tendency for a social cleavage to form, as people avoid painful disputes, separating this subculture from the surrounding community. Seen the other way around, without some degree of social separation, the subculture will find it difficult to sustain deviant norms and counteract the pressures to conform communicated through social relations with outsiders. In our future theoretical work, we will explore these issues more deeply. For now it is enough to explain that *deviant subculture* is a unitary concept, although we find it convenient to group its indicators under three headings.

There are two common standards against which we can measure deviance. First, we can follow a purely statistical approach, defining deviance as any significant departure from the average for the populations as a whole. Second, we can emphasize the importance of power and influence, defining deviance as any behavior characteristic that is scorned and punished by powerful elites in society. The problem with the first approach is that it may define an elite as deviant, even when the elite has the power to enforce its standards on others. To a great extent elites represent the society with which the sects are in tension. For our purposes the proper standard is a combination of the two approaches, an informed analysis that is interested in both the population average and in the norms set by elites.

In many of our tables, the low- and medium-tension denominations are in fact very close to the average for Protestants as a whole. In other cases, the low-tension group is somewhat far from the average, although the high-tension groups tend to be farther from the average in the opposite direction. Perhaps both ends of the distribution represent tension with the social environment? But this conclusion, following the purely statistical model of deviance, is unwarranted. Ours is a relatively secular society in which the otherworldliness of high-tension sects does not harmonize with the assumptions built into economic, political, and nonreligious cultural institutions. Many studies have shown that the denominations we label "low tension" are in fact most favorably placed in the class structure. This is true for the respondents in our study, as several analyses showed. For example, only 13 percent of members of the low-tension denominations identified themselves as working-class, while fully 40 percent of the sect members applied this label to themselves. Forty percent in the low-tension group had completed college, compared with 17 percent of sect members. Fifty-five percent of those in the low-tension denominations held high-status jobs: professional, technical, and similar workers, or propri-etors, managers, and officials. Half this proportion of sect members, 27 percent, said they held such high-status jobs. The low-tension end of the spectrum is anchored closest to the centers of societal power. This fact allows us to identify these denominations conclusively as the low-tension groups even when they depart somewhat from the average for the population as a whole. In a theocratic society, low tension might mean intense involvement in religion (of a certain kind), but in our secularized nation low tension means low levels of commit-ment to traditional religion.

DEVIANT NORMS, BELIEFS, AND BEHAVIOR

Johnson (1963:544) drew the connection between tension and deviance, saying "religions enforcing norms on their adherents that are sharply distinct from norms common in secular quarters should be classed relatively sectarian." At the other extreme, "bodies permitting their members to participate freely in all phases of secular life should probably . . . be classified as churches." We cannot specify *a priori* precisely which norms will be subjects of disagreement between high-tension groups and the rest of society, because sects will reflect the culture and the history of the particular societies in which they emerge. But in general we would expect that issues of personal morality will be the most common areas of dispute. If we wanted to identify sects in a society of which we had no previous knowledge, we would have to do a preliminary survey to identify norms concerning personal behavior that were foci of heated debate in religious circles. After that we could survey different religious groups to see which professed extreme minority views on these matters.

The survey data in hand primarily concern behavior *permitted* by secular society but *forbidden* by some religious groups. But we know that some kinds of behavior are prohibited by the larger society but encouraged by these groups. For example, several high-tension American sects encourage speaking in tongues, while such behavior would be considered psychopathological in a secular setting. Norms of mental health do differ significantly from one religious group to another, with fundamentalist groups showing the greatest disagreement with the standards of psychiatrists (Larson 1964, 1968). A few sects encourage ritual poison drinking and serpent handling, despite laws against these practices (LaBarre 1969). Several cults use hallucinogenic drugs despite their secular prohibition, including the Native American Church, the Rastafarians (Furst 1972), and the Love Family, which initiated members through drug-induced revelations. We have data on some relatively mild forms of religious behavior required by the sects, but the clearest starting point is to look at behavior *prohibited* by the sects.

Table 1 shows that members of sects and higher-tension denominations do disagree with the majority on a number of moral issues. Members of sects are more likely than others to feel that morals in this country "are pretty bad and getting worse." The most extreme differences in this table are in attitudes toward dancing and the moderate use of alcohol. The overwhelming majority of members of low-tension denominations tolerate such behavior, while the majority of sect members reject it. These huge differences demonstrate strikingly that the sects do reject normative standards that are accepted by the society at large, while churches accept these standards. But differences need not be this large before they are significant. Obviously, a number of factors other than religious concerns may influence individual opinions. For example, gambling may be opposed on purely practical and economic grounds. The majority in every Protestant group disapproves of gambling, but the proportion is 20 to 30 percentage points higher in the sects than in the total Protestant population. As groups, the sects reject gambling more strongly than do the low-tension denominations, even if a majority in all Protestant groups are opposed to this behavior.

Table 2 shows that high-tension groups hold a number of deviant beliefs, opinions that are distinctly different from secular standards, even if two of these opinions are accepted by more than half of our sample of respondents. Low-tension denominations do not reject Darwin's theory, nor are they convinced by stories about the devil, biblical miracles, or the Second Coming. Medium-tension denominations tend to accept the historical reality of biblical miracles, including the story that Jesus walked on water, but these two beliefs describe a distant past that need not have much relevance for participation in contemporary secular society. Beyond their utility as indicators of disagreement, the

Table 1
Deviant Norms

Percentage of each group giving the indicated response

	Denominations		Sect-like		Sects					Total Protestant (2,326)	Total Catholic (545)
	Low tension (1,032)	Medium tension (844)	Missouri Lutheran (116)	Southern Baptist (79)	Church of God (44)	Church of Christ (37)	Nazarene (75)	Assemblies of God (44)	Seventh-Day Adventist (35)		
The respondent feels that morals in this country "are pretty bad and getting worse."	41	47	53	71	66	73	71	84	83	48	43
The respondent disapproves of dancing.	1	9	28	77	77	95	96	91	100	18	1
The respondent disapproves of gambling.	62	67	81	96	89	100	92	98	97	69	27
The respondent approves of censorship of movies and books.	31	36	49	65	57	57	73	82	66	39	72
The respondent disapproves "highly" of someone who drinks moderately.	4	6	2	38	43	57	57	57	60	11	1
The respondent feels that drinking liquor would definitely prevent salvation.	3	3	1	15	30	38	39	30	46	7	2
The respondent is "rather concerned with trying to live as sinless a life as possible."	55	67	76	90	86	92	91	91	94	65	76
The respondent believes what we do in this life will determine our fate in the hereafter.	31	45	53	89	82	84	95	93	94	46	71

Table 2
Deviant Beliefs

| | Percentage of each group giving the indicated response | | | | | | | | | | |
| | Denominations | | Sect-like | | Sects | | | | | Total Protestant (2,326) | Total Catholic (545) |
	Low tension (1,032)	Medium tension (844)	Missouri Lutheran (116)	Southern Baptist (79)	Church of God (44)	Church of Christ (37)	Nazarene (75)	Assemblies of God (44)	Seventh-Day Adventist (35)		
Darwin's theory of evolution could not possibly be true.	11	29	64	72	57	78	80	91	94	30	28
It is completely true that the devil actually exists.	14	38	77	92	73	87	91	96	97	37	66
Biblical miracles actually happened just as the Bible says they did.	39	61	89	92	84	97	88	96	91	57	74
It is completely true that Jesus walked on water.	28	55	83	99	84	97	93	96	100	50	71
Definitely, Jesus will actually return to the earth some day.	22	48	75	94	73	78	93	100	100	44	47

five beliefs listed in Table 2 also represent tension because they indicate dissatisfaction with the world as it can by perceived by the human senses, studied by science, and analyzed by reason. Taken together, they indicate rejection of the world as it seems, or at least the feeling that the material world is not rich enough unless supplemented by the supernatural. All people probably desire more than life can actually give them, but in Table 2 we see that this dissatisfaction is probably much greater for the sects than for the low-tension denominations.

One of the disadvantages of survey research is that we must usually accept at face value whatever our respondents tell us. Sometimes attitudes and opinions are very poor reflections of social reality and fail to predict behavior (Schuman and Johnson 1976). Even self-report behavioral items may provide more direct evidence. Table 3 lists five such measures and has very much the same pattern of results as Table 1 and Table 2. Of course, the first one, frequent prayer, is not inherently deviant. Over two-thirds of our church-member respondents pray often or daily. But the sects are 25 percentage points above the low-tension denominations. High-tension groups have a somewhat higher norm for prayer, but much higher norms for saying grace, reading the Bible at home regularly, listening to religious programs, and spending evenings in church. Thus, high-tension denominations not only reject some important secular norms and hold deviant opinions, but also set unusual standards for positive religious behavior.

SECTARIAN REJECTION OF SOCIETY

High tension means not only *difference* from secular society, but also *antagonism* toward it. Table 4 lists four items that bear on particularism, "the belief that only one's own religion is legitimate" (Glock and Stark 1966:29). The first two items give special honor to Christians, saying that heaven and salvation are reserved for true believers in Jesus Christ. High-tension groups within the Christian tradition are especially likely to agree with these two items. The pattern of responses to the statement that Hindu religion would prevent salvation is not the simple reflection of the two previous items as logic would require it to be. It may be that rejection of Hindu religion by sect members is not stronger, because Hindus are not part of the surrounding American socio-cultural environment. The last item in Table 4, tithing, shows that the sects, unlike any of the lower-tension groups, demand sacrifice for the sake of the sect, a personal investment on the part of members that indicates that they value the sect highly. Taken together, the items in Table 4 show that members of high-tension groups place very high value on their own groups.

Table 5 describes the social struggle that goes on at the border of high-tension religious groups. Members of the sects frequently attempt to convert others to their faith and at the same time, are concerned about defending their religious group against outside influences. In part, conversion attempts may be public dramatizations of particularistic pride, but they are also based on hostility toward outsiders. Unless outsiders can be converted to the sect, sect

Table 3
Deviant Behavior

	Denominations		Sect-like		Sects						
Percentage of each group giving the indicated response											
	Low tension (1,032)	Medium tension (844)	Missouri Lutheran (116)	Southern Baptist (79)	Church of God (44)	Church of Christ (37)	Nazarene (75)	Assemblies of God (44)	Seventh-Day Adventist (35)	Total Protestant (2,326)	Total Catholic (545)
The respondent prays "quite often" or "regularly once a day or more."	63	71	80	87	89	92	85	91	91	70	76
Grace is said at all meals in the respondent's home.	16	25	41	53	66	65	69	80	77	28	22
The respondent reads the Bible at home regularly.	12	24	21	63	48	49	59	57	69	23	5
The respondent regularly listens to or watches religious services on radio or television.	7	10	13	28	18	22	33	34	40	12	6
In an average week, the respondent spends two or more evenings in church.	6	10	8	52	61	70	56	70	23	15	5

Table 4
Particularism

| | Percentage of each group giving the indicated response | | | | | | | | | | |
| | Denominations | | Sect-like | | Sects | | | | | Total Protestant (2,326) | Total Catholic (545) |
	Low tension (1,032)	Medium tension (844)	Missouri Lutheran (116)	Southern Baptist (79)	Church of God (44)	Church of Christ (37)	Nazarene (75)	Assemblies of God (44)	Seventh-Day Adventist (35)		
Only those who believe in Jesus Christ can go to heaven.	13	39	80	92	59	89	81	89	77	36	12
Belief in Jesus Christ as Savior is absolutely necessary for salvation.	47	71	97	97	96	97	93	100	94	65	51
Being of the Hindu religion would definitely prevent salvation.	4	15	40	32	32	60	35	41	17	14	2
Tithing is absolutely necessary for salvation.	8	12	7	18	52	43	45	39	69	14	10

Table 5
Conversion and Defense

	Denominations		Sect-like		Sects					Total Protestant (2,326)	Total Catholic (545)
Percentage of each group giving the indicated response	Low tension (1,032)	Medium tension (844)	Missouri Lutheran (116)	Southern Baptist (79)	Church of God (44)	Church of Christ (37)	Nazarene (75)	Assemblies of God (44)	Seventh-Day Adventist (35)		
Once or more the respondent has tried to convert someone to his or her religious faith.	38	50	63	89	86	84	83	86	83	50	40
Often the respondent has tried to convert someone to his or her religious faith.	5	8	10	32	32	32	27	36	34	10	5
The respondent sometimes prays to ask God to bring someone else to Christian faith and belief.	26	38	48	87	84	95	85	86	89	40	37
The respondent is "very interested" in knowing the religious affiliation of people he or she meets.	12	16	19	44	34	49	32	39	34	18	9
The respondent feels "we should not allow missionaries from non-Christian religions to spread their teachings in a Christian community."	17	27	35	41	36	41	41	55	23	25	23
The respondent says, "I tend to distrust a person who does not believe in Jesus."	19	27	34	53	46	51	47	55	33	27	22

members will have difficulty carrying on close relationships with them. Conversion appeals typically claim that the converting group is better than any other, and that the secular world is quite bad. Members of high-tension groups are more likely to distrust nonbelievers than to feel their community needs to be defended against non-Christian missionaries. For these people, the perimeter of their sect is a battlefront; the conversion struggle is a fight for acceptance from other persons, yet rejection of society as a whole. Interestingly, the Seventh-Day Adventist respondents are not especially worried about Hindus (Table 4) or about other non-Christians (Table 5). This unusual tolerance in a sect is probably the result of this group's experience of persecution in overseas missionary work, which resulted in dedication to norms of toleration for self-defense if for no other reason.

High tension with the societal environment is not merely a matter of strong options and deviant behavior. It is also manifested in patterns of social relations. In extreme cases, high-tension groups separate completely from the social life of the larger society and retreat into geographical isolation. Such extreme separation is not just an antique phenomenon affecting Hutterites, Amish, and Mormons. Even in the twentieth century, some high-tension groups have fled their societies of origin, wandered in the wilderness, and sought completely new sociocultural environments (Zablocki 1971; Bainbridge 1978). Table 6 shows six indicators of less complete separation.

The first two items show that sects are most likely to disapprove of marriages with members of other religious groups. In tension with the social environment, their relations with outsiders are strained. Conversely, relations with other insiders are favored. Members of sects are more than twice as likely to say they "fit in very well" with their church congregation than are members of low-tension denominations. The sect member's friends are much more likely to be fellow members of the same group. Social separation from outsiders and closer relations with other insiders are implied by each other. Together, they constitute encapsulation of the sect, isolation of each high-tension subculture as a distinct, closed social world.

In a sociometric study of Protestant ministers, Balswick and Faulkner (1970:310) found that sectarian ministers were bound together in a "fairly tightly knit clique" in comparison to ministers of low-tension denominations who had "the most loosely structured interrelationships." This finding suggests that not only the members, but also the clergy of high-tension religious groups tend to be socially encapsulated. Further evidence for this observation is reported in a recent survey study of 1559 Protestant clergymen by Harold E. Quinley (1974). Unfortunately, the sample did not include ministers of small, radical sects, but there were 131 Missouri Lutherans and 167 Southern Baptists, and 42 percent of the total described themselves as Fundamentalist or conservative. Quinley combined responses to several questionnaire items to produce a five-point index of religious orientation from "most modernist" to "most traditionalist." The 320 "most traditionalist" clergymen expressed views that place them at the high-tension end of the distribution. For example, they believed that "Jesus walked on water" and that "the devil actually exists." The questionnaire also asked how frequently they visited informally with other

Table 6
Social Encapsulation

	Denominations		Sect-like		Sects					Total Protestant (2,326)	Total Catholic (545)
Percentage of each group giving the indicated response	Low tension (1,032)	Medium tension (844)	Missouri Lutheran (116)	Southern Baptist (79)	Church of God (44)	Church of Christ (37)	Nazarene (75)	Assemblies of God (44)	Seventh-Day Adventist (35)		
Respondent disapproves of religious mixed marriages.	31	39	70	80	55	68	85	86	94	43	65
Respondent feels marrying a non-Christian would "possibly" or "definitely" prevent salvation.	9	16	22	20	46	51	68	73	57	18	27
Respondent says, "I fit in very well with my church congregation."	22	23	25	42	48	47	53	66	54	27	23
Half or more of the people the respondent associates with are members of his or her congregation.	29	37	36	51	77	59	72	75	69	38	47
Three or more of the respondent's five closest friends are members of his or her congregation.	22	25	26	49	61	65	65	66	83	29	36

ministers, either of their own denomination or of other denominations. Visits with fellow ministers of their own denomination did not vary significantly by religious orientation. Such visits were made less than once a month by 22 percent of the "most modernist" clergy and by 21 percent of the "most traditionalist." But there was a great difference in visits with clergy of other denominations. While only 28 percent of the "most modernist" clergy made such visits less than once a month, fully 52 percent of the high-tension ministers made interdenominational visits this seldom (Quinley 1974:249).

SOCIETAL REJECTION OF SECTS

We have shown that tension can be measured as rejection of the sociocultural environment by religious groups that have deviant norms, that struggle in conversion and defense, and that are somewhat socially encapsulated. It remains to be shown that the other side of tension, rejection by the larger society, can be measured and gives the same general results. The California survey included a few social distance items which allows us to compare public acceptance of seven religious groups. A recent Gallup poll also included social distance measures that bear on this point.

Table 7 summarizes social distance data from the California survey. The original question actually listed twenty-seven different categories of person, including such varied stimuli as "a German," "an alcoholic," "a conservative," "a liberal," and "a teetotaler." The respondent was asked to give his immediate reaction if he met someone about whom he know nothing but the indicated label. In Table 7 we give the percentage of each group that "would feel friendly and at ease" with each stimulus person. The most important data are the two columns for "total Protestant" and "total Catholic." These figures suggest how much each stimulus group is accepted or rejected by church members as a whole. The majority of all respondents say they would probably feel friendly and at ease with a Methodist, an Episcopalian, a Roman Catholic, or a Jew. That is, these church members find little problem with established conventional faith, even if this means a non-Christian faith. However, the Jehovah's Witnesses, the only sect among the stimuli, receives a *much* lower level of acceptance. Except for two fellow sects that show some warmth toward the Jehovah's Witnesses, there is rejection across the board. Atheists and Spiritualists receive even greater rejection, primarily because the higher-tension denominations are less likely to accept them than is the less-tension group. Spiritualists are the nearest thing to *cult* members included in the questionnaire in any way. Elsewhere we have explained that cults, like sects, are in high tension with the sociocultural environment; cults can be distinguished from sects by the fact that their culture is exotic or novel (Stark and Bainbridge 1979).

Comparable data were collected by a 1977 Gallup Poll of a national sample of about 1500 adults. Respondents were asked to indicate on ten-point scale how much they liked or disliked each of fifteen religious groups and three religious leaders. Because the respondents included people who were not church members, and because many may have felt inhibited from expressing

Table 7
Social Distance

Percentage of each group giving the indicated response

	Denominations		Sect-like		Sects					Total Protestant (2,326)	Total Catholic (545)
	Low tension (1,032)	Medium tension (844)	Missouri Lutheran (116)	Southern Baptist (79)	Church of God (44)	Church of Christ (37)	Nazarene (75)	Assemblies of God (44)	Seventh-Day Adventist (35)		
Would feel friendly and at ease with a Methodist.	82	86	83	82	87	70	80	82	86	84	57
Would feel friendly and at ease with an Episcopalian.	84	80	82	62	80	60	60	71	77	80	65
Would feel friendly and at ease with a Roman Catholic.	73	72	78	58	68	49	48	52	71	70	78
Would feel friendly and at ease with a Jew.	72	69	75	49	71	70	52	68	77	69	63
Would feel friendly and at ease with a Jehovah's Witness.	29	32	26	27	25	49	13	18	46	29	27
Would feel friendly and at ease with an atheist.	29	23	19	16	23	30	7	16	11	24	23
Would feel friendly and at ease with a Spiritualist.	26	22	22	18	16	43	9	5	3	23	25

a negative judgment of other citizens, we do not expect the levels of rejection to be very high. The number who failed to express any opinion at all varied from stimulus to stimulus, as we have removed them from our reanalysis, calculating the percentage of those holding a definite opinion who disliked the given group or leader. Only 6 percent disliked "Protestants," and the main Protestant denominations (Methodists, Lutherans, Presbyterians, Baptists, and Episcopalians) received low rejection scores, ranging from 4 to 8 percent.

Higher scores indicate some measure of rejection by the dominant groups in society. Catholics were disliked by 11 percent of the respondents, while between 12 and 15 percent rejected the following higher-tension groups: Southern Baptists, Eastern Orthodox, Evangelicals, Jews, and Quakers. Unitarians are disliked by 21 percent, Mormons by 25 percent, and Seventh-Day Adventists by fully 27 percent. It is interesting that Pope Paul VI received the same score, 11 percent, as did Catholics, the religious group he led. Billy Graham got an intermediate score of 15 percent, about the same as Evangelicals at 14 percent. Sun Myung Moon, the leader of the deviant Korean cult familiarly called the Moonies (The Unification Church), got an extremely unfavorable rating—93 percent of those familiar with him dislike him. This shows that his cult is in extremely high tension with the sociocultural environment.

The Gallup data also permitted us to look at how several of the groups judged themselves. Between 47 and 60 percent of members in major Protestant denominations and the Catholic church gave their own group a most highly favorable rating. Among the Mormons, relatively rejected by other respondents, fully 91 percent gave their own group the top score. As Gordon W. Russell (1975) has reported, Mormon respondents tend to see themselves as "the Chosen People." This reflects the pattern we have already found: high-tension groups are rejected by outsiders but evaluate themselves highly.

Although the main focus of our analysis has been comparison of low-tension and high-tension Protestant groups, attention should also be called to differences between the total Protestant and Catholic groups. Johnson suggests that "it is wise to classify Catholicism [in America] as somewhat more sectarian than most of the major Protestant bodies" (1963:545–546). Certainly, when it was a weak religious minority in a predominately Protestant country, as was the case decades ago, Catholicism experienced palpable tension with the sociocultural environment. For a variety of reasons, that tension has diminished over the years, but discrimination against members of the Catholic faith still exists in some sectors of important societal institutions (Greeley 1977a, b). The picture given by our tables is much simpler for the Protestant sects than for the Catholics. Often, the Catholic average is almost identical with the Protestant average. At other times, the Catholics are in the same direction from that average as are the Protestant sects, while occasionally the Catholics are on the side away from the sects. This pattern is not consistent with a simple description of Catholicism as a high-tension group. Rather, it reminds us that Protestantism and Catholicism are distinctly different traditions of religious culture. The best measures of Catholic tension in our data set are found in Table 6 and Table 7, where we see evidence of some social encapsulation and social distance separating Catholics and Protestants. Other tables were designed to measure the tension of sects within the Protestant tradition. We do not have the data to distinguish higher- and lower-tension groups within the Catholic tradition, nor to complete a definitive analysis of the relationship between American Catholicism and the sociocultural environment.

CONCLUSION

With Benton Johnson we have conceptualized the church-sect dimension in terms of *tension with the surrounding sociocultural environment*. This concept is equivalent to broad subcultural deviance marked by (1) *difference* from the standards set by the majority or by powerful members of society; (2) *antagonism* between the sect and society manifested in mutual rejection; and (3) *separation* in social relations leading to the relative encapsulation of the sect. These are *not* to be considered as three different axes of tension or as three dimensions of sectarianism. Each is an integral aspect of tension. One might think of these as the three moving parts by which tension is created and sustained. And, like a set of moving parts, they are conceptually distinguishable for purposes of measurement, but it would be folly to disassemble the set.

The data we have examined justify use of tension as the ordering principle of the church-sect axis. Groups we intuitively regard as more church-like or more sect-like displayed marked quantitative differences on the many different items we examined and did so in a very consistent way. Nevertheless, this paper is best regarded as no more than a successful reconnaissance. We have made do with items written for other purposes. Clearly, it would be possible to construct much more sensitive and appropriate measures of tension and thereby gain much greater precision in ranking various religious groups. Indeed, it would be desirable to consider measures based on policies, procedures, and structures of religious organizations as such, in addition to measures created by aggregating individual-level data. Some promising work along those lines has already been accomplished by Michael Welch (1977).

Whatever improvements in measurement that can be achieved, the important point, in our opinion, is established by our results. Theoretical use of the concept of tension is warranted: *tension can be measured*. This is extremely important, for no significant theories concerning the origins and transformations of religious movements can be tested *unless* it is possible to rank order religious groups in an unambiguous way. For example, it is impossible to test the hypothesis that the arrival of an adult generation of socialized members tends to transform sects if we cannot be sure that particular religious groups are (or are not) less sect-like at time two than at time one. This is a very old hypothesis. That it has not yet been tested is indicative of the impediment created by the multidimensional typological schemes that produced primarily unorderable mixed types. Tension opens the door to testing this and all the many other things we think we know about the church-sect process. And, clearly, it is time we got on with the job. Fifty years have now passed since H. Richard Niebuhr first made it evident that a church-sect theory was desirable and likely to be possible.

margaret m. poloma

THE ASSEMBLIES OF GOD
AT THE CROSSROADS

In 1971 the Assemblies of God reported 8,619 churches with a membership of 625,000 served by 11,677 ordained clergy (Jacquet 1971:18). Just ten years later the membership had increased by over one million persons to 1,629,000 served by 9,562 churches and 22,584 ordained clergy (Jacquet 1981:29).

Today the Assemblies of God has over ten thousand churches in the United States and the number of persons who identify with the church now exceeds two million (Jacquet 1988.) Its growth has extended beyond North American shores to over one hundred countries serving a constituency of some fifteen million believers . . . one of the fastest growing Christian organizations in the world.

CONSTRUCTING CHARISMATIC REALITY

Pentecostalism, as well as the larger charismatic movement, may be said to represent a case in which Weberian "affective action" replaces "rational action" in constructing a worldview. Rather than concentrating on the use of the most effective means to achieve a desired goal, more attention is given to "affectional sentiments" in pursuing "absolute ends." Affective action thus flows more or less from sentiment and is viewed as a less rational form of conduct than rational action. Although Max Weber's types of action are "ideal types" which are not found in their pure form, they can be employed as heuristic devices for discussing differences found in social action.

Weber's discussion of affective action centers around charismatic leaders. In other words, it is the leader who is defined as charismatic, or ruling on the basis of personal traits or gifts, with followers responding to the leader's giftedness. The Charismatic Movement departs from Weber's discussion in that the traits identified by Weber as being characteristic of affective action are diffused among leaders and followers alike (although admittedly they are more concentrated in leadership).

Weberian charismatic authority has four main components that are relevant to reality construction of those in the charismatic movement:

The Assemblies of God at the Crossroads: Charisma and Institutional Dilemmas *by Margaret Poloma, copyright © 1989, University of Tennessee Press. Reprinted with permission of the University of Tennessee Press.*

1.   It is outside the profane sphere of activity (1947:361).
2.   It is sharply opposed to both rational and bureaucratic authority (1947:361).
3.   It is opposed to traditional authority in its repudiation of the past (1947:361–362).
4.   Its legitimacy rests on personal charisma (1947:362) or on gifts of grace that are comprised of "magical abilities, revelation of heroism, power of the mind and of speech" (1971:175).

These four traits may be found in key characteristics of the Charismatic-Pentecostal movement: the norm of experiencing the sacred in the midst of a profane world; the norm of expecting divine guidance for both personal and institutional concerns, standing in contrast to rational and bureaucratic methods; a reticulate organization that refuses to immortalize tradition and the past; and personal participation of the vast majority of adherents in the charismata of the movement. The Assemblies of God, perhaps even more than many other Pentecostal sects, has valiantly resisted what sociological jargon terms the "routinization of charisma," attempting to keep alive the vitality of its charismatic traits. Each of these traits deserves further comment in relation to the protest against modernity.

THE NORM OF THE SACRED
IN A PROFANE WORLD

Gerlach and Hine (1968:34) have observed that Pentecostal ideology is intolerant of any ideal-real gap that characterizes most social institutions. This characteristic may be extended to note a rejection of the sacred-secular dichotomy that characterizes modernity. The sacred is not only "ideal" but "real" for charismatics. God is viewed as a miracle worker who not only grants spiritual life to the believer but whose power permeates the mundane as well.

The ideology that God's power fills the believer is translated into the expectation of regular religious experiences for Pentecostals involved in the Assemblies of God survey. Sixty-two percent believed they had experienced a miraculous healing within the past year (with another 12 percent reporting uncertainty about such an experience), 67 percent have at least on occasion spoken in tongues, and 91 percent reported either frequently or occasionally experiencing a "definite answer to prayer requests." Although only 30 percent have experienced giving a prophecy, nearly half (47 percent) reported being slain in the Spirit, half (50 percent) heard God speak to them through a dream or a vision, just over half (55 percent) have participated in deliverance services, and nearly all (91 percent) have received "personal confirmation" of scriptural truths.

Despite this normative experience of the paranormal, Assemblies adherents are no longer the "disinherited" (Anderson 1979). They represent all walks of life and all educational levels. Their belief in and experience of divine healing, for example, does not preclude the use of physicians and modern medicine. Although in earlier times the Assemblies of God was suspicious of both modern science and higher education, much of this suspicion has abated as the denomination has experienced upward mobility. Only 21 percent of the respondents, for example, agreed with the statement that "scientific discoveries should be viewed with skepticism." In many matters of education, use of technology, and orientation toward science, the denomination is thoroughly modern.

This present "goodness of fit" between the Assemblies and modern society may be as much due to the dominant American weltanschauung as it is to any recent modification of Assemblies of God thought. A one-dimensional worldview which glorifies technology and avoids critical and reflexive thought is part of the larger culture (Marcuse 1964)—a worldview which, I maintain, is little threat to most conservative churches. The Assemblies of God, standing squarely in the conservative church camp, continues to resist natural theology (and in this sense resists accommodation) while simultaneously modifying its cognitive style to adapt to a technologically advanced society (and in this way yielding to the accommodative process). . . .

The mediating factor that lessens potential tensions between the Assemblies of God and rational modernity is the experiential. As a result of ongoing religious encounters it appears that many contemporary charismatics, Pentecostals included, are able to *incorporate their belief in and experience of a personal and active God with a decidedly modern worldview in a manner that actually enriches the spiritually impoverished one-dimensional man.* In still other words, Pentecostals have not discarded the virtues of instrumental rationality but rather have attempted to integrate the strengths of both rational action and affective-intuitive action.

The instrumental rational reasoning process so characteristic of science and bureaucracy are absorbed into a more dominant sacred weltanschauung within the Pentecostal perspective. It is God who is credited with providing modern medicine, advanced technology, and higher education, as well as personal benefits of a particular job, safe travel, and even parking places. This sacred worldview attributes all things to God rather than relegating the sacred to a particular time slot on Sunday mornings! Such attribution makes adherents skeptical about the powers of pure reason and its cousin, bureaucratic authority. . . .

RETICULATE ORGANIZATION AS A SAFEGUARD AGAINST ROUTINIZATION

From its inception in 1914, the Assemblies of God has resisted organization; yet with a following of some fifteen million persons worldwide and over two million in the United States, organization is a sociological necessity. Perhaps nothing can be as succinctly noted to demonstrate the ideological resistance to organization as the insistence by its leaders that the Assemblies of God is a *movement* rather than a *denomination.*

The Assemblies of God has primarily a congregational form of government which allows for self-determination, a trait that is jealously guarded by local churches and pastors. . . .

PERSONAL PARTICIPATION IN CHARISMA

Gerlach and Hine (1968:32), in a discussion based on their classic work on Pentecostalism, noted: "Charisma, that quality traditionally assigned by sociologists and anthropologists only to magnetic leaders of emergent movements, flows freely through the ranks of Pentecostalism." What Gerlach and Hine observed in their research over twenty years ago is still visible today in the Assemblies of God. Although pastors, . . . hold the key to how much charisma may be manifested by followers, charisma is not limited to pastoral or organizational leadership in Pentecostalism as implied in the classic Weberian discussion.

It is my thesis that the Assemblies of God is currently experiencing vitality and growth because of its ability to encourage personal participation in charisma without jeopardizing its organizational structure. Such action is actually viewed (at least in word if not always in deed) as indicative of the work of the Holy Spirit. Pastors and adherents thus stress the importance of affective action within an organization that is decidedly modern. Remembering the stereotyped uneducated Pentecostal worshipping in storefront churches, the Assemblies of God is proud of its new status and new buildings. Yet most are struggling against the potential forces of organizational success for quenching the personal leadings by the Spirit.

FOLLOWERS IN FOCUS

Since demographic variables, particularly age, sex, and education, will be used as controls throughout our data analysis, it will be useful to present a demographic profile of our Assemblies of God congregational sample. In order to provide a benchmark for comparison, the results of similar demographic measures reported in a March 1984 Gallup Report on a national sample of Americans will be employed. This comparison and contrast will permit the reader to place this sample of 1,275 Assemblies of God adherents within the frame of Protestantism in the United States.

Table 1 provides a summary of some key demographic traits of our Assemblies of God respondents: age, education, marital status, and income.

Although caution must be taken in comparing our Assemblies of God sample with a national poll, such a comparison should help to dispel any lingering doubts about the socioeconomic status of Assemblies adherents. Clearly they are no longer the "disinherited"—the lower rung of the economic and education ladders. In terms of both education and income, our Assemblies respondents excelled over the "average American Protestant" of the Gallup Report. An Assemblies of God adherent is most likely to be married, between the ages of thirty and forty-nine, be earning an income in 1982 of over $15,000 annually, and have at least some college training. . . .

REVISITING THE DILEMMAS

The Assemblies of God, as part of a larger Pentecostal revival in Christianity, was birthed in a unique charismatic breakthrough. The resurgence of early

Table 1
Demographic Traits: Assemblies of God Sample Compared with
National Gallup Poll Data

Gallup*	Assemblies of God (%)	Percent
Sex		
Male	40	46
Female	60	54
Education		
College graduates	22	14
Postgraduate/professional school	10	—
Four-year college	9	—
Bible college	3	—
College incomplete	32	14
Trade/business school	9	—
Some college	23	—
High school graduates	29	40
Less than high school graduate	17	32
Age		
Total under 30 years	32	24
18–24 years	16	14
25–29 years	16	10
30–49 years	43	34
Total 50 and older	25	42
50–64	19	23
65 and older	6	19
Income		
Under $15,000	50	56
Below $4,000	9	—
$4,000–8,999	14	—
$9,000–11,999	16	—
$12,000–14,999	10	—
$15,000 and over	47	44
$15,000–19,999	20	—
$20,000–24,999	16	—
More than $25,000	15	—
Marital status		
Married	72	66
Single	18	17
Widowed	5	10
Divorced/separated	5	7

* Derived from George Gallup, Jr. *Religion in America*. Gallup Report no. 222 (March 1984):47.

Christian experiences—glossolalia, healing, prophecy, and miracles—proved to be a setback to the cold rationality that had engulfed much of Christendom. Although Pentecostalism represents but one of the revolts against rationalization and routinization that periodically punctuate human history, it is distinctive in two ways. Like other descendants of the Protestant Reformation, it called for a "priesthood of all believers," but it went further, opening the possibility of prophetic gifts for all who were Spirit-filled. Moreover, Pentecostalism proclaimed Christian charisma as the birthright of all believers who earnestly sought the Holy Spirit. To protect this continued flow of charismatic experiences, Pentecostalism vigorously resisted institutionalization and dogma.

Without ever having encountered the scholarly works of Max Weber, the early Pentecostals shared the sociological master's concerns about the iron grip of rationality, albeit for different reasons. Max Weber's account of human history was decidedly pessimistic, devoid of the lifegiving hope the Pentecostals found in the experience of the Holy Spirit. As Werner Stark (1965:205) has astutely noted about the Weberian outlook, "In the contest between religious life and religious death, death appears to him to have the last word." Weber's pessimism downplayed the periodic reawakening of charisma that has spawned reformations and revivals throughout history (including the Pentecostal Movement, which had its origins during the very time Weber was penning his classic theories of religion and modern society). Although Weber correctly recognized that routinization and organization commonly follow charismatic breakthrough, he erroneously intimated that such developments necessarily kill the charismatic spirit.

Charisma, if it is to endure over time in modern society, will be bureaucratized in some form. It may lead to a bureaucracy that subserves the original spirit (in which case charisma is fostered by the organization) or it may lead to an organization that uses charisma to further the organization (in which case charisma is overpowered by rationality and efficiency). As Stark notes (1965:206): "In judging a church, the question cannot be whether it has connected with a certain apparatus of bureaucrats, but whether this bureaucratic apparatus has completely overlaid and stifled the life which it was supposed to assist and to preserve. Only where the latter contingency has become a reality can we speak of a routinization of charisma." . . .

The Assemblies of God structure is sufficiently flexible for the continued presence of charisma. The siren of accommodative forces, however, can deafen believers to the whisper of charismatic voices, dreams, and visions. Waiting quietly and patiently for the leading of God is not readily compatible with contemporary American culture, where instant lottery winners are heroes and fast-food chains a main export. Worldly models of growth and success have subtly made inroads in this denomination that once sought to be separate from the world. While pragmatism, efficiency, wealth, and power continue to make significant accommodative gains unnoted by all but the most astute observers, attempts are made to curb other accommodative forces. Where it is able, the Assemblies of God continues its struggle to defend its basic Pentecostal creed and vestigial Pentecostal mores. Becoming increasingly evangelistic in profile, some of its leaders are venturing into political waters and joining the efforts of the Religious Right in the name of "morality." On many recognized and a few largely unrecognized issues of accommodation, the denomination has lost ground. Pentecostals are no longer a "peculiar people" in many matters that once separated them from their neighbors. Accommodation in dress, entertainment, and lifestyle as well as, more recently, the lure of political power have undoubtedly facilitated their move into the mainstream.

part four

CATHOLICISM

In sociological terms, the argument can be made that in this century, Catholicism in America has moved from a sect to a denomination. As Andrew Greeley (1972) points out, Catholicism in the nineteenth and early twentieth centuries had the tenor of an immigrant church that was significantly different from if not in actual opposition to the dominant (Protestant) culture. As a means of maintaining group identity and in reaction to the opposition they received from the culture, Catholics, at least until World War II, engaged in boundary maintenance and maintained a relatively high degree of tension with the environment.[1] After this time, Catholics began to make significant social, educational, and occupational progress. Because of or as a result of assimilationist processes, some of the barriers between them and the rest of American culture began to fall.

The movement from sect-like group to "denomination" was significantly accelerated by the election of John Fitzgerald Kennedy to the presidency and the reforms of the Second Vatican Council. By many estimates, the latter event was one of the most significant for Catholicism in the past hundred years. It was an attempt to make the church more relevant to the modern world and involved such sweeping changes as making the vernacular, instead of Latin, the language of the Mass; permitting greater involvement of the laity; and beginning the use of the "People of God" terminology with its more inclusive language. The change that had perhaps the greatest impact—and with which both of the articles included here deal—was the "freedom of conscience" document established by the council. Indeed, this principle of individual conscience was evoked by many Catholics in opposition to the Vatican's 1968 document *Humanae Vitae,* which prohibited all means of artificial birth control. With all these changes, the Catholic church in the United States became less distinctive, less mysterious to outsiders, and perhaps even a bit more "Protestant"—in other words, very much like an American denomination.

However, this loss of distinctiveness was a mixed blessing. Some saw and continue to see accommodation and similarity to other groups as a dilution of what it meant to be Catholic. As Margaret O'Brien Steinfels (1993:16) puts it,

> The prevailing individualism, the tempting congregationalism of American Protestant Christianity, and the pragmatic rationality of our economic and business systems are increasingly congenial to the mindset of American Catholics. All of these represent enticing alternatives to the communal, hierarchical and sacramental understandings that lie at the heart of Catholicism. Were we more distant from the social distance of our immigrant forbearers, we would more easily see that the tensions we feel as American Catholics have as much to do with being American as with being Catholic.

Steinfels also notes that, similar to the situation characterizing American Catholics before World War II, the church is once again an "immigrant" church; but this time the immigrants come from places such as Vietnam and Latin

America. The hierarchy of the church is dominated by white European males who descended from previous waves of immigrants. This composition presents a barrier to further inclusion of those who do not share the same cultural understandings as the dominant group (African-Americans, Hispanic-Americans, and women).

Two other well-documented problems affect American Catholics. As discussed by Ebaugh (1977) and Wittberg (1994), women's religious orders are plagued by a rapidly aging population, a lack of new recruits, and an increasing number of defections. These factors not only have an effect on the potential survival of religious communities but also may result in the loss of one of the defining symbols of Catholicism. Catholic religious orders helped found and run many schools and hospitals, and as Steinfels (1993:18) puts it, the loss of these people represents a "thinning out of life at the center" and "the loss of people and places that embodied particular charisms, fostered certain devotions and specialized in certain kinds of work."

The second problem has perhaps received more publicity. Richard Schoenherr and Lawrence Young, in their book *Full Pews and Empty Altars: Demographics of the Priest Shortage in U.S. Catholic Dioceses* (1994), present a striking picture of what Schoenherr termed "a priesthood in irreversible decline."[2] He notes that the number of Catholic seminarians in U.S. theologates (the final years of study before ordination) decreased 59 percent between 1966 and 1993. If that were not enough, the priesthood is also plagued by defections and a problem with retaining young priests. He points out that in the early 1970s, 95 percent of all newly ordained priests were needed to fill posts created by resignations. At the same time, the numbers of diocesan priests are declining (Schoenherr projects a 40 percent decrease in the priesthood population between 1966 and 2005) and the numbers of the laity are projected to increase 65 percent during that time. This changes the active priest-to-laity ratio from 1:1,100 in 1975 to 1:2,200 in 2005. One of the reasons cited by Schoenherr and others for this shift is the problem of mandatory celibacy for priests, which is seen as keeping younger men out of the priesthood. The strictures of celibacy are also seen as the reason for younger priests resigning shortly after ordination to marry.

In the following excerpt from his excellent book *Conscience First, Tradition Second: A Study of Young American Catholics*, Patrick McNamara reviews the empirical literature on post–Vatican II American Catholicism and evaluates the factors that have given rise to what he terms the "selective Catholicism" during this period. For younger Catholics, some areas such as birth control, attitudes toward sexuality, divorce, and abortion under certain circumstances are seen as matters for individual conscience and not subject to the dictates of external authorities. These same people may acknowledge the traditions and authority of the church in some areas, while leaving others to conscience. The former areas are what McNamara terms "devotional Catholicism" and include respect for the clergy and an experiential belief in the importance of ritual involvement for fostering a sense of community. Although both aspects are part of the sensibility of many contemporary Catholics, McNamara closes this section with some concern for what these trends might mean for the future of Catholic identity itself.

The research reported by Andrea Williams and James Davidson in their article "Catholic Conceptions of Faith: A Generational Analysis" expresses the same cautions as McNamara about the future of Catholicism. Their methodology is based on focus group interviews covering the way in which three different cohorts of Catholics approach matters of faith. Their three cohorts are those born on or before 1940, those born from 1941 to 1960, and those born from 1961 to 1976. In their estimation, there has been a shift in the way these various cohorts practice Catholicism, from "institutional" (in which participation in the church is an anchor for faith and the reason things are done a certain way) to "individualistic" (in which there is more of an emphasis on a personal involvement with God). As they see it, "a combination of societal and specifically Catholic changes has conspired to produce a shift from institutional to individual conceptions of faith." They link these "specifically Catholic" changes to the social and structural changes that have affected the United States in the past several decades. The shift in religious meanings from the corporate to the individual had an adverse affect on the participation rates of younger Catholics. The youngest cohort of Catholics exhibit much more individualistic patterns than the oldest cohort, who tend to be more "institutional." This individualism comes at a time when more authority is shifting to the laity, partially because of the decline in Catholic religious orders and the coming shortage of priests. Williams and Davidson express concern about the willingness or ability of younger Catholics to be able to step into the vacuum and provide a viable future for the Catholic church in America.

In sum, the Catholic church faces several problems similar to the ones facing many mainline Protestant churches, such as an aging population, an aging leadership, and a possible decrease in the intensity of religious feeling by its younger members. There are also problems that may be uniquely Catholic, such as the future role of the laity in leadership positions, the structure of the church hierarchy itself, and the inclusion of minorities in the life of the church. Although Catholicism is subject to the same structural forces that cause Protestant churches to examine their place and future, some solutions will have to be found to problems that are uniquely Catholic.

ADDITIONAL READING

GREELEY, A. 1990. *The Catholic Myth: The Behavior and Beliefs of American Catholics.* New York: Macmillan.
    This is an accessible, often humorous analysis about why American Catholics are as they are today.

patrick h. mcnamara

CONSCIENCE FIRST, TRADITION SECOND

THREADS UNRAVEL: VATICAN II AND *HUMANAE VITAE*

Just how the Second Vatican Council affected American Catholicism continues to generate lively debate. What seems to me incontestable is the fallout from the 1968 "birth control" encyclical letter of Pope Paul VI. *Humanae Vitae* set off a reaction in the American Catholic church that simultaneously affected two elements of devotional Catholicism: *authority* and *the sense of sin*. The unanticipated events following the declaration show dramatically how great numbers of American Catholics, in pursuing the American dream of upward social mobility, had shed the "ghetto" distinctiveness. . . . They were prepared to react like their Protestant and Jewish neighbors, with supreme regard for the individual conscience and a disregard of authority attempting to enforce norms in the name of a sacred tradition. No less than the meaning of "being Catholic" was suddenly and unexpectedly at stake. . . .

It is precisely this sense of "being Catholic" that constitutes a problematic legacy for younger Catholics today. How did the devotional Catholicism taken for granted by an older generation begin to unravel?

Between 1968 and 1969, Catholic laity were treated to the spectacle of those traditionally representing authority publicly dissenting from a solemnly pronounced papal teaching. Instead of bowing submissively, some clergy and even some bishops seemed, at least tacitly, to be saying, "make your decision according to your own conscience." Furthermore, had not the Vatican Council asserted the right of the individual conscience to be free from outside coercion in its *Declaration of Religious Liberty?* At stake was no less than authority of the church itself. In Dolan's trenchant summary, "The encyclical and the harsh reprisal against dissenting clergy undercut this *Declaration* and created a severe credibility gap for the church. Catholics were not only disappointed, but disillusioned. For these reasons, *Humanae Vitae* was a shattering blow to the euphoria that flourished after Vatican II" (Dolan 1985:436).

The sense of sin seemed to be diminishing as Catholics were exposed to dissent from within the ranks of the clergy themselves. The issue of divorce with remarriage soon joined that of birth control. While the proscription of divorce with remarriage was officially unchanged, bishops and priests were scarcely unaware of the growing numbers of Catholics divorcing and remarrying, or wishing to remarry. Soon ministry to the divorced, with an accompanying attitude of compassion, replaced for many clergy a former attitude of condemnation. Annulments grew. In 1967, the American church granted 700 annulments; by 1978, the number grew to 25,000. The departure of many priests and nuns from active ministry raised questions about the requirements of celibacy and the value of a life vowed to poverty, chastity, and obedience (Dolan 1985:436). Did Catholics sin in practicing birth control, remarrying after divorce, or leaving the priesthood and sisterhood? Could an authority command respect and obedience when, in 1966, it no longer required abstinence from meat on Fridays, whereas before this date, deliberately eating on meat on Friday was a mortal sin meriting eternal punishment?

In retrospect, it is hardly surprising that survey research conducted in the 1970s and 1980s demonstrates significant changes in beliefs and practices among American Catholics. Particularly affected were members of the baby-boom generation coming to maturity from the mid-1960s on. . . . "Selective Catholicism," or theological individualism, in which the individual considers himself or herself the final arbiter and judge of what is to be believed and practiced, is a stance frequently found among these younger American adults and their children.

YOUNGER CATHOLICS IN THE 1970s: THE RISE OF THEOLOGICAL INDIVIDUALISM

The massive research of Father Andrew Greeley and colleagues stands as the premier source of information on post-Vatican II American Catholics. As senior study director of the National Opinion Research Center (NORC) affiliated with the University of Chicago, priest-sociologist Andrew Greeley, both as author and coauthor with colleagues, has written a series of books, articles, and research reports which taken in toto constitute a detailed profile of American Catholic belief, worship, and practice over the last twenty years.

I now summarize briefly the findings I think best illustrate the concept of theological individualism, for it is this shift in religious consciousness that distinctively stamps the young Catholics profiled. . . .

A good place to start is Greeley's concept of "the communal Catholic." Survey findings from 1973 and 1974 showed Catholic laypersons distrustful of the church's teaching authority and unwilling to take it seriously. Yet, insisted Greeley, this lay alienation did not extend to a rejection of their Catholic heritage or identity. Young Catholics skeptical of church leadership were not switching from Catholicism to other denominations; "communal Catholics" did not forsake Sunday Mass. They would remain Catholic in self-chosen identity yet exhibit a "self-consciously selective style of affiliating with the Catholic tradition" (Greeley 1977a:272). Their social location was a well-educated younger stratum "who find themselves on the fringe of the nation's intellectual and cultural elites, either trying to gain admission or conscious of the barriers that bar admission" (Greeley 1977a:272).

By 1979, Greeley was focusing explicitly on younger Catholics. In *Crisis in the Church*, he returned to "the very serious problem of the Church's almost nonexistent credibility in the area of sexual ethics. Seventy-three percent of Catholics *under* thirty years of age approved of premarital sex among engaged couples; by contrast, only 30 percent of those *over* thirty lent their approval" (Greeley 1979:260). In fact, a Chicago archdiocesan survey indicated that among those under thirty who reported receiving Holy Communion weekly and praying daily, "approximately two-thirds . . . approved of premarital sex among the engaged and approved of divorce and birth control" (Greeley 1979:13).

In the 1981 publication of *Young Catholics*, based on a 1979 survey of American and Canadian Catholics under thirty, and authored by Joan Fee and colleagues, findings were in continuity with previous research: 25 percent of those eighteen to twenty-nine years old had left the church; 35 percent of the entire group (fourteen to thirty years old) attended Mass weekly, three-quarters went to confession once a year or less. Yet almost half of both current and former Catholics said they felt very or moderately close to God and approximately a third of each group reported praying daily (Fee et al. 1981:230).

The authors note that by the time young Catholics reach their late twenties, they tend to "drift back" to more regular religious practice. The drift, they suggest, is an aspect of "a more general alienation from all social institutions," while the return is linked with marriage, particularly if the spouse is also Catholic. This return is also associated with "warm religious imagery" and "a sexually fulfilling marriage with such spouses," as well as with Catholic schooling (Fee et al. 1981:230).

In 1985 came *American Catholics since the Council: An Unauthorized Report*. Four years later Greeley published *Religious Change in America*. Both books summarize previous survey research. By 1975, any decline in church attendance had leveled off. The dropoff between 1969 and 1975 did not signal a young generation of Catholics turned "irreligious" and remaining so throughout their lives. Catholics in their twenties are just like Protestant young men and women—slightly under a third attend church weekly. This percentage jumps into the high forties for both traditions if one adds "at least once-a-month" attenders. In fact, higher attendance accompanies each successive age grouping. By the time they are in their early forties, over half of Catholics attend every week, or almost so—a figure rising to 67 percent if one includes the "at least once-a-month" category. In other words, as young Catholics enter their thirties when marriage and the raising of children become responsibilities, their attendance "rebounds" a good deal (Greeley 1985:223, 1989).

CATHOLICS IN THE 1980s

The early 1980s are covered by *The American Catholic People*, a comprehensive view of Catholic beliefs, attitudes, and practices in the United States (Gallup and Castelli 1987). In 1987, *The National Catholic Reporter* sponsored a national survey conducted and analyzed by four sociologists, William D'Antonio, James Davidson, Dean Hoge, and Ruth Wallace. Their report, *The American Catholic Laity in a Changing Church*, appeared in the fall of 1989.

I turn first to the three major conclusions of the Gallup-Castelli study.

First, in an overall sense, the authors agree with Greeley's assessment: church attendance has been stable from 1975 through 1985. The so-called decline phenomenon was short-lived. In fact, Catholics are back to religious activities such as confession, saying the rosary, involvement in parish life, and Bible reading. Increases among young Catholics in these devotions parallel those among older Catholics. Catholics *do* expect "liberalizing" changes in their church: ordination of women and married men, permission to practice birth control, remarriage following divorce, and abortion under some circumstances (rape, incest, or a deformed fetus). Trend data supported these expectations: 47 percent of Catholics in 1985 supported ordination of women, as opposed to 29 percent in 1974 (Gallup and Castelli 1987:56). American Catholics still show respect for the priesthood and for nuns. The church, however, received low marks from its members on how it treats separated, divorced, and remarried Catholics (Gallup and Castelli 1987:50).

Second, of interest to the present study, Hispanic Catholics, 70 percent of whom are Catholic nationwide, are singled out for analysis. Hispanics surveyed in 1978 by the Gallup Organization would like to see more evidence of Hispanic culture and tradition in church services. This is less the case as the respondents' income and educational levels increase. Three-quarters would like to see more Hispanic priests, but "only 56 percent say they would want a son of theirs to become a priest. This drops to 46 percent among those age eighteen to twenty-four" (Gallup and Castelli 1987:147). Fifty-one percent would approve of a daughter becoming a nun. Hispanics are, the authors suggest, more vulnerable to recruitment by non-Catholic churches due to "weak institutional ties to Catholicism," e.g., 10 percent of those surveyed reported doing some kind of work currently for their church (though an additional 41 percent said they would be willing to do so if asked) (Gallup and Castelli 1987:148).

Third, young Catholics are *not* leaving the church for good. Gallup and Castelli agree with Greeley that lower rates of attendance are most likely life-cycle effects. College-educated Catholics are no less likely to be involved in the church; three-fifths of them rate the church as "excellent" or "good" at meeting their needs (Gallup and Castelli 1987:190).

The D'Antonio, Davidson, Hoge, and Wallace study indicated no turnaround from previous trends in the late 1980s. Younger Catholics (eighteen to twenty-nine years old), as contrasted with those age thirty and older, are less likely to say the church is an important part of their lives, to attend Mass weekly, and to read the Bible on a regular basis; they donate less money to the church (D'Antonio et al. 1989:47). On moral issues of sex and marriage (sexual relations outside marriage, homosexual behavior, remarrying without annulment, and practicing birth control), young Catholics were joined by those ages thirty to fifty-five (in contrast with those over fifty-five) in believing that "final moral authority" should lie "with the individual or with a collaboration of church leaders and individuals" (D'Antonio et al. 1989:88–89). This is perhaps the first indication from survey research suggesting that the parents of many of today's teenage Catholics are no less "liberal" in some issues relating to church authority than are their offspring. However, for all ages, frequent Mass attendance notably increases willingness to accept church authority.

While the authors found that Catholic laity wish to participate in joint decision making with church leaders ("working toward a model of Church as voluntary association"), they also discovered that

> never did more than one-third of the laity acknowledge that the ultimate source of moral authority (who should decide what is morally right or wrong) should rest with the hierarchy alone. Contemporary Catholics see themselves as the proper sources of moral authority, with or without the teaching of church leaders as an aid to guide them. Rejection of Vatican decrees is greatest among the young and better educated. (D'Antonio et al. 1989:188)

CATHOLICS AS "LESS INTENSELY RELIGIOUS"

While the preceding portraits carry no overwhelming message of mass defection from the Catholic church, some findings from the Gallup-Castelli study seem relatively negative and deserve further reflection. The two authors point to "a greater erosion of outward concern about religion among Catholics than among Protestants" (Gallup and Castelli 1987:13). This erosion they label "the intensity factor." It shows up on responses where Catholics find religion *less* important than Protestants; whereas Catholics were *more* pious than Protestants in the 1950s, they are less so today.

On a ten-point scale, for example, Catholics are less likely than Protestants to give high priority to helping those in need. Slightly less than half (49 percent) of Catholics give this moral ideal a nine or ten rating, while 64 percent of mainline Protestants and 74 percent of Evangelicals do so. Catholics and Protestants do not differ significantly on political self-description (left, right, or center). But using the same scale, Catholics are more liberal than Protestants "concerning values toward sex, morality, family life, and religion." Just 19 percent of Protestants placed themselves in liberal categories in these areas, while 29 percent of Catholics did so (Gallup and Castelli 1987:9).

Surveys also show Catholics to be tolerant as a group in attitudes toward nonbelievers, homosexuals, and unwed couples living together. In addition, "the Catholic worldview also asserts itself in attitudes toward other religions, as seen in the greater sensitivity toward Jews and the astonishing difference revealed in the fact that, unlike Protestants, a majority of Catholics would not be deterred from voting for a qualified presidential candidate who happened to be an atheist" (Gallup and Castelli 1987:65).

Catholics list salvation fourth in importance when ranking personal needs in life, while Protestants place it first (Catholics list physical well-being, love and affection, and a sense of meaning in life ahead of salvation).

Catholics are *less* likely than Protestants to say that:

1.   they have a personal relationship with God (though an overwhelming majority say they do, of course).
2.   deepening a relationship with God is "very important" to them.
3.   they have been influenced by a presence or power different from their everyday lives.
4.   a person can't be a good Christian without going to church (Gallup and Castelli 1987:14).

Seventy-two percent of Catholics agree that "God doesn't really care how he is worshipped as long as he is worshipped." Catholics are more inclined to view the devil as an impersonal force causing people to do wrong, whereas Protestants incline to see the devil as a personal being; just 51 percent believe that God will punish evil for all eternity (Gallup and Castelli 1987:15). Catholics are more "accepting" than Protestants, viewing fewer actions as sinful and believing that salvation is possible without belief in Christ. Grappling with problems in this world seems more important to Catholics who "are more likely to emphasize love of neighbor and to rank broader social concerns above personal evangelization"—in a word, a more private and less enthusiastic approach to spreading their faith to others (Gallup and Castelli 1987:24–25).

Yet another survey conducted in 1985 discovered that 25 percent of those claiming to be Catholics considered religion "largely old fashioned and out of date"; a further 27 percent had "no opinion" on the same question. Less than half (48 percent) of Catholics could bring themselves to state that religion was "relevant and did supply answers in their lives," compared with 66 percent of Protestants who found religion relevant and a mere 15 percent who termed religion "out of date" (Deedy 1987:72–73).

Fifty-two percent of Protestant teenagers consider religious faith to be a very important quality, whereas only 37 percent of Catholic teenagers feel the same way (Princeton Religious Research Center 1987:2).

These findings, like all survey results, lie open to a variety of interpretations. I think Gallup and Castelli are too benign in recurring to the metaphor of "intensity." They suggest that U.S. Catholics are simply more pragmatically accepting of the world around them; they are less "personal" in their approach to religion when compared to their Protestant neighbors. I would agree instead with author John Deedy that the United States contains large numbers of "cultural Catholics" or "individuals for whom Catholicism is not so much a compelling spiritual experience as it was a social circumstance, a shared history, an accident of birth rather an actual spiritual and intellectual choice" (Deedy 1987:74). Perhaps the holding of old orthodoxies means less than "keeping in touch with roots," so that being a Catholic is part of a distinct *cultural* identity rather than a mark of distinctive belief, worship, and morality. Devotional Catholicism, of course, emphasized almost exclusively the "orthodox" dimension and, in so doing, provided elements of a distinctive identity, as we have seen. But these findings suggest that whatever remains of devotional Catholicism has become ensconced in a strictly personal, private sphere, contributing little to spiritual identity or distinctiveness. To the extent this interpretation is plausible, it may reflect an upwardly mobile Catholic population tending to invest much more in occupational and educational identities than in "personally religious" ones. The latter assume less salience as "ghetto Catholicism" has receded and its symbols, once so forcefully inculcated by religious authority figures, are now less evocative of and indeed necessary for one's sense of security, place, status, and personal identity.

The meaning of being a Catholic, in short, has not just changed in content; it appears to have diminished in importance to Catholics. This is the sense in which I suggest that Catholic distinctiveness or "differentness" has receded over the past two decades. This development is yet another indication of a profound change in the *tradition* called Roman Catholic as believers understand and profess it. Catholics seem to have blended all too smoothly into what Herberg called "the Great American Way of Life." He is echoed by recent research on a broad spectrum of American Catholics. David Leege, a director of the Notre Dame Study of Catholic Parish Life, points to Catholic educational attainment in recent decades:

> The legitimacy accorded church authority is no longer traditional, but increasingly rational; Catholics have known both education and life away from ancestral parishes; they are accustomed in their jobs and daily life to means-end calculations and have to be won to the reasonableness of a policy. They live in a society and have been socialized through an educational system that seldom accords absolute authority to any human being. They are accustomed to owing loyalty to an institution while still accepting or rejecting specific policies of its leaders. They find no great inconsistency in accepting the central mysteries of the church and, in recent decades, rejecting some of its teachings. (Leege 1985:21)

SUMMARY

Recent survey evidence leaves no doubt that selective Catholicism, or theological individualism, continues visibly and firmly in the 1980s. Catholics "make up their own minds" and set church authority aside on certain issues. Problems of divorce, credibility on the issue of birth control, and on "everything related to sex" remain. "When it comes to sex, church leaders are preaching to an audience that is simply not paying attention" (Gallup and Castelli 1987:182).

I have reviewed this large body of research in some detail if only because it demonstrates empirically better than any abstract argument the substantial shifts in the tradition labeled "devotional Catholicism." I say "shift," because the changes clearly have been neither drastic nor totally transforming. Here survey research joins the contemporary experience of many Catholics to underline how much of devotional Catholicism remains intact: the clergy continues to be respected; sin and repentance are acknowledged, reduced though the list of sins may be; ritual involvement confers on many a sense of community and of comfort and some believers find the miraculous retains its force in their lives as prayers for "hopeless cases" are unexpectedly answered.

But tradition *has* eroded in some clear respects, particularly (though by no means exclusively) among younger Catholics for whom the principle of selectivity seems well entrenched in areas of birth control, sexual attitudes, abortion under certain circumstances, and divorce with remarriage. Catholics have simply defined these areas as outside the legitimate range of external authority. They are subject mainly to individual experience and judgment. Add to this the apparent loss of intensity pointed out by Gallup and Castelli and the question poses itself: is being a Catholic any longer a badge of distinctive identity? . . .

In sum, as the 1980s came to a close, survey research demonstrated the enthronement of individual conscience, particularly in the lives of younger Catholics, as the ultimate arbiter of what is believable or not believable, right or wrong, for each individual. "Selective Catholicism" seemed firmly in place. Catholic leadership appeared little inclined to challenge this phenomenon directly. Instead the American bishops in the 1980s took a leaf from another Vatican II theme, insertion of the church into the world's agenda of socioeconomic issues. Exhibiting their own brand of "historical consciousness," they urged American Catholics to bring their religious heritage to bear on questions of nuclear war and disarmament and on issues of social justice and the more equitable distribution of wealth within the American economy as well as to consider whether the pursuit of affluence and acquiring consumer goods is compatible with Christian values. How receptive younger Catholics, in particular, may be to these appeals is an issue of central importance if the bishops are not to be "playing to an empty house." Catholic leadership confronts a laity whose "time-space" context in late twentieth-century United States is one of rapid assimilation to middle- and upper-middle-class (professional) status. A key issue . . . is young American Catholics' receptivity to this new "prophetic thrust" articulated by their leadership.

andrea s. williams and
james d. davidson

CATHOLIC CONCEPTIONS OF FAITH
A Generational Analysis

Most observers agree that there is a great deal of diversity among American Catholics. While there was a certain amount of diversity in the 1940s and 1950s (Fichter 1951), the beliefs and practices of American Catholics have become increasingly varied since then. Studies done during the 1950s and 1960s indicated that there was more uniformity among Catholics than among mainline Protestant groups.[1] . . . More recent research, however, suggests that American Catholics' beliefs and practices are now more diverse than they were prior to the Second Vatican Council.

In this paper, we argue that one dimension of this shift from uniformity to pluralism has been a movement from an *institutional* to an *individual* conception of faith. We define an institutional understanding of faith as one in which a person sees the church as an essential mediating force in his or her relationship with God. Analogous to Kennedy's (1988) description of "culture one" Catholics, Catholic laity holding an institutional conception of faith are concerned with the teaching authority of the church, whether they agree or disagree with particular doctrines. They believe it important to participate in church rituals and ceremonies, such as attending Mass, receiving the Eucharist, and getting married in the church.

Laity maintaining an individual understanding of faith are similar to those whom Kennedy (1988) labels as "culture two" Catholics. Rather than being concerned with the teachings and rituals of the church, Catholics holding an individual conception of faith emphasize a direct, intimate relationship with God. They view faith as very personal, having little to do with pronouncements of the magisterium or participation in the sacraments.

Using focus group data, this paper explores a generational shift from institutional to individual understandings of faith. We argue that generational differ-

Andrea S. Williams and James Davidson, "Catholic Conceptions of Faith: A Generational Analysis," Sociology of Religion *57(3) (1996). Reprinted by permission of the Association for the Sociology of Religion and the authors.*

ences in conceptions of faith have resulted from both societal and specifically Catholic changes.

A GENERATIONAL EXPLANATION

Mannheim pioneered the study of cohorts in his 1952 essay "The Problem of Generations." He argued that persons are shaped and molded during their adolescence in ways that forever impact their behavior and attitudes. His point was that persons born during the same time period and in a similar geographical region share a collective understanding of the world. Having been exposed to similar historical and cultural phenomena during their adolescence, persons born during a specific time period share a worldview that is likely to be vastly different from those born during different time periods. Thus, Mannheim argued, persons belonging to particular birth cohorts have a shared vision of the world.

Since the publication of Mannheim's essay, researchers have relied on his theory of generations to explain the religious sensibilities of generations. . . . In his recent book, *Frameworks*, Walrath (1987) lays out his interpretation of Mannheim's theory. According to Walrath, persons are forever affected by the historical and cultural phenomena to which they are exposed between the ages of thirteen and twenty-two. When persons are in this age range, they are experiencing their "formative years." Thus, the political, economic, and social events occurring during a person's formative years continue to affect her worldview for the remainder of her life. In Walrath's (1987:35; italics in original text) words:

> [Persons] move chronologically through childhood, youth, and so forth on into old age like the generations that preceded them. But their experiences of the world are qualitatively very different at similar stages . . . they never let go of the experienced differences . . . they continue to perceive and define the world in terms of that unique framework as they progress through their lives . . . *they perceive the same experiences differently from those socialized previously, who are now side by side with them in the same period.* In important respects they never grow up to take on the same perspectives their elders hold. They become a "cohort."

According to Wuthnow (1976b:851), it is "events placing extra strain on the transition from family values to economic values [which] are likely to increase the chances of distinct generation units forming." Thus, those who experience events such as war and great economic depression (both of which affect persons' entry into the economic sphere and raise questions regarding gender roles) during their formative years are most likely to have similar worldviews that are different from those of other cohorts. But it is not just wars and economic depressions that influence the collective vision of a generation. The assassination of heroes, legal rulings, political scandals, and social events such as the introduction of MTV can all influence a generation's worldview. This paper focuses on events that have influenced the religious beliefs and practices of three generations of Catholics.

THREE GENERATIONS OF CATHOLICS

We use age cohorts to distinguish between three generations of Catholics. . . . The oldest cohort grew up in the 1930s and 1940s. The middle generation was a product of the 1950s and 1960s. The youngest generation came of age in the 1970s and 1980s.

These three generations have had very different experiences during their formative years (roughly age 13 to 22). Some experiences are societal in nature, uniting all members of the generation, regardless of their religious persuasions. Other experiences are specifically Catholic, setting Catholics apart from non-Catholics in the same age cohort. Together, we argue, these societal and specifically Catholic experiences foster a trend from institutional to individual conceptions of faith.

SOCIETAL INFLUENCES

Several writers . . . have observed a societal shift in recent decades from an institutional-collective worldview to a personal-individual emphasis. This cultural shift is associated with myriad social changes in American society.

Like all other Americans in their age cohort, Catholics who grew up in the 1930s and 1940s were influenced by the Great Depression and World War II. They knew what it was like to suddenly lose their jobs, incomes, and ability to provide for their families. They were called upon to defend their own nation from attack, and to defend the world against the evils of Nazism. They needed to pull together as a nation—to help one another economically and to win a world war. They turned to their families, government, and one another for help. They learned that their parents, political leaders, and other institutional authorities would do all they could to end economic hardship and bring peace. They complied when these authorities asked them to do their part in promoting the common good.

Catholics who grew up in the 1950s and 1960s experienced dramatic changes during their formative years. When they were coming of age, they knew both the tranquility of the postwar Eisenhower years and the radical social movements of the 1960s. During the 1950s, they learned to have confidence in established institutions; in the 1960s, they learned to challenge them. In the 1950s, they learned to respect authority; in the 1960s, they questioned it. These "baby boomers" went from acceptance of established institutions to insistence on individuals' right to determine their own lifestyles, including their own religious beliefs and practices.

Catholics who have grown up in the 1970s and 1980s have known political corruption from Watergate to Whitewater; scientific and technological debacles from Three Mile Island to Chernobyl and the *Challenger*; corporate downsizing and income polarization; increased divorce among their parents; the proliferation of drugs; and fear of AIDS. Disillusioned and fearing the future, members of so-called Generation X distrust institutional authorities and feel they only can depend on themselves.

In addition to these secular experiences, there have been at least two society-wide changes in the religious landscape that also promote a shift from institutional to individual conceptions of faith. Several observers . . . claim that in recent decades there has been a collapse of religion's collective importance. As religion's integrative role in American culture has declined, religion has largely become a personal matter. In Hammond's (1992:11) words, there has been a "significant increase in 'personal autonomy,' meaning both an enlarged arena of voluntary choice and an enhanced freedom from structural restraint." According to this perspective, the trend toward voluntarism is evident in all religious faiths (Roozen and Hadaway 1993), including Catholicism (D'Antonio et al. 1989).

There also has been a decline in confidence in religion as a social institution. Whereas older generations were taught to emphasize the functional importance of religion and to respect religious authorities, today's youth stress the prevalence of religious hypocrisy, using Jim Bakker, Jimmy Swaggart, and pedophilia in the Catholic church as evidence for their case. Disillusionment with religious authorities promotes individualism among young Americans, regardless of religious affiliation. "If religious leaders can't be trusted," young people say, "then we have no one to rely on but ourselves."

While these societal conditions lend themselves to a shift from reliance on institutions to reliance on self, they are not enough to account for a shift from institutional to individual conceptions of faith among Catholics. One also must appreciate the role that specifically Catholic experiences have had on members of the three generations we are examining.

SPECIFICALLY CATHOLIC INFLUENCES

Unlike most members of mainline Protestant denominations, Catholics growing up in the 1930s and 1940s were immigrants, or the sons and daughters of immigrants. They had limited educations, blue collar jobs, and modest incomes. They were distinctly working class. But, by the 1950s and 1960s, Catholics were upwardly mobile; they were making it into the American mainstream. By the 1970s and 1980s, there was no doubt that Catholics had achieved social, economic, and political parity with Protestants (Greeley 1990). With socio-economic success came assimilation into American culture, . . . one aspect of which is an emphasis on the freedom to pick and choose one's own religious beliefs (D'Antonio et al. 1989).

In the 1930s and 1940s, a vast network of specifically Catholic organizations protected Catholics against religious prejudice and discrimination; promulgated a distinctly Catholic worldview; stressed the importance of obeying church teachings; and produced levels of doctrinal orthodoxy and religious practice which exceeded those of most Protestant denominations. Catholics growing up in the 1930s and 1940s were socialized into a "ghetto mentality" which assumed that the world was a relatively hostile place, and that Catholics would be safe if they stayed in the church and participated in its large array of Catholic organizations. They learned a very collective, institutional approach to faith.

Baby boomers grew up with one foot in the "old church" and one in the "new church." In the 1950s, they were taught their faith by priests and nuns who relied heavily on the *Baltimore Catechism*. They learned a very institutional concept of church; individuals were always accountable to the church. They viewed the church as "the one true church." They were to do what the priests and nuns told them to do. When they did not, they were to go to confession seeking absolution for their sins.

Then came Vatican II, the most important event in the last one hundred years of Catholic history. Vatican II was a uniquely Catholic experience in the mid-1960s. No other American faith group experienced the anticipation, formulation, and implementation of such dramatic changes. No other group experienced the radical change in religious worldview that the Council promulgated. . . .

Catholics growing up in the 1970s and 1980s know relatively little about the council itself, but have had a very different type of religious upbringing because of it. Instead of memorizing the *Baltimore Catechism*, they have been taught that they are on personal "faith journeys" and that they must take responsibility for their own religious beliefs and practices. Instead of learning that the church is an end in itself, they have learned that it is a means to an end (it is there to help them along the way, providing sacraments which will sustain them on their journeys). Instead of a collective view, they have learned a very individualistic concept of faith (Markey 1994; O'Malley 1986).

Thus we contend, a combination of societal and specifically Catholic changes have conspired to produce a shift from institutional to individual conceptions of faith. If we are right, older Catholics who came of age during the pre–Vatican II years of the 1930s and 1940s should have the most institutional approaches to faith. Catholics who grew up in the 1950s and 1960s are likely to have the most conflicted (institutional *and* individual) views of faith. Catholics who have been raised entirely in the post–Vatican II church should be the most individualistic of all.

DATA AND METHODS OF RESEARCH

The data used for this paper are part of a larger study entitled the Catholic Pluralism Project. The goals of this project were to describe and explain the diversity of religious beliefs and practices among Catholics. The first stage of the project focused on Catholics in Indiana. The second stage included a national sample of Catholics. The study was coordinated by a team of sociologists, theologians, and advisors representing all five Indiana dioceses. The Catholic Pluralism Project included five types of data collection: (1) archival data concerning the church in Indiana; (2) individual interviews; (3) focus groups; (4) a statewide mail survey of Indiana parishioners; and (5) a national telephone poll of Catholics.

The data explored in this paper come from the fifteen focus groups moderated in the summer of 1993. Three focus groups were conducted in each of Indiana's five dioceses. One focus group in each diocese was made up of older persons who experienced their formative years prior to the Second Vatican Council; one included middle-aged Catholics who experienced both the pre–Vatican II church and the implementation of Vatican II while they were coming of age; and one consisted of young persons who grew up entirely after the changes of Vatican II.

The focus groups were audiotaped. Each focus group was presented with the same set of six topics: (1) religious upbringing; (2) the extent to which participants were raised in tightly knit Catholic communities and their feelings regarding such communities; (3) their understanding of the term "church," and what they see as the most positive and negative aspects of the church today; (4) why they identify themselves as Catholic and what this identity means to them; (5) the essentials of being a "good Catholic"; and (6) ways in which being Catholic has impacted their lives. The sixth item produced little response from focus group participants, so reactions to this item are not considered in this paper.

THE PARTICIPANTS

Names and addresses of prospective participants were obtained by telephoning parish pastors in each diocese. Pastors were asked to recommend persons who would ensure diversity within groups, such as active as well as less active parishioners, parishioners with different racial and ethnic backgrounds, and women as well as men.

Each layperson suggested to us received an invitation to participate in a focus group and was offered forty dollars monetary compensation for time, childcare, and travel expenses.

Actual participants included 45 pre–Vatican II Catholics, 43 Vatican II Catholics, and 47 post–Vatican II Catholics. The participants were more religiously committed than the average American Catholic (e.g., they attended Mass more regularly than most Catholics), a fact which increased their willingness to talk about the issues we posed and added to the quality of our data.

Almost all focus group participants had a high school diploma, and about 25 percent had attended college. There were, however, people from all walks of life: professionals such as lawyers and physicians participated, as well as factory workers and farmers. Males and females were equally represented in almost all the focus groups but not in three of the post–Vatican II generation focus groups, where women were overrepresented. Persons of differing racial ethnic and backgrounds were represented fairly in those dioceses (Gary and Indianapolis) which have the greatest racial and ethnic diversity.

METHODS OF ANALYSIS

In the first stage of analysis, all members of the research team listened carefully to each audiotaped focus group. Two researchers from each of the five dioceses listened to the tapes of the three focus groups that had been done in their diocese. The authors listened to all fifteen of the focus group recordings. Researchers took notes on frequently heard key words, memorable quotes and phrases, emerging themes and patterns, and specific responses to the six research questions.

Members of the research team then met to share notes and discuss overall impressions of cohort similarities and differences. There was general consensus in two areas: (a) the religious education and upbringing described by post–Vatican II Catholics was very different from that described by persons of the older cohorts; and (b) the youngest generation of participants was less institutionally committed to the church than either of the other two generations, with those belonging to the oldest cohort being the most institutionally committed of the three generations.

Williams then listened again to each of the fifteen taped focus groups twice. This time, specific responses to questions were categorized as indicating institutional or individual understandings of faith. Faith is defined as a perception of one's relationship with God. Institutional understandings of faith view the church as mediating the relationship between God and an individual; they define the institutional church as essential to one's relationship with God, often pointing to participation in the sacraments as a means of relating to God. Individual perceptions of faith do not regard the institutional church as an important factor in relating to God. Rather, they focus on the importance of a personal relationship with God which minimizes the importance of the institutional church and the sacraments.

Discussion items asking participants why it is that they are Catholic and how they go about strengthening their faith, as well as how they define what it means to be a "good Catholic," are the most useful for determining whether participants see their faith in institutional or individual terms. Responses emphasizing the importance of the church when explaining their Catholic identity were coded as institutional conceptions of faith. Examples of this include assertions by participants that they are Catholic because the Catholic church is the "one true church." Statements made by respondents downplaying the importance of having a Catholic identity and the church's role as a mediator with God were coded as expressing individualism. Assertions that faith is strengthened through participation in the sacraments or Mass attendance were recorded as reflecting institutional commitment, whereas statements that faith is strengthened though personal conversation with God and without the intervention of the church were coded as individual understandings of faith. Answers to the questions about what it takes to be a "good Catholic" were coded as expressing commitment to the institutional church if participation in the sacraments, financial contributions to the church, and obedience to church teachings were emphasized. Discussions of being a "good person" were seen as reflecting individualistic notions of faith.

FINDINGS

While expressions of individualism and institutional understandings of faith exist in all three generational cohorts, the findings also reveal the important cohort differences we expected.

RELIGIOUS UPBRINGING: GENERATIONAL DIFFERENCES

Catholics who experienced their formative years prior to Vatican II overwhelmingly stated that they had been taught the importance of the institutional church as children. Focus group participants who were raised in the 1950s and 1960s described their religious upbringing very similarly to those of the older generation. Participants of both generations talked of memorizing the *Baltimore Catechism* and being taught that the Catholic church is the "one true church." The majority of Catholics in these age groups stated that they had attended parochial schools at which nuns taught them the importance of attending Mass, confession, praying the rosary, and respecting the Holy Days of Obligation. Persons of these cohorts talked of "doing" their faith more than understanding it, stating that their religious training had been very "regimented." . . .

While there was little difference in the way these two generations described their religious upbringing, Catholics in the youngest birth cohort described their religious training very differently. Like people in the older generations, most post-Vatican II Catholics talked of attending Catholic schools or Confraternity of Christian Doctrine (CCD) classes. But unlike the older focus group participants, their discussions of what they were taught actually turned into discussions of what they were not taught. . . .

CONCEPTIONS OF FAITH: GENERATIONAL DIFFERENCES

PRE–VATICAN II GENERATION

In discussing their faith, most participants of this generation viewed the institutional church as an important mediating force in their relationship with God. When asked why they are Catholic, several members of this generation stated that it is because the Catholic church is the "one true church," with the implication being that the "best" way one can relate to God is through the Catholic church. One man expressed the sentiments of this generation when he said that "the Catholic church has the answers." Another participant said, "If you're going to be a Christian, you have to be a Catholic." It seems that to participants of this generation, their relationship to the church and self-definition as Catholic are central to their faith. . . . When asked about the essentials of being a "good Catholic," most participants of this age cohort answered with statements such as "participate in the sacraments," "abide by the commandments and rules of the church," and "be active in the church in some way." Almost all pre–Vatican II generation participants agreed that it is important to support the church financially and attend Mass regularly. The majority of participants in this cohort argued that it is important for a "good Catholic" to follow church teachings regarding premarital and homosexual relations, although some voiced disagreement with the birth control teaching. A pre–Vatican II male who accepts the birth control teaching said a good Catholic must

> accept the pope as our leader and take his word and follow what the pope teaches and what the church teaches. Do a minimum as far as receiving sacraments and obey rules. I don't think you can just do your own thing and still call yourself a Catholic. Follow teachings of the Catholic church . . . not pick and choose like a cafeteria . . . there are people who disagree with church teachings and call themselves Catholic, but they're not.

A participant in one pre–Vatican II generation focus group stated that she did not believe it to be important to be a "good Catholic." Rather, she argued, it is more important that a person be a "good person." Clearly this participant subscribes to what we have defined as an individualistic conception of faith, but her opinion differs greatly from the majority of participants her age. While her statement shows that individualistic understandings of faith exist among Catholics of the pre–Vatican II generation, the viewpoints generally expressed by this age group emphasize the importance of institutional commitment.

VATICAN II GENERATION

We expected participants of this generation to voice both institutional and individualistic understandings of faith. Vatican II Catholics experienced both the pre–Vatican II church and the council during their formative years, and therefore are likely to be ambivalent about the church's role in their relationship with God. We heard responses that varied from institutional to individualistic perceptions of faith. While some participants clearly reflected individualistic understandings of faith, others tended to give responses similar to those provided by pre–Vatican II participants. In addition to these individual differences, responses varied according to the question asked. While some questions elicited individualistic responses from most participants, others produced both individualistic and institutional responses.

Vatican II Catholics tended to define "church" in ways that differed from pre–Vatican II Catholics. In this age group, there was talk of "spirituality" and having a "personal relationship with God." Some persons of this cohort described their "religion" or "spirituality" as being separate from the church. As one woman summed up the sentiments of her generation, "The priest is the church, the way we relate to God is our religion or our spirituality. It's almost like they are two different things." Comments similar to these were heard in all five Vatican II focus groups.

When asked what the church can do to foster commitment among Catholics their age, one participant mentioned that the church should "move toward a spiritual church, one which has a direct relationship between you and your God or your higher power." Another person agreed, saying that the church should put more emphasis on "the spiritual aspect, rather than doctrine." She then asked, "If you don't have a personal relationship with God, what does everything else mean?" . . . Clearly, these participants view their faith in largely individualistic terms, downplaying the need for mediation of the church in their relationship with God. As one group member said, "My spirituality is more important to me than my religion, and I can be spiritual anywhere. In fact, I am more spiritual walking in the woods than I am walking down the main aisle of the church."

When asked why they are Catholic, however, some Vatican II generation Catholics voiced explanations that were very similar to those given by the pre–Vatican II generation participants. For example, some focus group members stated that they are Catholic because Catholicism is the "best" or "true" religion. These participants strongly embrace their Catholic identity. One participant stated that he is Catholic because he is "convinced that the Catholic church is going to get [him] to heaven." The articulation of opinions such as these indicate that some persons of this generation do view the church as a central component to their faith. Many others in this age group, however, voiced opinions which differ greatly from those commonly heard from the pre–Vatican II participants. For example a few participants stated that they could be just as happy belonging to some other faith tradition. They just "happen" to be Catholic; they were born and raised Catholic and remain Catholic out of convenience. Several other participants stated that their "personal relationship with God" is more important to them than their Catholic identity. A female participant explicitly stated what we have defined as an individualistic understanding of faith when she said, "Faith is my relationship with God, personally."

Responses to the question of what is required for a person to be a "good Catholic" indicate that while some participants maintain institutional conceptions of faith, others believe that a person's faith is not dependent on institutional commitment. . . .

POST–VATICAN II GENERATION

Of the three generations, the participants of the youngest cohort were most likely to express individualistic views of faith. This was evident in the number of times post–Vatican II Catholics emphasized that being a "good person" is more important than commitment to the church. When asked what it takes to be a "good Catholic" many participants said that participation in the sacraments, Mass attendance, and contributing to the church financially are unimportant. . . . These respondents argued that they do not want to judge others according to criteria set forth by the church because "what really counts is what's in your heart," that what is important is "that you're doing the right thing for you," and that "whether a person is a good Catholic or not is between the person and God." . . .

The majority of participants stated that they are Catholic because they were born and raised Catholic and have never considered being anything else. However, this did not mean that they are committed to the Catholic identity or the institutional church. . . . Another woman summed up the sentiments of many post–Vatican II participants saying that "Your religion is within you . . . it's your relationship between you and God . . . it doesn't matter if you're Catholic, Jewish, or Protestant."

When discussing the issue of strengthening faith, most participants gave vague responses. While many stated that they think it is important to strengthen faith, they said little about how they go about doing it. . . . The majority seemed to agree with the opinion of one woman, who said, "You don't have to go to church all the time . . . you can pray at home." Like those who came of age in the 1950s and 1960s, post–Vatican II participants used the word "spirituality" when discussing their faith and responding to questions about strengthening it. . . .

While the post–Vatican II generation emphasized a personal relationship with God, there were participants who are clearly committed to the church as an institution. . . . Others expressed concern over the church's teaching against artificial forms of birth control. While most participants of this age group said they do not care about the church's view of birth control, most wished the church would reconsider its position. Despite this, even those who espoused commitment to the institutional church maintained that "being a good person" is more important than attending Mass, contributing to the church, or participating in the sacraments.

CONCLUSIONS

Although there were some intragenerational variations, our focus group data indicate significant intergenerational differences in the way Catholics think about faith. Catholics who experienced their formative years prior to Vatican II view their faith primarily in institutional terms. For Catholics of this generation, the church is seen as a mediating force in their relationship with God. Persons of this cohort indicate that a Catholic identity, participation in the sacraments, and overall commitment to the church are essential to relating with God. They see little difference between involvement with the church and relating to God because the two are deeply interconnected.

This is certainly less true for Catholics who came of age during Vatican II. Many describe their faith as being less institutionally based than those who came of age before them. Others reflect institutional notions of faith that are similar to the views of pre–Vatican II Catholics.

The post–Vatican II generation maintains the most individualistic views of faith. Concern with whether an individual is a "good person" dominates their discussions. Most members of this age cohort place great emphasis on having a "personal relationship with God" and do not describe the church as an essential component of their faith. If the committed young Catholics in our focus groups do not view the institutional church as an important mediating force in their relationship with God, young Catholics who are no longer attending Mass certainly do not.

These findings suggest that birth cohort is a powerful predictor of the ways in which American Catholics view their faith. These findings strengthen the similar conclusions of researchers. . . . Although our findings show that intragenerational variation exists, these variations can likely be explained by other variables such as ethnicity, gender, and family upbringing.

Our findings support the argument that differences between young and old Catholics are due, in part, to a "cohort effect," not just an "age effect" as argued by other researchers (e.g., Greeley 1989). In our focus groups, the youngest cohort of Catholics described religious upbringings which differ greatly from those described by pre–Vatican II and Vatican II Catholics. Rather than detailing for us what they learned in CCD classes and in their religious education courses in Catholic schools, they told us that they learned little about what it means to be Catholic. Instead of learning church teachings, their religious education consisted of learning to be a "nice person." Because they were taught to view faith as "having a personal relationship with God," and were not taught to emphasize institutional aspects of the church, it seems unlikely that today's young Catholics will take on the views and practices of their elders as they get further into the life course. Replicating the focus groups in five to ten years using the same participants would certainly help determine whether those belonging to the post–Vatican II generation will embrace more institutional views of faith as they get older, or if they will continue to maintain individualistic religious sensibilities.

Although our focus groups were conducted within one state, feedback we have received from lay Catholics and clergy in other parts of the country suggest that our findings can be generalized beyond Indiana. . . .

IMPLICATIONS FOR THE FUTURE

. . . Well-documented declines in priestly vocations and religious orders . . . seem even more ominous when listening to the post–Vatican II generation. As the shortage of priests, sisters, and brothers suggests a need for greater participation of lay persons in active leadership roles, one is left wondering whether today's young Catholics will be willing to take on such institutional responsibilities. Our research, of course, cannot conclusively answer this question. While it appears that post–Vatican II Catholics do not embrace institutional commitment to the church, instead preferring a more personal brand of faith, there is diversity within the generation. D'Antonio (1996) has found that women and persons with the most Catholic schooling are the most highly committed members of the post-Vatican II generation, but they also are more likely to disagree with church teachings than men and Catholics with less

Catholic schooling. This paradox suggests that today's young Catholics who are most likely to profess an interest in working to maintain the institutional church will also present challenges to the hierarchy and conventional understandings of what it means to be Catholic.

One thing is certain: the hands of time cannot be turned back. Societal changes, as well as changes occurring within the church, leave no doubt that tomorrow's Catholics will be very different from previous generations. The children of post–Vatican II Catholics will receive their religious education from those who never read the *Baltimore Catechism*, and are likely to know little about the changes brought about by Vatican II. The conceptions of faith post–Vatican II Catholics are apt to pass on to the next generation will look decidedly individualistic in nature.

part five

JUDAISM

In 1840, there were approximately 15,000 Jews in the United States. By 1914, that number had grown to 2 million, and presently, by the reckonings of the *American Jewish Yearbook*, there are some 5.8 million (Singer 1994). The four major Jewish groupings in the United States are (in size order) Conservative, Reform, Orthodox, and Reconstructionist.[1] The Reform movement was started in the United States in the nineteenth century by German rabbis influenced by the rationalism and humanism of the Enlightenment. They sought to "modernize" Judaism to make it a better fit with modern culture and emancipate Jews from some of the limitations of traditional Judaism. It was an attempt to set aside some of the "unenlightened" customs of Judaism that kept Jews apart from the cultural mainstream. For example, Blau (1976) notes that in Reform synagogues, "some of the prayers were reworded to avoid expressions of Jewish particularism that might have been considered unpleasant or even offensive by sensitive and enlightened people."

At the end of the nineteenth century, the Conservative movement arose as a reaction to the assimilationist modernism of Reform. Conservative Judaism is seen as the wish to return to the strength of Jewish tradition without returning to Orthodoxy. Conservative Jews maintain the basic practices of Judaism (Sabbath observation, the importance of Hebrew in Jewish life, and many of the dietary laws) without being strict observers of every nuance of *Halacha* (the code of Jewish practice).

Another attempt to synchronize Judaism with modern times was the Reconstructionist branch, which was begun in the United States in 1922 by Mordecai Kaplan. Similar to Reform, Kaplan sought to eliminate "outdated" doctrines such as divine revelation and Jewish particularism but, unlike the Reformers, he sought to keep a great deal of the tradition for social rather than religious purposes. In this formulation, "Jews were most centrally a people, not a religious group" (Davidman 1991:36).

By contrast, Orthodox Judaism represents a resistance to all the encroachments of modernity on religious life. Orthodox Jews[2] adhere most strictly to the demands of *Halacha*. Davidman maintains that this belief in the "obligatory nature of religious law" is what distinguishes the Orthodox from the other branches.

In her book *Tradition in a Rootless World: Women Turn to Orthodox Judaism*, Lynn Davidman provides a fascinating look at the women of Lincoln Square Synagogue and Bais Chana Synagogue, who incorporate elements of modernity (pluralism, rationalization, and the changing nature of women's roles in the larger culture) yet stay true to an ancient and revitalized tradition. Davidman chose to study two Orthodox congregations that were attempting to make their way in the modern world without losing Orthodox identity. The truth-claims and thus the attraction of Orthodoxy were that it was "true" because it had stood the test of time and survival. This truth-claim provided an attractive rootedness for secular Jews who were in daily encounter with secularizing trends. Instead of shutting themselves off from the world (as the ultra-Orthodox did), these particular groups selectively incorporated elements of modernity into their interpretation of the religious tradition. This not only reconstructed the tradition but also made it appealing to modern secular Jews. Bais Chana and Lincoln Square offered, in the chance to "return" to Orthodoxy, answers to some complex questions. These included clarity about gender roles and guidelines for nuclear family life. A solution was thus provided for Jewish women without the requirement of having to lead sequestered lives. One of the answers was the idea of "equity, . . . of separate but equal roles." This emphasis legitimated the desires of contemporary women for revitalized "traditional" roles as an anchor in modern life.

A Time for Healing: American Jewry since World War II is part of the massive five-volume *The Jewish People in America*. In it, Edward Shapiro addresses some specific problems of the Jewish community in America. Some of the problems are similar to those faced by mainline Protestants (e.g., high divorce rates, low birth rates [except among certain Orthodox groups], and an aging population). The problem of intermarriage is particularly important to the Jewish community because it involves larger questions of assimilation and Jewish identity. After World War II, intermarriage increased as overt antisemitism decreased. Social mobility and acceptance rose for American Jews. As cultural acceptance of intermarriage grew (Shapiro notes that by the 1970s two-thirds of Gentiles approved of marriage between Christians and Jews), an older Jewish generation was unable to oppose the intermarriage of their children to Gentiles. Intermarriage exploded. In Shapiro's estimation, before 1960 only one in fourteen Jews intermarried; by the 1980s, the number was one in three nationally. In communities such as Denver, the number approached three out of four. Thus many began to doubt the long-term survival of Jewish identity in America.

Consistent with these descriptions, intermarriage was less common among Orthodox groups and most common among Reform groups. Consequently, Shapiro notes that Reform groups were also the most involved in dealing with the problems that intermarriage raised. The most important question, of course, was that of the identity of the children of such marriages. Were they Jewish or were they not? Traditionally, the question was answered by matrilineal descent. It was considered the only way to be "truly" Jewish. In 1983, however, a decision was reached by the Reform synagogues that a child from a union in which *either* parent was Jewish would be considered a Jew if formal acts of identification were performed. This established the premise for either patrilineal or matrilineal descent. Jewish identity was thus made as much a matter of identification as lineage. Of course, not all groups accepted Reform's formulations. This very vital debate continues.

ADDITIONAL READING

BASKIN, J. (ed.). 1991. *Jewish Women in Historical Perspective*. Detroit: Wayne State University Press.

Chapter 12, "Spiritual Expressions: Jewish Women's Religious Lives in the Twentieth Century U.S.," provides a good overview of the religious trends of Jewish women in the twentieth century.

lynn davidman

TRADITION IN A ROOTLESS WORLD

Women Turn to Orthodox Judaism

WOMEN, JUDAISM, AND MODERNITY

The sweeping social structural changes that constituted "modernization" had a profound impact on the European Jewish communities, beginning in western Europe. Following the French Revolution, male Jews were granted full citizenship in the French state, marking the beginning of the breakdown of the walls of the ghettos that had confined Jews since the Middle Ages. New opportunities for geographic and economic mobility emerged, and Jews, primarily men, began to enter the wider society in many of its various occupational, educational, social, and cultural spheres. Not surprisingly, changes in religion were soon to follow.

Even though Jews have to some extent always modified their religious practices in response to the influence of surrounding cultures, the opportunity for integration into the wider society presented Jews with new opportunities and challenges. One way they attempted to meet these challenges was by reconstructing their religion so that they could maintain their religious participation without attracting unwanted attention to their differences from their neighbors.

The first significant attempts at reform began in Germany in the early nineteenth century. Young, intellectual Jewish men, who had finally had the opportunity to receive university educations and had studies with philosophers such as Kant and Hegel, attempted to create a Judaism that would be more suitable for modern life (Goldscheider and Zuckerman 1984:68). Following the lead of the eighteenth-century German-Jewish philosopher Moses Mendelssohn, they sought to transform those aspects of synagogue worship and ritual observance that set Jews apart, thereby facilitating Jews' integration into the mainstream society (Raphael 1984:5). The first Reform synagogue was founded in 1810 to establish a contemporary Jewish service in which rituals, customs, and prayers that were unenlightened or unaesthetic would be eliminated; this service would demonstrate that Judaism was "as progressive, modern, and enlightened an expression of the common religion of humanity as any other faith" (Raphael 1984:7). The Reform Judaism that began in the Jewish communities of Germany spread throughout Europe and in the 1820s took root in the United States as well.

This new variety of Judaism, created in response to the challenges of modernization and the Enlightenment, represented an extreme form of accommodation. The founders of the Reform movement in the United States, like their European counterparts, attempted to fashion a brand of Judaism that would be more in turn with the sensibilities of their Christian neighbors. These reformers eliminated or modified the traditional practices and doctrines that had established and reinforced Jews' uniqueness, such as kashrut (the dietary laws), observance of the Sabbath, the idea of the divine origin of the Bible, the belief that Jews were "the chosen people," and Hebrew language services. Today Reform Judaism is the second largest denomination: 29 percent of U.S. Jews identify as Reform.

In the twentieth century, two additional forms of Judaism were developed in the United States: Conservative and Reconstructionist. The founders of Conservative Judaism were Reform rabbis who, while no longer committed to strict observance of every detail of traditional Jewish law, nevertheless reacted against the seeming disregard for tradition in Reform Judaism. These men sought to create a variety of Judaism that would attract Orthodox and Reform Jews by offering the perfect combination of tradition and change (Raphael 1984:8; Sklare 1972). In the early 1900s a group of rabbis espousing this orientation founded their own rabbinical academy, the Jewish Theological Assembly, and then their own congregational organization, the United Synagogue of America.

In contrast with Reform rabbis, Conservative leaders generally agreed on the need to maintain such basic practices as the dietary laws and Sabbath observance and such essential doctrines as belief in Jewish nationalism and the importance of Hebrew in Jewish life (Rudavsky 1967:321). They were also willing, however, to modify or discard some of the other laws, such as the traditional Jewish divorce laws, which relegated women to a passive role. Conservative Judaism is the largest U.S. denomination; 34 percent of U.S. Jews identify themselves as Conservative.

Reconstructionist Judaism, which claims only 2 percent of the U.S. Jewish population, represented yet another approach to constructing a Jewish religious alternative that suited the times. It was founded by Mordecai M. Kaplan, who in 1922 broke away from the Orthodox synagogue of which he had been rabbi to form a new congregation, the Society of the Advancement of Judaism. He felt that the other branches of Judaism were notoriously unsuccessful in attracting and keeping adherents. Therefore, Judaism needed a new approach. His major treatise outlining his vision of a "reconstructed" Judaism was published in 1922 under the title *Judaism as a Civilization: Toward a Reconstruction of American Jewish Life.*

Like the Reformers, Kaplan eliminated "outdated" doctrines such as supernatural revelation and divine "choosing" of the Jews. In contrast to the Reformers, however, he sought to maintain many of the traditional customs, rituals, ceremonies, and festivals. He specified that these were to be retained not because they were divinely ordained but because they provided rich opportunities for spiritual experience. Judaism, in this view, served primarily a social function: Jews were most centrally a people, not a religious group. Kaplan conceptualized Judaism in its broadest terms as including a variety of religious and secular components (Raphael 1984:180–182).

Whereas Reform, Conservative, and Reconstructionist approaches have to varying degrees accommodated the secular society, Orthodox Judaism represents the other end of the continuum of responses to modernity and adheres most strictly to the tenets of Halacha. Most Orthodox Jewish communities—which in premodern Europe represented the norm and thus did not need the special label *Orthodox*—attempt to resist modernization encroachments on traditional religious ways of life. Orthodox's leaders and members share the belief that the Torah is of divine origin; therefore, all of its commandments must be obeyed. This acceptance of the obligatory nature of religious law is what distinguishes the Orthodox from the other branches.

Nevertheless, even within this seriously committed branch of the religion, there are enormous variations that reflect the myriad stances to the modern world adopted by Orthodoxy's many subgroups. The scope of this intragroup variation can be seen in the areas of training and governance: whereas Reform, Conservative, and Reconstructionist Jews each have one rabbinical academy that trains their leaders, and one religious assembly that governs the group, Orthodox Jews may be ordained in numerous different seminaries and yeshivas or even by individual rabbis, and the congregations may belong to one of several synagogue assemblies.

Although these Jewish responses to modernity offer interesting possibilities of research, this study focuses on Orthodox Judaism because as the most fundamentalist form it seems to represent the most unlikely choice for individuals on modern society. By choosing the most unusual case I am able to see in high relief the various ways in which a group that is committed to tradition but nevertheless exists in a modern society can attract modern people and deal with the conflicts produced by the ongoing tensions between tradition and modernity. . . .

RELIGIOUS INSTITUTIONS' STRATEGIES FOR SURVIVAL IN MODERNITY

For Lincoln Square Synagogue and Bais Chana to attract newcomers to their Orthodox worlds, their representatives had to find ways of reaching out into the wider society and recruiting among the contemporary generation of secular Jews. The most important strategy for accomplishing this goal was to present what these representatives claimed to be a traditional religious way of life in terms that clearly reflected engagement with modern culture. The Orthodox religious groups reinforced their credibility to new recruits by emphasizing the longevity of the tradition. In contrast to so many of the recently constructed available means for finding oneself—the various self-help groups popular in large cities and imported Eastern religions such as the Hare Krishnas and the Moonies—the rabbis claimed that Orthodox Judaism was true because it had survived the test of time. Its validity and strength rested on the fact that it was ancient and unchanging.

But the leaders at Lincoln Square and Bais Chana actually introduced modern features into their interpretation of the religious tradition. They reached out into the modern society and incorporated elements of it in order to reconstruct the tradition and make it appealing to modern secular Jews. The rabbis and representatives of these communities engaged a great deal with the secular world. They know about feminism, evolutionary theory, and contemporary psychology, and they used this knowledge to enhance their communities' appeal. Nevertheless, they staked their legitimacy on their claims to traditional religious authority. In the context of a constantly changing society, a religion presented as ancient and unchanging could indeed be appealing. The religious world they constructed represented two distinct types of new religious forms whose validity was reinforced by reference to the weight and authority of tradition.

Although both institutions legitimated their authority by emphasizing their traditionalism, the meaning of tradition was interpreted and reconstructed differently in each religious community. The representatives of Lincoln Square Synagogue and Bais Chana each devised their own strategies for creating a religious world in the face of the challenges of modern society. They developed unique approaches to contemporary secular society that ranged along a continuum from accommodation to resistance. Their different degrees of engagement with the larger society affected all aspects of the religious worlds they constructed, such as their teachings, forms of social organization, and types of religious authority. . . .

I have analyzed each group's responses to modernity through a close examination of the ways they dealt with several challenging features of contemporary life: differentiation, pluralism, individualism, rationalization, and the changing of women's roles. What we have seen is that instead of being eroded by these difficult features of modernity, each institution found a way to directly deal with them and utilized them to its own advantage in attracting new recruits.

The religious leaders at Lincoln Square Synagogue created a mode of existence in the modern secular society by constructing a religious world that accommodated many features of contemporary life. The representatives of this community did not resist differentiation, pluralism, rationalization, or the changing of women's roles. Instead, the rabbis openly acknowledged all these features of modern life and incorporated them into their presentation of Orthodoxy. For example, they offered newcomers an Orthodox religious way of life in which differentiation was still possible. The synagogue made available numerous opportunities for newcomers and members to adopt the religion as the central focus of their lives. But the rabbis also acknowledged and accepted the recruits' commitment to a continued differentiation of their lives into occupational, residential, social, and religious spheres.

Similarly, the rabbis minimized the threat of pluralism by acknowledging that Orthodox Judaism was indeed one choice among many available options. The women who came to this community had exercised their choices and constructed reasonably stable lives within the freedoms of modern society. Thus, instead of negating the idea of choice and challenging the dominant individualism and functional rationality of our culture, the rabbis appealed to their urbane, secular audience by actually emphasizing mainstream middle-class U.S. values: freedom, choice, and the power of reason.

The leaders and members of the Lubavitch community, in contrast, inter-acted to produce a contemporary Orthodox world that attempted in many ways to resist the encroachment of modernity. They created an alternative to the differentiation of life in secular society by establishing structures in which all recruits' and members' needs were met within the confines of the community. The rabbi challenged pluralism and individualism and appealed to women who had gotten "in trouble" making the wrong choices by asserting that individuals were not really free to make their own life-shaping decisions. Instead, their essential selves were predetermined. He negated the element of choice in the women's attraction to Orthodoxy and instead asserted that this transformation was inherent in, and demanded by, the women's own inner beings. Thus, the representatives of this community vigorously opposed rationalization: they did not present the women with rationales for the various observances but instead claimed that they were to be followed simply because God so commanded.

The particular approaches to tradition and modernity in the two communi-ties were especially visible in the rabbis' teachings about gender. At Lincoln Square Synagogue they accommodated contemporary feminist ideals by pre-senting a religious definition of women's roles that supported women's activity in the workplace, if the woman desired it, even while emphasizing the impor-tance of women's roles in the home.

In contrast, the Lubavitch teachers' positions on sexuality, women's roles, marriage, and the family resisted many contemporary liberalizing trends. The teachers downplayed the importance of romantic love as the basis for successful marital relationships and instead promoted the women's commitment to the proper fulfillment of their roles. The rabbis taught that women, by nature, were meant to be exclusively mothers and wives and derogated the feminist empha-sis on women's career advancement. Nevertheless, their arguments against feminism revealed some knowledge of and engagement with it, a necessary consequence of their existing and attracting newcomers within the modern secular society.

The attention devoted in these Orthodox communities to questions about women's roles, gender definitions and norms, and the nuclear family was a reflection of the centrality of these concerns in the general culture. The rabbis were well aware of contemporary trends and capitalized on them by offering solutions to these most difficult dilemmas.

The religious communities in this study each claimed to offer one type of solution—a "traditional" one—to the issues that were problematic for the *ba'alot teshuvah* [a woman who adopts Orthodox Judaism as an adult]: the need for clarity about gender, guidelines for nuclear family life, and, for the women at Bais Chana, an end to sexual exploitation. Many recent studies of religious communities have also found that the provision of "traditional" solutions to these modern dilemmas was a significant dimension of their appeal (Ammerman 1987; Kaufman 1985, 1987; Neitz 1987; Rochford 1985; Rose 1987). These groups offered models of gender, sexuality, and family that competed with those prescribed by most feminists. Instead of the feminist program of broader gender definitions and options, sexual liberation, an emphasis on careers, and the acceptance of a variety of family patterns, Orthodox Judaism proposed clearly circumscribed gender norms, the control of sexuality, assistance in finding partners, and explicit guidelines for nuclear family life.

Both religious communities offered their own version of a distinct alternative to the liberal feminist goal of equality: that of equity, the idea of separate but equal roles. The religious groups were attractive to some contemporary women precisely because they legitimated the women's desires for the "traditional" identity of wives and mothers in nuclear families. The rabbis told the recruits that women's role was highly valued in Orthodoxy and that woman's primary place in the home, where a majority of the rituals took place, gave her special status within the Jewish religious world. In addition, Orthodox Judaism's emphasis on the nuclear family and women's place in it actually provided the women with an additional benefit: they gained support for a conception of men's roles that placed great stress on men's involvement in the home and with their families.

Although the conception of women's roles in these two Orthodox communities was conventional, their vision of masculinity and prescriptions for male roles were actually modern. Achieving men's increased involvement in the family has been a goal of many feminists. The Lubavitch and modern Orthodox attempts to construct "traditional" religious responses to contemporary gender ambiguity reveal the significant influence of modern social norms.

Religion acts a mediator between the public and the private spheres. In modern society we are often taught to seek a great deal of our satisfaction within the private sphere because the public realm has become too institutionalized and bureaucratic. But we are simultaneously surrounded by signs of trouble in the private sphere, such as family violence, the rising rates of divorce, drug addition, and the difficulty of maintaining stable relationships. Even though modern individuals seek solace within private life, many of them find that the private realm has become fraught with ambiguity and emptiness. The women profiled in this book found it hard to create the kinds of family lives they wanted. They sought an institutional context that would legitimate their desires and help to achieve them. The Orthodox Jewish communities represented here, and other religious groups like them, thus offer solutions, difficult to find elsewhere, to the dilemmas of modern life.

edward s. shapiro

A TIME FOR HEALING
American Jewry since World War II

The growing rate of intermarriage was the most troubling aspect of contemporary American Jewish life for Jewish survivalists. Intermarriage presented an insoluble dilemma since it stemmed from diminishing antisemitism and rapid social and economic mobility, which Jews welcomed. With Jews now living in suburbia, attending residential colleges rather than urban commuter institutions, and working in corporate and academic bureaucracies, social contacts with Gentiles became closer and more frequent. Surveys taken in the 1980s revealed that a large majority of Jews had close relationships with Gentile colleagues and neighbors and that they had a more positive attitude toward non-Jews. No longer did Jews perceive all Gentiles to be closet antisemites. In such an atmosphere, an increase in intermarriage was inevitable. Jews who decried intermarriage proposed such panaceas as improving Jewish education and strengthening the Jewish family. None of these held out much prospect for slowing the rate of intermarriage, particularly since those most prone to intermarriage were the least likely to be enrolled by their parents in Jewish schools or to be the products of intensely Jewish families (Liebman and Cohen 1990:53–54).

Jewish parents were often unable to convey to their offspring the reasons for their opposition to intermarriage. The ethnic and religious loyalties that they took for granted did not resonate to the same extent among their children. Furthermore, the liberalism that Jewish parents had passed down to their children encouraged intermarriage. Liberalism warned against intolerance, encouraged people to judge others as individuals and not as members of a group, and argued that religious and ethnic differences were anachronisms. How could liberal Jews attribute to antisemitism the reluctance of Gentiles to marry Jews and at the same time oppose Jews selecting Gentile spouses without appearing to be bigots themselves? The answer that many Jews gave to their children for opposing intermarriage was sociological and psychological.

Marriage was difficult even in the best of circumstances, they argued, and marriage across religious and ethnic lines reduced the possibility for its success. The mental health of the couple and not the threat to Jewish survival became the basis for rejecting intermarriage. Such an argument was self-defeating when it became apparent by the 1980s that the success or failure of a marriage often had little to do with religious and ethnic differences. When this became evident, parents were left without an effective weapon for opposing intermarriage. For the young, intermarriage simply took the liberalism of their parents to its logical conclusion, and they viewed parental opposition to intermarriage as hypocritical, particularly in those cases when their parents had not previously exhibited any strong religious or ethnic attachments.

Another reason for the Jewish difficulty in opposing intermarriage was that it was a by-product of a development that Jews otherwise favored—the willingness of Gentiles to have closer social relationships with Jews. A Gallup poll in the 1970s revealed that over two-thirds of Americans approved of marriages between Jews and Christians. . . .

Until the 1960s, few American Jews saw intermarriage as a threat to Jewish survival, in part because the intermarriage rate was low. Less than one out of fourteen Jews who married prior to the 1960s had a non-Jewish spouse. It was also due to the expectation that antisemitism would prevent widespread intermarriage and that Jewish community norms would continue to discourage it. Surveys indicated that the overwhelming majority of Jewish parents strongly opposed intermarriage. . . .

The intermarriage rate increased so dramatically that by the 1980s few Jewish families, except for the Orthodox, had not been affected by it. Over one-third of American Jews who married in the 1980s had a non-Jewish spouse. In New York City the figure was lower, while in the hinterland the intermarriage rate was higher. In Denver, nearly three-quarters of the Jews had wed non-Jews. Jews did not know how to deal with what David Singer in 1979 described as "the single most pressing problem confronting the organized Jewish community" (1979:48). As intermarriage snowballed, Jews were less willing to object to it, particularly when many of the leaders of America's most prominent Jewish organizations and their children were themselves intermarried. If intermarriage was not viewed as a curse, neither was it viewed as a blessing. American Jews, Singer noted, were now condemned to "living with intermarriage." . . .

The writings of Marshall Sklare, the most distinguished American sociologist of American Jewry, reflected the growing concern of American Jewry with intermarriage. There was not one reference to intermarriage in his famous 1957 anthology, *The Jews: Social Patterns of an American Group*. Sklare's 1964 *Commentary* article, "Intermarriage and the Jewish Future," was among the first significant examinations of what up to that point had not been a decisive aspect of American Jewish sociology. It appeared in the same year that *Look* magazine published its famous cover story, "The Vanishing American Jew" (Morgan 1964:42–46). Sklare noted that Jews had a reputation for resisting intermarriage, that the Jewish rate of endogamy was far higher than that of any other white ethnic or religious group, and that American Jewish leaders and scholars complacently believed the threat of intermarriage had been contained. The most widely accepted figure for the rate of intermarriage at that time was a low 7.2 percent (Morgan 1964:42–46). . . .

In 1964, Sklare was not yet convinced that the situation was irreparable, and he did not rule out the possibility that the threat of intermarriage could be countered. This hopeful note was missing from Sklare's next *Commentary* article on intermarriage, which appeared in 1970, one year before a major study revealed that the current Jewish intermarriage rate was over 31 percent. Sklare's essay bore the far more somber title "Intermarriage and Jewish Survival" and argued that, despite some hopeful signs of American Jewish renewal, the survival of the American Jewish community was imperiled. Sklare was concerned here not only with the increase in the intermarriage rate but also with its growing acceptance within American Jewry. The stance of parents of Jewish spokesmen toward intermarriage was in the process of changing from opposition to accommodation. "The Jewish community as a whole is soon bound to find itself embroiled in a bitter debate over what this new development portends for its survival as a distinctive group" (1970:51–58). . . .

This crisis particularly affected the Reform movement, because intermarriages were more prevalent among its members than within Orthodoxy or Conservatism. Orthodox and Conservative rabbis would not officiate at an intermarriage since it was a violation of Jewish law. Although the Reform movement did not accept the binding power of Jewish law, it nevertheless had opposed intermarriage. As late as 1973, the Central Conference of American Rabbis, a Reform organization, reaffirmed this position. This resolution, however, was not binding on the CCAR's members, since no sanctions were imposed on dissenting rabbis. This was in keeping with the Reform movement's tradition of allowing its rabbis the autonomy to interpret Jewish tradition as they saw fit. Furthermore, the 1973 resolution was not a manifestation of any increased opposition to exogamy. Rather it was a last-ditch effort to hold the fort against the increasing sentiment within the Reform rabbinate in favor of participating in intermarriages (Rosenberg 1985:171–172).

The growth in the intermarriage rate and the desire of the prospective Jewish spouse and his or her parents to have a rabbi participate resulted in Reform rabbis receiving an increasing number of requests to solemnize such marriages. This presented them with a dilemma. On the one hand, they realized that participating in an intermarriage was viewed as aberrant by the majority of their colleagues and that it ran counter to Jewish tradition. On the other hand, they sympathized with the idea of having a Jewish presence at an intermarriage, and they were often pressured by their congregants to participate in such weddings. They also feared that a refusal would lessen the possibility that the couple would ultimately identify with the Jewish community. Thus Rabbi Irwin Fishbein urged his colleagues in 1973 "not to slam a door that may be only slightly ajar" by refusing to officiate at intermarriages. Fishbein claimed that "rabbinic participation in mixed marriages is in the best tradition of reform Judaism. It is an attempt to respond in a positive way to the increasing incidence of mixed marriage in a mobile and open society" (Wertheimer 1989:93). As a result, not only did the number of Reform rabbis willing to perform intermarriages increase, but they also become less defensive about doing so. By the time of the 1973 CCAR convention, at least 10 percent of America's approximately one thousand Reform rabbis were willing to officiate at intermarriages, and their numbers would escalate rapidly over the next two decades. One survey in the late 1980s estimated that half of Reform rabbis participated at mixed marriages (Singer 1979:50).

The Reform movement responded to a sense of despair regarding the demographic hemorrhaging of American Jewry in other ways as well. Rabbi Alexander Schindler, a leading Reform spokesman, proposed that Jews abandon their traditional resistance toward conversions and embark on a vigorous missionary campaign. In 1983, the Reform movement established the Commission on Reform Jewish Outreach to encourage "both the non-Jewish parents in mixed marriages and their children, along with the 'unchurched,' to convert to Judaism to become Jews by choice" (Rosenberg 1985:132–133). Soon American Jews were distinguishing between "Jews from birth" and "Jews by choice." Orthodox and Conservative leaders opposed these proselytizing efforts. They feared that persons responding to a Reform-sponsored missionary program effort would be lukewarm Jews at best and that their conversions would not be conducted according to Jewish law. . . .

Even more controversial than the Reform's decision to undertake a proselytizing campaign was the 1983 resolution of the Central Conference of American Rabbis that a child with one Jewish parent would be classified as Jewish if the child, "through appropriate and timely public and formal acts of identification with Jewish faith and people," indicated a wish to identify with Judaism and the Jewish people. These acts included attending religious school and participating in religious services. By implication, a child with a Jewish mother and a Gentile father would not be considered Jewish if these "formal acts of identification" were not performed. The 1983 decision resulted in part from pressure on the part of the Reform lay leadership that such children—their own children and grandchildren—not be written off. The Reform rabbinate was also eager for these children to remain with the Jewish community and the Reform fold, and it wished to eliminate from Judaism distinctions based on gender. The patrilineal decision was not a radical break with Reform practice since in many Reform congregations the children of non-Jewish mothers were already considered "cultural" Jews. Ideologically, however, it was a sharp break with the conventional definition of a Jew based on matrilineal descent or traditional conversion (Wertheimer 1989:106).

Conservative and Orthodox rabbis, as well as a minority of Reform rabbis, feared that the patrilineal decision could split American Jewry. They warned that this sharp break with Jewish tradition would force Jews to investigate the family pedigree of prospective spouses to ensure that they were actually Jewish. They also asserted that the 1983 decision granted a certain legitimacy to intermarriages. Finally, they noted that it had delegitimized children with Jewish mothers and non-Jewish fathers who were unwilling, for whatever reason, to perform "formal acts of identification." Jewish law had always considered such persons to be Jewish based on the principle of matrilineal descent.

Jewish survivalists were concerned both with the quantitative and qualitative aspects of intermarriage. Intermarriage reduced the size of the American Jewish populations. Furthermore, the Jewish identity of intermarried families was not as strong as that of endogamous families. Handwringing regarding intermarriage generally missed the point: intermarriage was not the cause of acculturation and assimilation but its result. Jews did not intermarry in order to assimilate; they intermarried because they were already largely assimilated. This triumph of love over tradition indicated the extent to which they were Jewish Americans rather than American Jews. . . .

Previously in American history, immigration had boosted the Jewish population, but this had not taken place to the same extent after 1945. The postwar waves of Jewish immigrants were small in comparison to those of the nineteenth and early twentieth centuries, and the Jewish identity of the Israelis and Soviets who made up the majority of the Jewish immigration of the 1970s and 1980s was often attenuated. Much to the amazement of American Jews, many of the Israeli and Russian immigrants were Jewish in name only. The most important waves of immigration to America during the 1970s and 1980s were from Latin America and Asia, and these contained few Jews. Even if the Jewish and non-Jewish birth rates had been comparable, the percentage of Jews in the general population would have declined because of immigration. By 1990, there were more Asians living in the United States than Jews (Gutman 1966:354).

American Jews were ignoring the first commandment of the Bible to "be fruitful and multiply." Since the 1930s the Jewish birth rate had been approximately one-quarter to one-third less than that of Gentiles, and this disparity continued into the 1960s, when the birth rate among Jews declined to below the zero population growth (ZPG) rate of 2.1 births per woman. The Jewish birth rate remained below ZPG throughout the 1970s and 1980s. "For American Jewry," sociologist Chaim I. Waxman said, "the issue is not that of zero population growth, but of negative population growth" (Waxman 1983:168). The prognosis was particularly bleak because the intermarriage rate was increasing, and intermarried couples have fewer children. Furthermore, every year more Jews were becoming part of that segment of society that has a low fertility rate—the college-educated, upwardly mobile, affluent residents of metropolitan regions (Schmelz and Dellapergola 1989:75–76).

Some American Jews were not only troubled by the overall low Jewish birth rate but also by the disparity between it and the much higher birth rate of the Orthodox. If the current trends in birth rates continued into the twenty-first century, the power of the Orthodox in the United States (and in Israel) would inevitably increase. This was not a comforting prospect for those fearful of Orthodox hegemony within American Jewry. . . .

The low birth rate of Jews helped account for another significant element in the American Jewish demographic crisis—the graying of American Jewry.

American Jews were considerably older than the rest of the population and, as a result, their mortality rate was higher. In 1980, 15.5 percent of the Jewish population was over sixty-five, compared to 11.8 percent for the total American white population. In response to the growth of the Jewish elderly, Jewish federations established new vocational, social, and medical programs to service the aged, and Jewish old-age homes were expanded and new residential facilities were constructed (Glazer 1989:10). . . .

During the 1970s and 1980s, the divorce rate among Jews approached that of Gentiles, and the percentage of Jewish children living in one-parent families rose steadily. In addition, the Jewish marriage rate decreased. For the first time in its history, American Jewry had a large number of singles. According to one study, in 1965 73 percent of Jewish adults in Boston were married. Only 56 percent were married ten years later (Waxman 1983:162). "It's a huge problem," Sylvia Barack Fishman of Brandeis's Cohen Center said. "People in general are marrying later, but Jewish people are marrying even later. This works against the communal interest. It becomes a Jewish issue because whatever may be adaptive in the general community, may be maladaptive in the Jewish community, a minority community which already suffers from intermarriage" (William Petschek National Jewish Family Center 1987:5). Between 1967 and 1979 the percentage of never-married Jews in their thirties increased by over two and a half times, and the percentage of separated and divorced Jews in the same age group quadrupled. One survey of over six thousand Jewish males found that half of all the men under forty were either intermarried or divorced, and many of the remaining men were single. This, of course, was one element in the low Jewish birth rate. . . .

Most Jewish sociologists prior to the 1980s were gloomy regarding the future of American Jewry. In the 1940s and 1950s they worried that the vicissitudes of the business cycle and antisemitism threatened American Jewry, while during the 1960s and 1970s they emphasized the threat of affirmative action, acculturation, and assimilation. In his 1985 *Commentary* essay "On Jewish Forebodings," Nathan Glazer asserted that, while Jews would continue to identify as Jews, "little by way of custom, belief, or loyalty will be assumed as a result of their identity as Jews. . . . The sociologists who have persistently feared for the American Jewish future may . . . have feared for the wrong reasons; but I believe they have been right to be fearful" (1985:36).

In the 1980s, however, a few Jewish sociologists dissented from this pessimism. The most important aspect of the study of contemporary American Jewish sociology during the 1980s was the debate between transformationists such as Steven Cohen, Calvin Goldscheider, and Alvin Zuckerman, who believed the American Jewish community was in the process of being transformed but not weakened, and assimilationists such as Charles Liebman, Marshall Sklare, William B. Helmreich, and Glazer, who asserted that American Jewry was assimilating culturally and declining numerically.

The transformationists acknowledged that America had greatly modified Jewish life during the twentieth century, but they argued that this did not threaten Jewish continuity. They claimed that new criteria must be used for judging the vitality of American Jewish life, criteria that were appropriate for Jews living in modern rather than premodern times. The ebbing of the customs and observances that Jews brought with them from Europe and the Arab lands has been counterbalanced by the emergence of new practices, such as the celebration of Hanukkah, and of new concerns, such as Russian Jewry and the security of the state of Israel.

Thus the transformationists were not unduly disturbed by the low percentage of American Jews who observed the Sabbath and maintained a kosher household. The transformationists also argued that intermarriage was actually increasing the Jewish population because of the many Gentile spouses who converted to Judaism and because, they contended, at least half of the children in intermarried families were being raised as Jews. These assertions were highly problematic. Even more important for the transformationists was that Jews even into the fourth generation continued to identify themselves as Jews, to live in Jewish neighborhoods, and to have Jews as their closest friends. Finally, the transformationists were not convinced that Jewish schools had failed in imparting a sense of Jewish identity to their students.

The bête noire of the transformationists was a sociological paradigm that argued that modernization was incompatible with the maintenance of strong ethnic and religious loyalties. This paradigm was strongly challenged, particularly by Goldscheider and Zuckerman in their *The Transformation of the Jews* (1984). For them, the modernization process had modified but not attenuated Jewish identity. Industrialization, urbanization, and nationalism had undermined traditional religious mores, but they also led to the emergence of new religious ideologies, to the birth of modern Zionism and then Israel, and new bases of ethnic and religious cohesion such as Jewish cultural organizations and Jewish suburban neighborhoods. According to Goldscheider and Zuckerman, modernization had actually strengthened Jewish cohesion.

As modern social scientists, the transformationists relied on survey research for their information. The transformationists' critics were skeptical of the accuracy of sampling techniques, since individuals disaffected from the Jewish community would probably not be reached by such surveys. Even more important was the transformationists' reliance on computer printouts. Statistics can measure, but they cannot evaluate. Thus they could reveal how many Jews attended a Passover seder, but they could not disclose what took place at the seder and what significance it had for those attending. Statistics could also not distinguish between peripheral and important Jewish involvements. Lighting Hanukkah candles was put on the same level with riding on the Sabbath since both are ritual observances. But observing the Sabbath connoted a depth of Jewish commitment that was far greater than lighting candles.

For the transformationists, the key issue was cultural cohesiveness and survival. For assimilationists such as Glazer, the key issue was whether there was anything worth preserving in American Jewish culture. From the assimilationist perspective, the manner in which the transformationists framed their questions and defined Jewish identity confirmed their fears that American

Jewish culture had been trivialized. In the final analysis, the difference between the transformationists and the assimilationists did not concern the
question merely of whether the glass of American Jewish identity was half
empty or half full. It also involved the issue of whether the liquid was worth
drinking in the first place.

part six

RELIGIOUS MOVEMENTS

Left, Right, and Nonconventional

Part of the story of religion in America has been about the struggles of various groups to move from the outside to the inside. There are various inner circles (full participation, equality, and political participation) toward which people move and various barriers they have to transcend to reach those goals. This section examines the paths followed by three broadly conceived religious movements as they move from the margins to positions of greater prominence and fuller participation in various arenas.

Matthew Moen, in his article "From Revolution to Evolution: The Changing Nature of the Christian Right," summarizes the existing literature on the "new Christian Right." He also suggests that the sociological evaluation of the rise of this phenomenon may have told only part of the story. As he points out, many analysts have written on the political resurgence of Evangelical Protestantism in the 1970s, but most have focused on how politics has been changed by the advent of the Christian Right. At the same time, not many have written on the changes within the Christian Right in the past quarter century (i.e., how politics has changed this group). Similar to Melton's analysis, Moen contends that the choice of metaphors and analytic strategies used by certain scholars in describing the Christian Right has caused them to disregard significant changes occurring within these organizations. The theory was that such groups were single-minded (if not simple-minded) in the pursuit of their crude political goals. It followed logically that once some modicum of political influence was obtained, the groups would recede into the background or would eviscerate themselves via political blunders. In Moen's analysis, the evolution of the Christian Right has been much more subtle, and its path can better be understood with reference to developmental periods or phases.

The first period (1978–1984) was the "Expansionist," characterized by the emergence of politically unpolished organizations such as the Moral Majority, headed by Fundamentalist pastors. The "Transition" period (1985–1986) was characterized by retrenchment and the merging or disappearance of organizations that had either overreached themselves or lost some of their initial impetus. Paradoxically, some organizations shut down because of a modicum of success on local issues. These local issues being solved and the cachet of national causes waning, such organizations lost their raison d'être. This was also the period when many analysts assumed that the Christian Right had run its course. The last period is the "Institutional" (1987–present), characterized by stable and well-funded organizations. In Moen's estimation, it is this phase during which existing organizations examined their successes, evaluated their political strategies, and retooled to be able to compete in the broader realm of political ideas. Moen notes that this phase is also marked by a shift in the political rhetoric from casting every issue in terms of its moral import to the adoption of the language of classical liberalism and speaking in terms of "rights, equality, and opportunity."

The proper role of and for women vitally concerns virtually every organized religious group. Christianity and Judaism, in their various incarnations, have been involved in either aiding the struggle of women for full participation or legitimizing continued inequality by the overlay of religious tradition and symbolism. In a society that is increasingly pluralistic, "nonconventional" religions (primarily those with an Eastern or Asian pedigree) make up a greater part of the American religious mosaic. Because of their "exotic" practices and antagonism to the dominant culture, these groups have received significant opposition by being stigmatized (and feared) as "cults." For these nonconventional religions, the price of not fitting in has been to be derided as irrational by the mainstream.

In the article "The Feminist Critique in Religious Studies," Rosemary Ruether sketches the involvement of Judaism and Christianity in perpetuating and legitimating the subordination of women. She writes of the difficulty of finding an academic and theological space for women to do religious studies in an environment heavily influenced by patriarchal understandings and metaphors. She maintains that the symbolism of religion establishes the supposed inferiority of women as a social fact, which only continues their inequality. She sketches three varieties of feminism that might act as a counterbalance to the limitations placed on women by patriarchy.

The first group, which she identifies as "Evangelical feminists," work within a given tradition with the idea that the message of Scripture is essentially egalitarian, and that better understanding of the true role for men and women comes via better exegetical understanding of those texts. The second group she characterizes as "liberationists." Theirs is an iconoclastic perspective, focusing on the prophetic elements of the Christian and Jewish message to challenge "oppressive and self-serving religion." Sexism is defined as "a failure to measure up to the full vision of human liberation of the prophetic and gospel messages." The last group, in Ruether's estimation, is those who believe no adequate alternative can be found within the Jewish or Christian traditions. They wish to abandon them as altogether unsalvageable and seek sources of meaning outside those traditions. Ruether concludes that the patriarchal subordination of women "has been so massive and prevalent that to begin to take women seriously will involve a profound and radical transformation of our religions."

By any estimate, the 1960s were a time of social and cultural upheaval in the United States. They were also ostensibly a time during which younger people left organized religions and there was an influx of Eastern religions whose teachers, gurus, and masters offered to provide those answers younger people could not find in the older, traditional places. The decade also saw the rise of a counterculture that called for the rejection of the system and excoriated conventional churches for their role in supporting the system. At least, this is the popular and sometimes the scholarly view of the situation. In the view of many sociologists of religion, this cultural upheaval—combined with the rise of the counterculture and the defection from mainstream religion—provided the soil in which nonconventional and Eastern religions took root. Some of the most notable writings dealing with "cult" formation or participation are Beckford (1985), Bromley and Hammond (1987), Tipton (1982), Bromley and Shupe (1981), and Anthony et al. (1983). The theme of the creation of or adherence to new religious movements as a reaction to crisis seems to run through all of them.

In his article "Another Look at New Religions," J. Gordon Melton, the author of *The Encyclopedia of American Religions,* provides a strikingly different interpretation of the genesis and development of new or "nonconventional" religions in the United States. Melton makes the point that earlier uses of the term *cult* by social scientists reflected the bias that was common in the popular media. Because such groups were tarred by the brush of association with the "counterculture," they were often seen as a threat to established religion and accused of kidnapping and brainwashing impressionable young people. Nonconventional religions were seen as weak, ahistorical groups without linkage to a parent body that suddenly sprung up in America. Melton indicates instead that most of these groups are offshoots of established groups in other cultures. "What in the West are considered nonconventional religious alternatives . . . are primarily denominations of the mainline dominant religion in another country." In the literature, "cults" were seen as centered around a charismatic leader whose special powers held some sway over his or her followers. If this were the case, once that person died, the group would be expected to fall apart owing to an inability to "transfer charisma" to later generations.

In Melton's longitudinal analysis, however, this was not seen to be the pattern for nonconventional groups. Many of these groups, in his estimation, were established in the 1950s and still exist despite several changes of leadership. He attempts to debunk the "cult formation as a reaction to crisis" model by use of two testable propositions. First, if the reaction-to-crisis model is accurate, the number of new groups formed should show a direct correlation with the time of greatest social unrest (i.e., the 1960s). Second, recruitment and growth of those groups should show a decline as distance from the time of upheaval increased. In his empirical analysis, there was no "explosion" of cults in the 1960s, as growth of nonconventional groups has been steady for the past four decades. Also, most of the groups formed in the 1950s and 1960s did not fade away, although many have undergone some reorganization to boost recruitment. Melton's ideas provide new insight into the common social scientific wisdom and the formation and future direction of marginal and nonconventional religious groups.

If we have learned anything from the study of American religious movements, it is that nothing is certain but change. There are very few groups so exotic or threatening by the standards of today that they may not be a "normal" part of the religious mosaic of tomorrow.

ADDITIONAL READINGS

ALBANESE, C. 1993. "Fisher kings and public places: the old new age in the 1990's." *Annals of the American Academy of Political and Social Science* 527:131–143.

This article evaluates "new age" practices as a recurrence of much older religious forms.

RICHARDSON, J., J. BEST, AND D. G. BROMLEY. 1991. *The Satanism Scare.* New York: Aldine de Gruyter.

This volume of collected essays provides social scientific evaluation of the reality and hysteria of the phenonemon of satanism in the United States.

matthew c. moen

FROM REVOLUTION TO EVOLUTION
The Changing Nature of the Christian Right

The principal objective of this essay is to explain change in the Christian Right over time; the central argument is that the Christian Right has gradually reconciled and adjusted itself to the secular norms and practices of American politics. Stated alliteratively, the Christian Right has forsaken revolution for evolution, abandoning its quixotic quest to "put God back in government" (Ogintz 1980) for a calculated campaign to infiltrate and influence carefully selected repositories of political power. It has done so on its own rhythm, rather than on the cycle presidential politics, as one might reasonably surmise from the exhaustive research on the presidential elections of the 1980s and 1992 (Johnson and Tamney 1982; . . . Johnson and Burton 1993).

With a few exceptions (. . . Moen 1992), scholars have not really focused on how political activism has shaped the Christian Right, preferring instead to concentrate on how the Christian Right has influenced politics. Neglecting one side of that causal relationship has skewed the literature; scholars know much about the Christian Right's voting behavior, campaigning, and lobbying, but comparatively little about its internal dynamics over time. Yet, it is important to understand the movement's machinations, both for the sake of explanation and prognostication. This essay is a small step in that direction; I deliberately sketch the big picture, providing references along the way to works containing the details.[1]

A subsidiary objective of this essay is to examine popular and scholarly understanding of the Christian Right. This task is approached in a constructive spirit, with the hope of fostering dialogue among scholars; it is not meant to suggest that only my interpretations are correct, nor to replicate solid review essays of the existing literature. . . . The time is ripe to assess the state of affairs, in the wake of the Reagan-Bush era and of events that captured the attention of scholars, such as the closure of Moral Majority . . . and the candidacy of Pat Robertson. . . . Many words were penned about the Christian Right during the

Reprinted from "From Revolution to Evolution: The Changing Nature of the Christian Right" by Matthew C. Moen, Sociology of Religion 55(3):345–357 (1994). *Reprinted by permission of the Association for the Sociology of Religion and the author.*

1980s and the 1992 elections, making it an opportune time to reflect on some of the things written.

THE RISE OF THE CHRISTIAN RIGHT

The rapid rise of the Christian Right in the late 1970s astonished observers of American politics. Journalists were among the most surprised, writing only two articles during the time the movement was crystallizing (March 1979–February 1980), as measured by the *Reader's Guide to Periodical Literature*. Many politicians were also caught off guard. The "born-again" Baptist president, Jimmy Carter, did not sense the depth of unrest among conservative Christians until it became too late to make amends (Hastey 1981). The whole situation was aptly described years later by Kenneth D. Wald (1987:182): "Of all the shifts and surprises in contemporary political life, perhaps none was so wholly unexpected as the political resurgence of evangelical Protestantism in the 1970s."

The rise of the Christian Right is a familiar story that has been told by historians, sociologists, theologians, and political scientists, among others. . . . Common to those discussions is that the Christian Right arose in response to a complex array of liberal and secular trends, ranging from the eradication of religion in the schools, to easy availability of abortion, to tax policies that adversely affected the traditional family.

The rapid rise of the Christian Right spawned a potent and sometimes mean-spirited counterattack from those far removed from the conservative Christian subculture. Liberal activists created groups like People for the American Way as platforms for personal attacks on Christian Right leaders; intellectuals mocked the Christian Right's concerns by penning a "Secular Humanist Declaration"; theologians drew unflattering biblical analogies, with the Rev. William Sloan Coffin suggesting that Christian Right leaders were "jackasses"; government officials reflexively described Moral Majority as a white racist group, and compared Jerry Falwell to the Ayatollah Khomeni, as if one could casually ignore the legal, cultural, and theological schisms separating an American Christian from an Iranian Muslim (Nyhan 1980). . . . Scholars opposed to the Christian Right also succumbed to the temptation to overstate matters, with one historian comparing the Christian Right of the 1970s to the European Fascism of the 1940s (Linder 1982). The shrill rhetoric and simplistic comparisons shaped the tone of public discourse in the early 1980s, just as opponents hoped. The Christian Right was caricatured as a collection of hillbillies bent on creating a theocracy, and evidence that this view was assimilated by the public could be found in its negative assessment of the Christian Right's leaders, issues, and organizations (Shupe and Stacey 1983). . . .

Researchers certainly did not create the negative perceptions that took root; the Christian Right's opponents and even its own leaders accomplished that task, through their miscalculations and mistakes (Moen 1989). Yet, once scholars started explaining the rise of the Christian Right, they contributed to the perception that the movement was suspect. Hadden and Swann (1981) laid the groundwork for many subsequent studies by suggesting that the Christian Right was a technologically driven movement spawned by master manipulators. They identified the modern "televangelist" as the force behind the surge of traditional religiosity. While a plausible explanation, it blinded other observers to the possibility that the Christian Right was more of a grassroots protest than a technological artifact; moreover, such a "top down" explanation implicitly trivialized the concerns of social conservatives, by casting those concerns as the baggage of unsophisticated followers being duped by clever elites.

Journalists subsequently portrayed the "televangelists" label and the "top down" paradigm as gospel, occupying themselves with unmasking the conservative preacher conspiracy afoot. Their work reached its apogee years later, when they blithely associated ministers barely connected to the Christian Right but tainted by scandal, such as Jim Bakker and Oral Roberts, with those responsible for creating the key Christian Right groups (Martz et al. 1987; Ostling 1987). Many journalists never grasped the distinctions among ministries and objectives, equating Jim Bakker's quest to build the ultimate Pentecostal amusement park with Fundamentalist Jerry Falwell's mission to remake America. (Some still insist on stereotyping conservative Christians, demonstrated by a *Washington Post* article calling evangelicals "uneducated and easy to command"; see Moen 1993.) Given this lack of understanding of the conservative Christian community, and the inculcation of the "top down" paradigm, is it any wonder that the "resurgence" of the Christian Right circa 1992 surprised many writers?

Scholars fed the perception that the Christian Right was suspect in another way—by using frameworks that suggested some sort of personal or social strain. For instance, Wald and his colleagues (1989a) borrowed from the psychology literature to examine empirical support for "authority-mindedness" in the Christian Right; other scholars used the status politics and lifestyle defense paradigms toward a similar end . . . (Wald et al. 1989b). Those paradigms drew criticism for their explanatory power. . . . (Moen 1988), and also for their presumption of pathological problems among Christian Right supporters (Jelen 1991).

The larger point is that the Christian Right was placed very early into established frameworks that often reflected a liberal understanding of the conservative mindset. The concerns of Christian Right supporters were explained as the by-product of authoritarian personalities or symbolic crusades, rather than taken at face value. One unfortunate result of pigeonholing the Christian Right was that scholars circumscribed their research agendas. They neglected fruitful lines of inquiry, while debating the fine points of value-laden frameworks—the academic equivalent of fiddling while Rome burned. For instance, scholars virtually ignored the Christian Right's infiltration of state Republican party organizations until the Reagan era was over . . . (Hertzke 1993). Those missed opportunities are not easily recompensed because the Christian Right has undergone dramatic changes over time.

PERIODS OF DEVELOPMENT

The Christian Right has passed through two distinctive phases since its rise in the late 1970s, and is in the midst of a third (Moen 1992). This periodization scheme is embellished and refined here to provide a picture of how the Christian Right has evolved. While such a framework is open to criticism, it may serve to synthesize major changes in the Christian Right, including its reorientation to the traditional norms and practices of American politics.

EXPANSIONIST PERIOD (1978–1984)

As the label implies the dominant characteristic of the Christian Right during the expansionist period was steady growth. The National Christian Action Coalition was launched in 1978 and became the first national organization of the Christian Right. It was followed by the Religious Roundtable, Christian Voice, Moral Majority, and Concerned Women for America (1979), the Freedom Council (1981), and the American Coalition for Traditional Values (1983). The proliferation of organizations and their concomitant division of labor signaled steady growth (Hatch 1983).

Reliable membership estimates for each specific organization were difficult to obtain. Christian Right leaders dispensed data, but they had every incentive to exaggerate their constituency's size. Independent assessments varied considerably. With Moral Majority, for instance, scholars suggested membership figures that ranged from 482,000 to 3,000,000; journalists estimated its voter registration campaigns netted 200,000 to 3,000,000 new voters (Liebman 1983). . . . When scholars documented the unpopularity of Moral Majority's issue positions, they implicitly confirmed the lower estimates, although they mostly refrained from such conjecture (Shupe and Stacey 1983). . . . Based on Moral Majority alone, though, one can reasonably conclude that the Christian Right consisted of several hundred thousand (if not millions of) citizens. It grew at a remarkable rate early on.

The geometric growth of the Christian Right created a high public profile. Journalists wrote hundreds of stories about its leaders and organizations (Hadden and Shupe 1988), with 75 percent of that coverage coming within three years after an organization was launched (Moen 1992). Since seven of the eleven national organizations composing the Christian Right formed during the expansionist period, the early 1980s were a publicity bonanza.

Owing to rapid growth and high visibility, the Christian Right successfully influenced the political agenda. It helped shift the congressional agenda in fundamental ways, winning votes on constitutional amendments to ban abortion and to permit prayer in schools in the 98th Congress (1983–1984), as well as securing passage of an array of lesser objectives . . . (Moen 1989). It also altered the public dialogue. The Christian Right placed a cluster of issues involving conventional morality and the traditional family at the political forefront, simultaneously bumping off items that offended, such as the Equal Rights Amendment . . .(Wald 1992). Some observers missed those indices of influence. Pressman (1984) and D'Antonio (1990), for instance, defined success for the Christian Right in absolute rather than relative terms—it should win elections and final passage of bills, not just alter the terms of debate. Those questionable standards contributed to the erroneous assessment that the Christian Right was spent by the mid-1980s.

Ironically, the Christian Right's agenda-setting success was costly. It convinced many lawmakers that it was time to consider new issues, since key Christian Right objectives were voted upon by the 98th Congress (1983–1984). Concurrently, Christian Right leaders made a host of mistakes while lobbying on Capitol Hill that created a less hospitable environment in the future. Their political amateurishness was yet another defining characteristic of the expansionist period, and it abetted the demise of the early groups.

The expansionist period is also distinguishable by the overt and pervasive religious underpinnings of the Christian Right. It was led by a clique of fundamentalist pastors and laypersons, such as Bob Billings (National Christian Action Coalition), Ed McAteer (Religious Roundtable), Jerry Falwell (Moral Majority), Beverly LaHaye (Concerned Women for America), and Tim LaHaye (American Coalition for Traditional Values). They attracted most Fundamentalist supporters, who are very conservative and often intolerant of their Evangelical and Pentecostal brethren (Shupe and Stacey 1983). . . . The presence of Fundamentalists was most evident at the 1980 National Affairs Briefing, where leaders made pronouncements grounded in a literal interpretation of the Bible that jarred many Americans, such as God not hearing the prayers of Jews (Jorstad 1981).

The predominance of Fundamentalists during the expansionist period was also evident in the way that leaders handled political issues. They focused on issues with strong moral overtones, such as gay rights, abortion, and pornography; moreover, they declared the correct position on those issues according to Scripture, and attacked alternative views as misguided biblical interpretation or secularism (Heinz 1983). Christian Right leaders also used moralistic language, speaking freely about the need to restore "moral sanity" (Falwell 1980), and defining issues like abortion and pornography in terms of sin. Taking stock of the Christian Right's rhetoric and early activities, Jorstad (1981:8) stated: "The theme brought home in every speech, every sermon, every pamphlet, every request for funds was that of saving Americans by a return to what the leaders called its traditional morality." The early Christian Right was long on morality, but sort on skill.

TRANSITION PERIOD (1985–1986)

The critical transition period is often overlooked by scholars intent on explaining the rise of the Christian Right in the early 1980s or assessing its activities in the wake of Moral Majority and Pat Robertson's presidential bid. The distinguishing feature of this period was retrenchment. . . .

The breadth of change is striking. Nearly every organization suspended its work, merged with another, or dissolved. (The only new group formed during this time was the Liberty Federation in 1986, which was Jerry Falwell's vehicle for absorbing the Moral Majority and then exiting politics in 1987.) The principal reason for retrenchment was the erosion of a direct-mail base during the mid-1980s (Diamond 1989:59). It was caused by an odd combination of agenda-setting successes that defused the anger of conservative Christians, along with tactical blunders that sapped their confidence in their leaders. Local supporters become weary of constant monetary appeals to fight distant national battles (Moen 1992:27).

Interestingly, this wholesale transformation went virtually unnoticed. *The New York Times* carried only sixteen stories about the Christian Right during the transition period (focused mostly on Pat Robertson's budding presidential candidacy), compared to 132 stories in 1980–1981. The decreased visibility seemed to reflect the institutionalization of the "top down" and symbolic crusade paradigms, which assumed that Christian Right supporters would decrease their activism once they vented their frustrations. The media were so certain that the Christian Right was fading away that they paid scant attention at all, let alone to subtle changes in progress.

As in the expansionist period, one change fostered others. The organizational retrenchment eradicated natural platforms for Christian Right leaders to speak out on issues, and consequently eroded their ability to shape the legislative and public agendas. The retrenchment also destroyed some of the inventiveness that the Christian Right exhibited in its earliest years, when it was on the cutting edge of issues, such as the impact of the tax code on families and the quality of the public schools. Christian Right leaders were relegated to the role of apologists for controversial Reagan administration positions, including South African sanctions and aid to the Nicaraguan Contras. The movement's agenda withered along with its early organizations, tempting observers to write a political obituary. Yet, Christian Right leaders were using this time of retrenchment to advance a strategic reorientation already in progress. The rapid collapse of organizations and a political agenda simply hastened that process.

INSTITUTIONALIZATION PERIOD (1987–PRESENT)

The distinguishing feature of the institutionalization period is the existence of several stable and well-positioned organizations. Space constraints preclude a discussion of the role of Christian Right elites in retooling the movement; suffice it to say that during the transition period, they examined their mistakes, assessed the existing political situation, commissioned polls to outline appropriate strategy, then restructured the movement in major ways (Moen 1992). The present characteristics of the Christian Right contrast sharply with previous periods, and explain why the movement is better positioned today.

One characteristic is a more predictable financial situation. The early organizations banked on direct mail for their financial support, an unpredictable well-spring because of the ease with which contributors can turn off the flow (Godwin 1988). It is as easy as tossing out repetitive third-class mail. Cogni-

CONCLUSION

Evidence and reason suggest that the Christian Right will march down the same path it has followed since 1987. The forces driving the Christian Right's reorientation in the first place still remain, such as an unfriendly political environment in the nation's capital and a climate of popular opinion that disdains moralism. The Christian Right will continue to offer liberal language and to operate at the grassroots, where its prospects are quite good. It has experienced leaders and ample funds, in part because it draws upon the extensive resources of the Rev. Moon, Pat Robertson, and now James Dobson (Shupe 1990) . . .; it is engaged in an intense cultural war that motivates followers; it operates outside the realm of a Democratic majority in Washington. Its work would proceed quietly, except for the clamor created by its opponents, who realize that in many ways it is better positioned today than in earlier eras.

At the same time, the Christian Right faces major challenges. It lacks a titular leader who can command immediate attention, like Jerry Falwell could in 1981–1982. It lacks a galvanizing issue comparable to the tax-exempt status of religious schools, the one that ignited Fundamentalists in the late 1970s. It still suffers from personal rivalries (Jelen 1991), and now is often blamed for the Republican party's poor performance in 1992 (Leege 1993:23). It faces the same dilemma of virtually all other interest groups: retaining its fervent supporters while trying to broaden its base of support. Striking a balance between purity and pragmatism will remain problematic for a movement containing political and theological cross-currents.

rosemary radford ruether

THE FEMINIST CRITIQUE
IN RELIGIOUS STUDIES

EFFECTS OF WOMEN'S EXCLUSION
ON THEOLOGICAL CULTURE

The exclusion of women from leadership and theological education results in the elimination of women as shapers of the official theological culture. Women are confined to passive and secondary roles. Their experience is not incorporated into the official culture. Those who do manage to develop as religious thinkers are forgotten or have their stories told through male-defined standards of what women can be. In addition, the public theological culture is defined by men, not only in the absence of, but against women. Theology not only assumed male standards of normative humanity, but is filled with an ideological bias that defines women as secondary and inferior members of the human species.

Many examples of this overt bias against women in the theological tradition can be cited. There is the famous definition of women by Thomas Aquinas as a "misbegotten male." Aquinas takes this definition of women from Aristotle's biology, which identifies the male sperm with the genetic form of the embryo. Women are regarded as contributing only the matter or "blood" that fleshes out the form of the embryo. Hence, the very existence of women must be explained as a biological accident that comes about through a deformation of the male seed by the female "matter," producing a defective human or woman who is defined as lacking normative human standing.

Women are regarded as deficient physically, lacking full moral self-control and capacity for rational activity. Because of this defective nature women cannot represent normative humanity. Only the male can exercise headship or leadership in society. Aquinas also deduces from this that the maleness of Christ is not merely a historical accident, but a necessity. In order to represent humanity Christ must be incarnated into normative humanity, the male. Only the male, in turn, can represent Christ in the priesthood.

Rosemary Radford Ruether, "The Feminist Critique in Religious Studies," Soundings: An Interdisciplinary Journal *64.4:388–402 (1981). Reprinted by permission of* Soundings.

traditions about women and the roles women have actually managed to play. For example, evidence is growing that women in first-century Judaism were not uniformly excluded from study in the synagogues. The rabbinic dicta against teaching women Torah thus begin to appear, not as a consensus of that period, but as one side of an argument—that eventually won—against the beginnings of inclusion of women in discipleship.

Similarly the teachings of I Timothy about women keeping silence appear, not as the uniform position of the New Testament church, but as a second-generation reaction against widespread participation of women in leadership, teaching, and ministering in first-generation Christianity. Indeed the very fact that such vehement commandments against women learning the teachings were found in the traditions would have been a clue to the existence of widespread practices to the contrary. Otherwise, the statements would have been unnecessary. But because the documents were used as Scripture or normative tradition, rather than historical documents, this was not realized.

The participation of women in early Christianity was not simply an accident of sociology, but a conscious expression of an alternative anthropology and soteriology. The equality of men and women in the image of God was seen as restored in Christ. The gifts of the prophetic spirit, poured out again at the Messianic coming, were understood, in fulfillment of the Messianic prediction of the prophet Joel, to have been given to the "maidservants" as well as the "menservants of the Lord" (Acts 2:17–21). Baptism overcomes the sinful divisions among people and makes us one in the Christ: Jew and Greek, male and female, slave and free (Galatians 3:28). Thus, the inclusion of women expressed an alternative theology in direct confrontation with the theology of patriarchal subordination of women. The New Testament now must be read, not as a consensus about women's place, but rather as a conflict and struggle over two alternative understandings of the gospel that suggested different views of male and female.

This alternative theology of equality, of women as equal in the image of God, as restored to equality in Christ and as commissioned to preach and minister by the Spirit, did not just disappear with the reassertion of patriarchal norms in I Timothy. It can be traced as surfacing again and again in different periods of Christian history. The strong role played by women in ascetic and monastic life in late antiquity and the early Middle Ages reflects a definite appropriation by women of a theology of equality in Christ that was understood as being applicable particularly to the monastic life. Celibacy was seen as abolishing sex role differences and restoring men and women to their original equivalence in the image of God. As the male church deserted this theology, female monastics continued to cling to it and understood their own vocation out of this theology. The history of female monasticism in the late Middle Ages and the Counter-Reformation is one of a gradual success of the male church in suppressing this latent feminism of women's communities. It is perhaps then not accidental that women in renewed female religious orders in Roman Catholicism today have become militant feminists, to the consternation of the male hierarchy. . . .

TRANSLATION OF WOMEN'S STUDIES IN RELIGION INTO EDUCATIONAL PRAXIS

Obviously women cannot affect an educational system until they first secure their own access to it. It has taken approximately one hundred and twenty-five years for most schools of theological education to open their doors to women and then to include women in sufficient numbers for their concerns to begin to be recognized. Women began to enter theological schools of the congregational tradition beginning with Oberlin in the 1840s and Methodist institutions in the 1870s. Only in the 1970s have some Roman Catholic and Jewish seminaries been open to women. Moreover, even liberal Protestant institutions did not experience any "critical mass" of female students until the 1970s.

Usually, access to theological education precedes winning the right to ordination. Winning the educational credentials for ordination then becomes a powerful wedge to winning the right of ordination itself. It is for that reason that there may be efforts to close Roman Catholic seminaries, at least those directly related to Rome, to women. Rumor has it (as of this writing) that a decree has been written but not yet promulgated in Rome forbidding women to attend pontifical seminaries (which would include all Jesuit seminaries, but not most diocesan and other seminaries). Women's tenure in professional schools of theology cannot be regarded as secure until they win the right to ordination. Only then can they develop a larger number of women students and attain the moral and organizational clout to begin to make demands for changes in the context of the curriculum.

Generally, demands for feminist studies begin with the organization of a caucus of women theological students. They then begin to demand women's studies in the curriculum and women faculty who can teach such courses. In many seminaries, particularly in U.S. liberal Protestant institutions, there has been some response to these demands: some women faculty have been hired, and some women's studies incorporated into the curriculum. It is at this point that we can recognize several stages of resistance to the implied challenge to the tradition.

One standard strategy of male faculty is to seek and retain one or two women on the faculty, but to give preference to women who are "traditional scholars," not feminists. This is fairly easy to do by the established rules of the guild, while, at the same time, appearing to be "objective." Feminist studies are nontraditional. They force one to use nontraditional methods and sources and to be something of a generalist. Their content is still in flux and experimentation. Rare is the person who can fulfill the expectations of both traditional scholarship and feminist scholarship equally well. So it is easy to attack such persons as "unscholarly," and to fail to tenure them in preference to those women who prefer to be "one of the boys." As of this writing there is an alarming erosion of feminist faculty talent in theological education through precisely this method. This has forced feminist scholars in theological education to band together in a new national organization, Feminist Theology and

Ministry, in order to defend the employment of feminists in existing institutions of theological education.

Efforts are also underway to create new, alternative settings for women's studies in religions. For example, groups in the Boston-Washington corridor and in Chicago (largely, but not exclusively, Roman Catholic) are seriously considering the development of autonomous feminist theology schools for women, since the existing (especially Roman Catholic) institutions have proved so unfavorable to their interests.

In some other settings a decade-long struggle for women's studies in religion is beginning to bear fruit. For example, at the Harvard Divinity School, bastion of "traditional" education, a pilot program of graduate assistants in women's studies in various fields has continued for some eight years, for much of this time under constant threat of liquidation. However, a study of the program located one of its chief flaws in the lack of prestige and respect given to the women's studies teachers by the tenured faculty. As a result, a new level of funding has been developed to allow this program to be continued and eventually to be converted into a permanent research center for women in religion, with five full-time junior and senior faculty appointments. It remains to be seen whether this expanded "prestige" will not result in some of the same pressure to prefer traditional over feminist scholars.

In the development of feminist studies in the curriculum, most institutions move through several stages. The first stage is a grudging allowance of a generalist course on women's studies in religion that is taught outside the structure of the curriculum and usually by a person marginal to the faculty. The male faculty tend to feel little response for the content of the course (about which they generally know nothing) or its instructor, and no commitment to its continuance as a regular part of the curriculum.

The second stage is when faculty begin to acquire women in one or more regular fields who are both respected as scholars and prepared to do women's studies. Women's studies courses can then be initiated that are located in the various regular disciplines of the curriculum, such as biblical studies, church history, theology, ethics, pastoral psychology, preaching and liturgy, or church administration. These courses, however, are taught as occasional electives. They attract only feminist students, mostly females and a few males. The rest of the student body is not influenced by them. Most of the faculty ignore them. The new material in them does not affect the foundational curriculum. In other words, women's studies in religion goes on as a marginal and duplicate curriculum. There is now a course in "systematic theology" and a second one of "feminist" theology. The foundational courses continue as before. Therefore, implicitly, they claim the patriarchal bias in theology as the "real" or "true" theology.

The third stage would come when feminist studies begin to affect the foundational curriculum itself. Here we might detect two more stages. The third stage would be when foundational curricula continue as usual, except for an occasional "ladies' day" when women's concerns are discussed. Thus, for example, one would teach twelve weeks of traditional male church history, and then one week in which "great women" are considered. The fourth and optimum situation would be reached when feminist critique really penetrates the whole foundational curriculum and transforms the way in which all the topics are considered. Thus, it becomes impossible to deal with any topic of theological studies without being aware of sexist and nonsexist options in the tradition and bringing that out as an integral part of one's hermeneutic. Thus, for example, one would understand St. Paul as a man whose theology is caught up in ambivalent struggle between various alternatives: between an exclusivist and a universal faith, between an historical and an eschatological faith, and between a patriarchal and an integrative faith. The way he handled the third ambiguity, moreover, conditioned fundamentally the way he handled the first two ambiguities. Thus, one cannot understand Paul as a whole without incorporating the question of sexism into the context of his theology.

Generally we can say that most seminaries who have dealt with women's studies at all are somewhere between stage one and stage two, usually at stage one. A few have done an occasional "ladies' day" in the foundational curriculum. Few have even begun to imagine what it would mean to reach the optimum incorporation of feminism into the foundational curriculum, as a normal and normative part of the interpretive context of the whole. Moreover women's studies in religion has not yet matured to the point where it is able to offer a comprehensive reconstruction of methodology and tradition in various fields. For example, a genuine feminist reconstruction of systematic theology is yet to be written.

Even further down the road is the "retraining" of male faculty who are able to take such work into account. There are exceptions. Occasionally one finds that prodigy, a male professor who early recognized the value of the feminist critique and has been able, easily and gracefully, to incorporate it into his teaching with a minimum of defensiveness or breast-beating. In general, however, one would have to say that women's studies in theological education is still marginal and vulnerable. The conservative drift of the seminaries means that increasing numbers of women students themselves are non- or antifeminist. Cadres of explicitly hostile white male students are emerging. Constant struggle is necessary to maintain momentum or even to prevent slipback. The recent publication of the book *Your Daughters Shall Prophesy* (Pilgrim Press, 1980), reflects on this ten-year struggle for feminist theological education in several major educational settings.

ALTERNATIVE VIEWS OF FEMINISM AND RELIGIOUS STUDIES

Finally, we must say that feminists in religion are by no means united in what they understand to be the optimum feminist reconstruction of religion. We also have to reckon with the fact that religion is not simply an academic discipline. It is an integral part of popular culture. Concern with it has to do with modus vivendi of large numbers of people in many walks of life. It shapes mass institutions, the church and the synagogue, as well as alternative religious communities that emerge to fill people's need for life symbols. Thus, the interest in feminism and religion has an urgency, as well as a rancor, that is different from that in academic disciplines.

There are several different lines that are emerging both in academics and across the religious institutions and movements of popular culture today. One group, who could be identified as Evangelical feminists, believe that the message of Scripture is fundamentally egalitarian. Scripture, especially the New Testament, proposes a new ideal of "mutual submission" of men and women to each other. This has been misread as the subjugation of women by the theological tradition. These feminists would hope to clean up the sexism of Scripture by better exegesis. It would be incorrect to interpret these Evangelical feminists as always limited by a precritical method of scriptural interpretation. Their limitations are often more pastoral than personal. They are concerned to address a certain constituency, the members of the Evangelical churches from which they come, with the legitimacy of an egalitarian understanding of biblical faith. They sometimes limit themselves to this kind of exegesis because they know it is the only way to reach that constituency.

A second view, which I should call the "liberationist" position, takes a more critical view of Scripture. People with this view believe there is a conflict between the prophetic, iconoclastic message of the prophetic tradition, with its attack on oppressive and self-serving religion, and the failure to apply this message to subjugated minorities in the patriarchal family, especially the women and slaves. The vision of redemption of the biblical tradition transcends the inadequacies of past consciousness. It goes ahead of us, pointing toward a new and yet unrealized future of liberation whose dimensions are continually expanding as we become more sensitive to injustices which were overlooked in past cultures. Liberationists would use the prophetic tradition as the norm to critique the sexism of the religious tradition. Biblical sexism is not denied, but it loses its authority. It must be denounced as a failure to measure up to the full vision of human liberation of the prophetic and gospel messages. A third group, we mentioned earlier, feel that women waste their time salvaging positive elements of these religious traditions. They take the spokesmen of patriarchal religion at their word when they say that Christ and God are literally and essentially male, and conclude that these religions have existed for no other purpose except to sanctify male domination. Women should quit the church and the synagogue and move to the feminist coven to celebrate the sacrality of women through recovery of the religion of the goddess.

Although I myself am most sympathetic to the second view, I would regard all these positions as having elements of truth. All respond to real needs of different constituencies of women (and some men). It is unlikely that any of these views will predominate, but all will work as parallel trends in the ensuing decades to reshape the face of religion.

The Evangelical feminists address themselves to an important group in American religion who frequently use Scripture to reinforce traditional patriarchal family models. Evangelical feminists wish to lift up neglected traditions and to give Biblicist Christians a basis for addressing the question of equality. They will probably get the liberal wing of these churches to modify their language and exegesis. The first creation story of women's and man's equal creation in the image of God will be stressed rather than the second creation story of Eve from Adam's rib. Galatians 3:28 will be stressed in Paul rather than Ephesians 5, and so forth. They might get some denominations to use inclusive language for the community and maybe even for God.

The liberationist wing would want churches to take a much more active and prophetic role in critiquing the sexism of society, not only on such issues as abortion rights, gay rights, and the ERA, but also on the links between sexism and economic injustice. They would press churches with a social gospel tradition into new questions about the adequacy of a patriarchal, capitalist, and consumerist economy to promote a viable human future.

The impact of the separatist goddess religions is more difficult to predict. Traditional Jews and Christians would view these movements as "paganism," if not "satanism." The goddess movements are likely to respond in a equally defensive way and to direct their feelings against feminists who are still working within churches and synagogues. A lot depends on whether some mediating ground can be developed. On the one side, there would have to be a conscious rejection of the religious exclusivism of the Jewish and Christian traditions and a recognition of the appropriateness of experiencing the divine through female symbols and body images. The goddess worshippers, in turn, might have to grow out of some of their defensiveness toward their Jewish and Christian sisters and start thinking about how we are to create a more comprehensive faith for our sons, as well as our daughters.

This is not to be construed as a call for such feminists to become (or return) to Judaism or Christianity, but rather a growth toward that kind of maturity that can recognize the legitimacy of religious quests in several kinds of contexts. As long as "goddess" feminists can only affirm their way by a reversed exclusivism and denial of the possibility of liberating elements in the biblical tradition, they are still tied to the same exclusivist patterns of thought in an opposite form.

A creative dialogue between these two views could be very significant. Countercultural feminist spirituality could make important contributions to the enlargement of our religious symbols and experiences. We might be able to experience God gestating the world in Her womb, rather than just "making it" through a divine phallic fiat. We would rediscover the rhythms that tie us biologically with earth, fire, air, and water which have been so neglected in our antinatural spiritualities. We would explore the sacralities of the repressed parts of our psyches and our environmental experiences. Many worlds that have been negated by patriarchal religion might be reclaimed for the enlargement of our common life.

It is not clear what all this might mean. It might well be the beginning of a new religion as momentous in its break with the past as Christianity was with the religions of the Semites and the Greeks. But if it is truly to enlarge our present options, it must also integrate the best of the insights that we have developed through Judaism and Christianity, as these religions integrated some (not all) of the best insights of the Near Eastern and Greco-Roman worlds. What is clear is this: the patriarchal repression of women and women's experience has been so massive and prevalent that to begin to take women seriously will involve a profound and radical transformation of our religions.

j. gordon melton

ANOTHER LOOK AT NEW RELIGIONS

A generation ago we thought we understood the phenomenon of marginal religions. On the edge of the religious community there was a handful of different kinds of religions, some exotic, some explosive, and a few troublesome. They were a problem only to a few sociologists who were trying to place several different leftovers into their typology of religious groups and Evangelical Christians disturbed by their unorthodox teachings. Through the first seven decades of the twentieth century, the term "cult" had come to be applied to these marginal religions. Yinger summarized what was known about the cults in his oft-quoted statement of the mid-1950s:

> The term cult is used in many different ways, usually with the connotations of small size, search for a mystical experience, lack of an organizational structure, and presence of a charismatic leader. Some of these criteria (mysticism, for example) emphasize cultural characteristics that are inappropriate in our classification scheme; yet there seems to be the need for a term that will describe groups that are similar to sects, but represent a sharper break, in religious terms, from the dominant religious tradition of a society. By a cult, therefore, we will mean a group that is at the farthest extreme from the "universal church" with which we started. It is small, short-lived, often local, frequently built around a dominant leader (as compared with the greater tendency toward widespread lay participation in the sect). Both because its beliefs and rites deviate quite widely from those that are traditional in a society (there is less of a tendency to appeal to "primitive Christianity," for example) and because the problems of succession following the death of a charismatic leader are often difficult, the cult tends to be small, to break up easily, and is relatively unlikely to develop into an established sect or denomination. The cult is concerned almost wholly with the problems of the individual, with little regard for questions of social order; the implications for anarchy are even stronger than in the case of the sect, which is led by its interest in "right behavior" (whether the avoidance of individual sin or the establishment of social justice) back to the problem of social integration. The cults are religious "mutants," extreme variations on the dominant themes by means of which

J. Gordon Melton, "Another Look at New Religions," The Annals of the American Academy of Political and Social Science *527:97–112 (1993). Copyright © 1993 by Sage Publications. Reprinted by permission of Sage Publications, Inc.*

men try to solve their problems. Pure type cults are not common in Western society; most groups that might be called cults are fairly close to the sect type. Perhaps examples are the various Spiritualist groups and some of the "Moslem" groups among American Negroes. (1957:154–155)

As social scientists were absorbing this understanding of cults as small, ephemeral marginal groups, the culture was also grasping a shift in the nature of America's religious establishment. Herberg (1955) suggested that the Protestant establishment of the previous generation had been replaced by a new establishment of Protestants, Catholics, and Jews. We seemed to have comprehended the basic structures of the religious community, at least in the United States.

As we were accepting this more plausible religious universe, however, forces somewhat outside of our vision were already at work to render it obsolete. Along with its destruction, World War II also spurred such an improvement in transportation and communication as significantly to shrink the world and launch new waves of international shifts in populations and religious ideas. For the West, the most important shift was the arrival of Eastern ideas. Certainly, since the 1890s, some Eastern thought had slipped through the significant legal barriers that had been erected to keep it out. However, immediately after the war, European countries began to invite outsiders into Europe to rebuild the labor market. With no thought to the religious ideas they would bring with them, western Europe welcomed Chinese Buddhists, Turkish Muslims, and Indian Hindus. And with a new consciousness of the world, Westerners began to travel to the East not just as explorers of their geography but as seekers in the spiritual terrain. Upon making a great discovery, these new explorers returned to open Japanese-style zendos, Sufi enclaves, and incense-filled ashrams.

Then in 1965, the major barrier to the entry of Eastern and Middle Eastern ideas into the American religious mix fell. Diplomats pursuing global political maneuvers in southern Asia had encountered a minor problem: Asians were insulted by American immigration policies. New friends in Asia demanded changes if America expected cooperation in the Southeast Asia Treaty Organization. With the immigration bill that was produced in 1965, barriers to Asian immigration were dropped. Asians and Middle Easterners, Asian and Middle Eastern religious teachers, and Asian and Middle Eastern religious ideas started a flow that to this day shows no sign of slowing and every sign of increasing.

The impact of change brought by the dropping of the immigration barrier was somewhat hidden by a diverting sideshow. The postwar baby-boom generation was reaching adulthood in a culture that was not prepared to absorb it. With insufficient openings in the culture, baby boomers came to create a counterculture that looked for alternatives everywhere—art, politics, economics, living arrangements, and religion. Among the alienated of the counterculture were the first converts to the new Asian religions.

Such ferment as the 1960s witnessed had parallels in American history, but now a new factor had been added. For the first time, a variety of Asian teachers, not just books, placed the full spectrum of Asian belief practice systems before a public seemingly hungry for new wisdom. A set of new ideas from the East, from the Sikhism of a Yogi Bhajan to the interesting variation on Christian themes by Korean evangelist Sun Myung Moon, presented themselves accompanied by teachers ready and eager to instruct a generation of seekers of alternative religious truths.

The coincidence of the beginning of the wave of Asian teachers with the counterculture's reaching its climatic stage had several dramatic, and I would suggest, distorting effects on our perception of what was happening. First, the scholars who initially called our attention to the burst of new religious activity, especially on the West Coast, were also individuals enthused with the counterculture and they erroneously tended to see the new religious impulse as a product of that counterculture. Thus as the counterculture died, they stopped tracking the continual influx of new religions, which has persisted unabated to the present.

Second, the movement of the first new religions among participants in the counterculture produced an intense reaction that took form as the anticult movement. While there is every reason to believe that some reaction to the growth of new religions would have developed, among Evangelical Christians, for example, the virulent form it took was directly related to the peculiarities of the counterculture. During the summers of the late 1960s and early 1970s, numerous college-age youths dropped out of school to spend time in California among the street people. Many, at the end of a summer in the counterculture, simply never returned their old ways. Some of these people were recruited by one of the new religions and when seen again, in the glowing enthusiasm of their new faith, appeared to parents, family, and former friends as religious fanatics. What could explain such a change? It had to be some illegitimate influence that had entered the lives of their sons and daughters. By the time the counterculture had died, and the new religions had moved on to more visible and recognizable recruitment techniques, a philosophy of destructive cults, brainwashing, and deceitful recruiting had entered the popular mind.

The combination of the continuing emergence of new religions for the last thirty years and intense controversy caused by the reaction of the anticult movement to their presence has had among its results a flowering of scholarship. Where, in 1960, one could hardly find a specialist in nonconventional religions, today several hundred can be found in the United States alone. As might be guessed, this flowering of scholarship has allowed a reexamination of all of our assumptions concerning the so-called cults. The rest of the article will attempt to bring together the major insights concerning what has been learned about the new religions and propose a new perspective as to how they may be viewed in the future.

TOWARD A NEW BASE FOR THE STUDY OF NONCONVENTIONAL RELIGION

Through the 1980s, the Institute for the Study of American Religion conducted a broad survey of American religious groups in preparing the text for the third edition of the *Encyclopedia of American Religions* (EAR3), published in December 1988, a 1991 supplement and, more recently, the fourth edition of EAR.

The EAR first appeared in 1979 as the focus of a continuing project to gather data on every primary religious body—denomination—that now operates or has ever operated in North America, and it is the only single source containing such data. As part of the survey, besides assembling basic descriptive material of a historical and theological nature, the institute made an attempt to gather information that could at a later date be quantified.

The survey has centered upon the 1,586 different religious groups that appear in EAR3, including over 700 nonconventional religious groups. For the purposes of this article, the groups in the original sample of 1,586 were identified as either mainline Christian churches or sectarian Christian churches. . . . Those religious bodies serving primarily an ethnic and/or immigrant membership—Jewish groups, the Buddhist churches of America, Arab Muslim associations, and so on—were deleted while at the same time recognizing the important role that the ethnic-immigrant groups play in the development of nonconventional religions. The deletions left 755 groups to be included in the survey. Supplementing the sample of 755 groups from EAR3 were an additional 81 nonconventional groups about which research has been completed and that either appeared in the EAR3 supplement or are slated to appear in EAR4. Also among the 755 groups were fifty groups whose date of origin could not be determined within a decade, though most had been formed since 1940.

Table 1 presents a breakdown of the total of 836 nonconventional religions, considered in fifteen groupings and showing how many individual new nonconventional religious groups of each type were formed decade by decade since 1940. As the table shows, prior to World War II, 169 cults had been formed. Thirty-five additional nonconventional religious groups were formed in the late 1940s, 88 in the 1950s, 175 in the 1960s, 216 in the 1970s, and 103 thus far have been located that were formed during the 1980s. The Adventist churches, while more properly considered sects rather than cults, have nevertheless been included in the survey, since a number of prominent Adventist groups have frequently been labeled as cults—the Seventh-Day Adventists, the Jehovah's Witnesses, the Worldwide Church of God, and the Identity churches. The overall conclusions of the survey are not changed by their inclusion.

The large sample of new religious groups allows us to move beyond some of the earlier studies of new religions, which based their generalizations about new religions on exceedingly small samples. Popular texts by Beckford (1985), Bromley and Hammond (1987), Bromley and Shupe (1981), Levine (1984), Tipton (1982), and Wallis (1984) based their theoretical conclusion upon direct reference to the same small sample of ten to fifteen contemporary cults with only passing and perfunctory acknowledgment that hundreds of others also existed.

THE EPHEMERAL NATURE OF NONCONVENTIONAL RELIGIONS

In the 1950s, Yinger characterized cults as short-lived groups, generally taken to be one generation in duration. Yinger, with no attempt to pose in scholarly

Table 1
Nonconventional New Religions Included in This Survey

	Date of formation					
	Before 1940	*1940s*	*1950s*	*1960s*	*1970s*	*1980s*
Adventists	24	6	8	8	20	9
Atheism	5	2	1	6	6	1
Mail Order				1	5	4
Mormon	17	3	6	1	10	3
Communal	11	2	4	9	4	1
Metaphysical	20	1	5	8	6	2
Psychic	36	10	25	48	23	18
Ancient Wisdom	29	3	14	14	16	8
Magick	2	2	2	24	45	29
Islamic	3	1	3	4	14	4
Other Middle East	4		1	2	1	
Hindu	10	1	6	24	33	10
Other Indian	1	1		4	6	2
Buddhist-Taoist	5	3	11	16	255	10
Miscellaneous	2		1	2	4	5
Total	169	35	88	175	216	103

Date of origin unknown: 50
Number of groups: 836

Source: Melton, *Encyclopedia of American Religions.* 3d ed. (1989). Data for the 1980s are only the first half of the decade.

Note: In the case of groups that have migrated to North America from other countries, the date of establishment in North America has been used as the date of origin.

neutrality, pictured nonconventional religions as small unstable groups at the opposite extreme from the ideal ecclesia. They were, to use his term, "mutants." He cited the Spiritualists and the Black Muslims as examples. This ephemerality of new religions was among the first elements of the common understanding of nonconventional religions to be challenged.

In the 1960s, Geoffrey K. Nelson attacked the issue in his important study, *Spiritualism and Society* (1969). It should be noted that Nelson used an entire movement as the subject of his research. Spiritualism (in contrast to, for example, a single Spiritualist group such as the National Spiritualist Association of Churches or the Church of the White Eagle Lodge) is analogous to the New Thought Metaphysical Movement (in contrast to any particular group such as the United Church of Religious Science or the Unity School of Christianity). Nelson's argument, however, did not distinguish between Spiritualism as a movement and any one of its prominent components. Spiritualist organizations have survived for over a century, and the more prominent ones show no sign of demise. The two major Black Muslim organizations, cited by Yinger, have survived since 1926 and 1929, respectively, and both seem destined to survive for many decades to come.

Table 2
Nonconventional New Religions Reported as Defunct as of 1990

Date formed	Number formed	Number defunct
Before 1940	169	38
1940s	35	7
1950s	88	8
1960s	175	29
1970s	216	30
1980s	103	2
Unknown	50	11
Total	836	125
Number of nonconventional religions in survey: 836		

Source: Melton, *Encyclopedia of American Religions.* 3d ed. (1989). Data for the 1980s are only the first half of the decade.

In like measure, the survey of currently existing nonconventional religions shows a decade-by-decade growth in the number of additional religious groups and no rapid decline of groups after their allotted generation. Of the 836 groups surveyed, only 125 are now defunct. Of the 125 defunct groups, only thirty-eight are among those groups formed prior to 1940 (see Table 2). Thus approximately 200 nonconventional religious groups—that is, those formed prior to 1950—are in at least their third generation. Many, such as Jehovah's Witnesses, Theosophy, and Christian Science, have a firmly established place in America's religious landscape and have become the seedbed from which a number of variations have sprouted. While a few nonconventional religions do in fact come and go quickly—thirty of the 216 groups formed in the 1970s have already ceased to exist—and while most pass through unstable phases, especially in their first generation, the great majority of those that survive the first decade continue to become stable organizations with a lasting place in the religious ecology of their communities.

Thus the data currently available suggest, contrary to the understanding of nonconventional religions as ephemeral phenomena, that they are permanent religious phenomena that will tend to grow and evolve through the same normal stages of development as seen in the culturally mainline religions as they move from more informal organizations to a bureaucratic structure. Given the large number of individuals who are either religiously unattached—still representing millions, even though a relatively small percentage of the population—or loosely attached—an even larger group available for entirely new religious affiliation—new religions are never lacking for potential recruits.

This observation concerning the longevity as opposed to the transitory nature of nonconventional religion makes a direct comment upon the failure of the secular anticult movement to reach one of its stated goals. It has worked on the tacit assumption that the nonconventional religions were less than genuine religions and that with a combination of social pressure and legal force they could be destroyed. They were considered unstable cancer cells that could be surgically treated with some due attention. The opposite seems to be the case, however. The anticult movement, while bringing much pain to individuals and causing some groups to divert resources to defend themselves, has had no measurable effect on the development of the nonconventional religions, which, in the decade since Jonestown, have continued to grow, consolidate gains, and expand.

THE AHISTORICITY OF NONCONVENTIONAL RELIGIONS

If new religions are ephemeral, it can be—and frequently is—assumed, though rarely stated, that they can be treated apart from their history. Thus individual nonconventional religions are rarely considered with reference to like groups (do they exist?) or to predecessor groups (do these exist, since the current groups were developed by the singular religious visions of the founder?). Thus the Hare Krishna movement is considered apart from any reference to the centuries-old Vaishnava tradition of Bengal and the Gaudiya Math out of which it developed, not to mention the growing Indian American community, which now supplies it with much of its support. The Divine Light Mission is treated quite apart from the Sant Mat tradition and the role of the guru in that tradition. The Church Universal and Triumphant is treated as the product of its founders without reference to the Theosophical tradition, from which it derived most of its traditions, and the "I AM" Religious Activity, which served as an immediate predecessor. Unidentified flying object contactee groups can be treated without reference to the Theosophical and Spiritualist groups upon which they have modeled their life.

The truncated perspective of a nonconventional religion apart from the larger religious context within which it operates significantly distorts not only our understanding of it but our assessment of its impact as part of a larger integrated religious movement. While the Hare Krishna movement, in and of itself, may have little overall impact on middle America, as part of the larger Hindu and Asian religious incursion into America, it is participating in the reorientation of American religious life away from an exclusively Western Jewish-Christian format. Thus much of the distortion of our estimate of the significance and future of nonconventional religions derives from the disregard of the tradition that grounds and supports individual groups and supplies them with multiple avenues of influence.

In examining the various nonconventional religions currently operating in the United States, it was found that almost every group was related to a number of quite similar groups from which it had derived and/or with which it shared common roots. As William Sims Bainbridge (1985) put it, "In modern society, cults are born out of older cults, and most of them are known to cluster in family lineages." That is, "nonconventional" ideas and behavior patterns originated either in a culture—Japan, India, Turkey—in which they were normative or, in the case of homegrown religions, in a subgroup—the metaphysical occult community—where they were supported by a larger grouping of sympathetic people. Such diverse ideas can then be tested and refined over a period of decades, if not centuries, through the interaction of a cluster of groups that can be seen to constitute a movement.

Thus the concept of prosperity consciousness as currently espoused by, for example, the United Church and Science of Living Institute originated in the nineteenth-century metaphysical community. The ideas and practices associated with prosperity consciousness were then processed by the numerous metaphysical churches and practitioners only to be passed to the United Church's flamboyant pastor, Rev. Ike, in the 1960s. Rev. Ike's message is shared by over twenty metaphysical church groups that existed before he came on the scene and was discussed in over 200 books by different metaphysical authors. His contribution has not been in the generation of new ideas but in his forceful presentation of these ideas to the African-American community.

Thus, contrary to the popular understanding of cults as new innovative religious impulses, current data suggest that nonconventional religions fall within a relatively small number of long-standing religious families and traditions. Not only do the particular groups grow and develop, but the family of similar groups evolves much as the more conventional religions do. The Methodists are now divided into over thirty denominations and the Baptists into over sixty. What in the West are considered nonconventional religious alternatives—the Hare Krishna movement, Zen Buddhism, the Sufi orders—are primarily denominations of the mainline dominant religion of another country. Like the great majority of Christian bodies, these individual groups exist as schisms and variations within their long-standing particular religious tradition.

THE PROBLEM OF SUCCESSION IN NONCONVENTIONAL RELIGIONS

It is generally assumed that nonconventional religions, as ephemeral ahistorical groups, have a problem of succession on the death of their founder-leader. Drawing upon the discussion of charismatic leaders that originated with Max Weber, Yinger proposed what has become another truism about nonconventional religions, namely, that the death of the founder or charismatic leader of the group is experienced as a traumatic near-fatal event, "because the problems of succession following the death of a charismatic leader are often difficult, the cult tends to be small, to break up easily, and is relatively unlikely to develop into an established sect or denomination" (1957:155). More recently, Larry Shinn, in his discussion of the Hare Krishnas, noted, "A critical juncture in a charismatic community's history is the death of its founder" (1987:24). This truism concerning leadership succession derives from the earlier discussion in Weber of the problem of transferring the informal charisma attached to a founding person or persons to a formal, routinized structure.

Among scholars, while little has been written on the succession question, the strongly held opinion remains that the death of a leader is a crisis event of major proportions for a new religion. The dearth of written material on this point may be due to the virtual nonexistence of incidents of succession problems. In recent years, for example, we have witnessed the death of the founder-leader of the Church of Scientology, the Way International, the Worldwide Church of God, the Church Universal and Triumphant, the International Society for Krishna Consciousness, the Alamo Christian Foundation, the International Buddhist Meditation Center, the Zen Center of San Francisco, and ECKANKAR, to name but a few prominent examples. Each group passed through a brief period of mourning, analogous to that commonly acknowledged by older, more established churches following the death a beloved bishop or respected leader. In each case, there was a relatively smooth transition to a previously designated leadership, though there were certainly some power struggles.

The defunct nonconventional religious groups listed in EAR3 were examined to see if their demise could be tied to the founder's death. The largest percentage of defunct groups died after only a few years, long before the death or even retirement of the leader. Among recently defunct groups, correspondence has been continued with their founders. Others survived their leaders' death only to die after several generations of vital life. We are currently watching the Shakers die out completely. Of 125 defunct groups, less than ten showed any relationship between their founder's death and their demise. These groups were all quite similar in that they were organized as personal ministries of a single person who, for doctrinal and/or personal reasons, refused to mobilize followers as a church. Margaret Laird, for example, carried distrust of organization with her upon leaving the tightly organized Church of Christ, Scientist. Psychiana's founder briefly organized local groups but soon disbanded them. Unable to find a suitable successor, he allowed the movement to die with him. These few groups that died with their leader were all organized as personal ministries and possessed a strong antidenominational bias. They were not groups that failed simply because of succession problems.

One might think that if the natural expected death of a leader would not be traumatic, then the unexpected death of a leader by assassination certainly would. In one case, that of the Bishop Hill community in Illinois, whose leader, Eric Jannson, was shot by a disgruntled member, this seems possibly to have been the case. In numerous other cases, however, the groups survived and either still exist or survived for many generations. The Mormons have experienced the largest number of leader assassinations: Joseph Smith, James Jesse Strang, Joseph Morris, Joel LeBaron, to mention a few. But, except for the Morrisites, who died out in the mid-twentieth century, these Mormon groups have survived to this day.

Three reasons can be offered as to why succession is a minor to nonexistent problem. First, we can point to Max Weber's concept of the routinization of charisma. The routinization of charismatic authority should properly occur during the leader's lifetime, so that by the time of his or her death, the organization has completed the shift of focus. For example, the initial stages of the transfer of authority from L. Ron Hubbard to somewhat anonymous church officials of the Church of Scientology can be seen to have occurred as early as 1966, when Hubbard resigned all official positions in the church. While he informally continued to play an important role, his charismatic authority had already largely been transferred to his writings and to the organization by the time of his death a few years ago.

Second, the problem of succession was largely the product of an inaccurate picture of nonconventional religions. Cults were pictured as ephemeral ahistorical products that arose only in the immediate past, without significant roots in previous religious traditions. Such is not the case. Overwhelmingly, nonconventional religions are merely individual examples of a larger religious tradition. From their tradition, be it Hindu, Buddhist, Islamic, or the occult, the group has inherited models for transferring authority through a succession of leaders, as in the dharma transmission among Buddhists, the institutionalization of mediums as pastors among Spiritualists, or a succession of elected corporate officers as adopted by most occult groups over a century ago.

Adding to the distorted picture of nonconventional religions has been the inappropriate superlative language used in describing charismatic leaders. Echoing the rhetoric of the anticult movement, scholarly observers have frequently ascribed almost superhuman abilities to religious founders as they interpret the allegiance, devotion, and respect of group followers to be an intensely dependent relationship. I would suggest that while a highly dependent relationship between founder and followers sometimes exists, it is never total, even though it can occasionally contribute to the performance of illegal actions and even, on very rare occasions, under exacting circumstances, lead to a follower's death. Fieldwork on contemporary nonconventional religions corroborates the many accounts by exmembers that reveal patterns of doubt in individual members and ongoing critical review of leaders by the numbers of supposedly totalistic groups. In the case of the Unification Church, the Church of Scientology, and the Hare Krishnas, continued internal critical review has forced major changes in both structures and practices. We might also make note of those groups such as the Process Church of the Final Judgment and the Alive Polarity Fellowship who removed their charismatic leader-founder from office when that leadership proved unacceptable.

Third, even if we grant that at one time succession might have been a problem for first-generation religious groups, such is no longer the case simply because of the import of new legal demands upon new religions. Increasingly over the last two generations, during which time over half of all currently existing religious bodies have been formed, tax laws have forced almost all of them to organize or reorganize on a corporate model and, as a not-for-profit corporation, to place major legal powers—that is, the real powers—especially title to property, in the hands of a stable board of directors. While it is possible to exist as a religious organization without so incorporating, it is most difficult, and few groups follow that option, even for a short period.

Given the corporate stable legal structure apart from any charismatic leader, upon the leader's death or retirement, the group's board of directors immediately assumes its assigned role and oversees the smooth transfer of authority. To date, no treatment of the significant, powerful, but largely hidden role of boards of directors has found its way into the discussion of the life of nonconventional religions. Similarly, no treatment of the implications for religious groups of the subtle restructuring of American religion as a result of government fiat has found its way into church-state discussions.

UNCONVENTIONAL RELIGION AND SOCIAL UNREST

No issue has been so discussed and seemingly found so much agreement among social scientists as has the assertion of the connection between social turmoil and the emergence of new religions. While this assertion has been frequently made by religious sociologists and anthropologists throughout the century, it reappeared frequently in discussions of the new nonconventional religions in the West because of the early connection made between new religions and the disturbance associated with the counterculture. Thus, as many observers juxtaposed the emerging religious situation of the 1970s beside their vivid encounter with the campus-centered turmoil and the street people of the 1960s, the social upheavals of the 1960s offered themselves as the immediate and logical explanation of the religious ferment. Thus Tipton could speak of "getting saved from the sixties." Possibly Anthony, Robbins, and Schwarz summarized the position best when they wrote, "The emergence of new religions can be interpreted as the effects of a widespread perception in certain western societies on the inadequacy of scientific-technical rationalism alone to orient contemporary social life" (1983:7). This perception, it can be argued, lies behind what emerged as political radicalism in the 1960s and now continues in some of the new movements that can be viewed as the surviving remnants of the 1960s counterculture in modern societies. Wuthnow, writing in the mid-1980s, defined the period of the most vigorous new religious movement activity as the period from the 1960s to 1973, noting that "the Vietnam War which brought the religious and cultural unrest to a climax did not end until 1973" (1986:1–28). The big story of this era was the rise of new religions, which grew until 1975 or 1976 and then went into a period of stability and decline. Beckford saw the new religious movements in the West as directly tied to the period of social turmoil—the years of the early 1960s through early 1970s—and concludes simply that "rapid social change in the twentieth cen-tury is associated with the rise of a large number of new religious movements. They are both a response to change and a means of contributing to it" (1985:xv).

If the emergence of the noticeable number of nonconventional religions is but an overflow from the social unrest of the 1960s, then we should be able to expect (1) that the number of new groups formed should show a distinct relationship to the era of greatest social unrest and (2) that the recruitment and growth of those groups so formed should show a distinct decline as distance from the tumultuous time increased.

The exact opposite seems to be the case, however. As Table 1 reveals, a marked rise in the number of new religions began in the 1950s (with eighty-eight new groups reported as opposed to only thirty-five in the previous decade). The number of new groups showed a marked increase in the 1960s (175) and through the 1970s (216). So far, with data essentially from the first half of the 1980s, the number of new nonconventional religions being formed continues to be on the increase.

Thus, as the distance from the 1960s grows ever greater, the number of new nonconventional religions continues ever upward, and there is no indication that that rate of increase will slow in the foreseeable future. It is difficult to predict which families of religions will continue to expand, but the occult and Eastern groups show no loss of popularity.

Second, as new nonconventional religions emerge, older groups have shown an amazing staying power. Of more than 500 groups formed since 1950, less than 100 have become defunct, and twenty-one of those were small Neo-Pagan covens and groves, which have been quickly replaced. During this same period, while some groups have experienced significant ups and downs, most of the older groups have shown a pattern of continued high-level recruitment of new members, net growth, and geographical spread. The most successful have developed centers in Europe, Asia, the Caribbean, and South America.

Contrary to expectations, the pattern of growth shown by nonconventional religions treated in this study reveals no relation to social unrest or lack thereof and provides significant disconfirmation of the social unrest theories. The pattern of growth also provides additional disconfirmation of the image of nonconventional religions as ephemeral religious phenomena confined to the margin of culture.

Besides the overall pattern of religious growth, special note should be made of the growth of specific kinds of religious groups. Asian religious groups have shown a remarkable growth since the late 1960s. During the 1970s, they were a major reference point for social unrest theorists. However, it is to be noted that their growth began in the 1950s, with the emergence of Buddhism among soldiers who experienced life in Japan after World War II, which accounts for the emergence of Buddhism in America a decade earlier than Hinduism. More rapid growth began after the passing of the new immigration laws in 1965, which for the first time allowed many Asian teachers to migrate or spend long periods of time in the United States. That first burst of real growth of Asian religion has continued unabated as immigration continues.

The growth of Spiritualist and Ancient Occult Wisdom religions began immediately after World War II—wars have usually spurred Spiritualist activity—and new groups developed steadily through the 1960s. Slowing during the 1970s, they again revived, with the New Age Movement, and in the 1980s they reached new levels of acceptance in America.

Neo-Paganism, a form of popular magic religion, was imported to the United States in the mid-1960s. It emerged before the end of the decade and has enjoyed two decades of steady growth. It also seems to have a bright future, in spite of forces in the culture that continue to confuse it with Satanism.

Additionally, the overall growth pattern of new nonconventional religions within North America fits comfortably into the overall growth pattern of religion in general. During the twentieth century, Christianity has shown a steady rate of growth, more than twice that of the population. The problems of a few of the large, older, prominent denominations, which have experienced a period of decline over the last few decades, were more than compensated for by the growth of Roman Catholicism, the Southern Baptists, the Assemblies of God, and a number of other denominations that experienced a period of rapid expansion. At the same time, there has been a steady decade-by-decade appearance of new Christian denominations, the number of which grew from approximately 150 in 1900 to more than 600 by 1980. The appearance of new Christian sects continued unabated through the 1980s and also gives no indication of slowing or stopping.

The overall growth pattern of both conventional and nonconventional religion in America during the twentieth century suggests that religion is an independent force active in the world of economics and politics and must be considered in its own right, not as a mere child of economic forces, social unrest, and/or ephemeral shifts of political mood. I suggest that in the modern world, while the larger social climate may temporarily alter the immediate program of religious groups—thus creating variations in such things as recruitment tactics and social priorities—lead to adjustments in theological rhetoric and emphases, and change public perceptions of religious activity, religion as a whole continues on its own course in spite of either the social climate or the monetary expansion or decline of any particular group.

A NEW PERSPECTIVE ON NONCONVENTIONAL RELIGION

If the model of nonconventional religions as a set of small, ephemeral, deviant, weird, and largely irrelevant religions on the margin of culture is inadequate and the major building blocks of that perspective unsubstantiated by the data, what perspective does most adequately fit the data? A more global model should be developed that, first of all, sees North America and the West as participants both in the almost universal growth of religion around the world and in the immense diffusion of the older religions from their traditional geographical bases. During the twentieth century, Christianity has continued its penetration of customarily non-Christian lands, but its mobility has now been matched by Hinduism, Buddhism, Sikhism, Jainism, Baha'ism, Zoroastrianism, Islam Sufism—all the world's religions—which have become equally mobile through the migration of missionaries and adherents. As noted earlier, most of those groups that have been labeled cults in the West are simply representative denominations of these older religious traditions that are rapidly being established in the Western nations, are adapting to Western culture, and are initiating programs of recruitment in their new host countries.

Second, as the older religions have extended their following globally, the West spawned and/or revived several additional alternative religious traditions that during the last half century have matured, shown an amazing growth potential, and are now being exported around the world along with Christianity. Many of these new traditions, created in nineteenth-century America, include the Metaphysical tradition, which grew out of the thought and work of such people as Ralph Waldo Emerson, Mary Baker Eddy, and Emma Curtis Hopkins; the occult tradition, which reemerged through the likes of Andrew Jackson Davis, Madame Blavatsky, and Pascal Beverly Randolph; the Mormon tradition, which began with Joseph Smith; and the Adventist movement, initiated by William Miller. Each of these traditions represents a new gestalt in American religious life. Moreover, apart from the truth claims of any particular religious group, that is, by any objective scholarly standard, each of these traditions is just as valid and each possesses just as sophisticated a body of religious wisdom as do the several mainline Christian traditions or Judaism.

Third, just as Christianity, in spite of the decline of several of the older denominations, has experienced a steady growth in North America for the past century, a growth in both the numbers of adherents and the number of new denominations, so the new religions have experienced a steady growth during the same period of time. The rate of that growth was significantly increased in 1965 by the passing of new immigration law that allowed a host of new Asian teachers into the country and the subsequent growth of several hundred new Eastern-based religious bodies. The addition of new religions should continue at an even higher rate given the immigration law of 1990, which increases limits on immigration from Asia by 60 percent annually. While what we have thought of as alternative and nonconventional religions show no sign of becoming the majority in North America, they have established themselves as significant and stable minorities and are bringing about a new pluralistic religious environment in which each urban area will have a medley of all of the world's major religions and many of its lesser ones.

NOTES

PART ONE   RELIGION AND SOCIETY: EXPLORING THE RELATIONSHIPS

1. The excerpt included in this volume is from the 1995 translation by Karen Fields, which is, in my estimation, more lucid and friendlier to English speakers than the 1915 translation by Joseph Ward Swain.

2. The word *profane* comes from the Latin *pro* (before or outside) and *fanum* (temple). Something that is profane then is something outside of the temple or secular.

3. For a well-known quasi-functionalist analysis of the threat that death and contact with the dead poses for the solidarity of a group, see Bronislaw Malinowksi's (1925) analysis of the taboos among islanders in the South Pacific in "Magic, Science and Religion."

4. See the Symposium on Civil Religion by Carroll Bourg in *Sociological Analysis* 37(2):141–149, 1976.

5. For a good bibliography on American civil religion, see Gehrig (1981).

6. For example, Williams and Alexander (1994).

7. In a later essay, Bellah defended himself against charges that his analysis of civil religion was a glorification of the nation state. He stated, "I think it should be clear from the text that I conceive the central tradition of the American civil religion not as a form of national self-worship but as the subordination of the nation to ethical principles that transcend it and in terms of which it should be judged" (1970:168). He stated that his choice of the term *civil religion* may have led to some of the confusion about the issue.

8. This prophetic role for civil religion with its idea of challenge and calling to a higher ethical purpose is more clearly developed in Bellah's 1975 work *The Broken Covenant*.

PART TWO   MAINSTREAM PROTESTANTISM

Iannaccone, "Why Strict Churches Are Strong"

1. I am using the word *commitment* to denote the value that one attaches to involvement in the group. I do not assume that highly committed people are any less rational than others or that they are less inclined to free ride. They participate more only because they derive greater utility from participation.

2. Hoge surveyed expert opinion in an effort to identify the empirical determinants of church growth. In the current context, his data provide something approaching a

"double-blind" experiment, since neither he nor his subjects anticipated using the results to predict church attendance, contributions, or other individual-level behaviors.

3. One might wonder whether the experts' judgments simply mirrored the conventional denominational ranking. But the experts ordered the denominations quite differently when asked about their strength of ethnic identity and their style of governance (Hoge 1979).

4. Weber introduced the church-sect distinction to sociology (1958, 1963). Adam Smith introduced virtually the same distinction to economics more than a century earlier. Smith contrasted "established churches" and "small sects" at length in *The Wealth of Nations* (1965:740–766).

5. For the purposes of the analysis it does not matter whether these demands take the form of explicit consumption restrictions, such as dietary laws, or behaviors that isolate or stigmatize members so as to restrict their interactions with nonmembers.

6. The patterns in Table 1 are not unknown to the sociology of religion, although Figures 1 to 4 do provide a new view of the data. Numerous surveys of Protestant Christian groups find that denominations tend to fall into distinct types (Stark and Glock 1968; Roof and McKinney 1987). The present analysis builds on the work of Johnson (1963:542, 544; see Johnson 1971) who defined "churches" as religious organizations that "accept the social environment," embracing the norms and values of the prevailing culture, and contrasted them to "sects" that "reject the social environment."

7. The results in Table 2 come from the first truly random sample of American Jewry, the 1990 Jewish National Population Survey, gleaned from an initial survey of more than 100,000 Americans (Goldstein and Kosmin 1991). For similar results based on a 1970 survey of American Jews, see Lazerwitz and Harrison (1979).

8. Traditional church-sect theory does not generate this sort of a prediction. At best, it provides a *definition* of the sect as a "type" of religion that separates itself from society *and* maintains high levels of participation *and* draws its membership from society's poor.

9. Iannaccone, "Why Strict Churches Are Strong," *American Journal of Sociology* 99(5):1198–1200, prints the regression results.

10. The key regression result remains robust despite: (a) changed samples (e.g., Protestants only, whites only, married respondents, or the exclusion of extreme sects); (b) different estimation techniques (OLS, tobit, or logit); (c) alternate time frames (1984–1990, 1972–1983, or 1972–1990); (d) alternative denominational measures (1990 distinctiveness ranking, 1979 ranking, and denominational dummies that distinguish "liberal Protestants," "moderate Protestants," "conservative Protestants," "sect" members, and Catholics), and (e) the inclusion of additional explanatory variables (political orientation and a variety of attitudinal measures).

11. Some researchers have claimed that Kelley's observations concerning the "institutional" determinants of participation, commitment, and membership were biased by a neglect of "contextual" factors, such as the average age, income, education, and birth rate within the membership of various denominations (Hoge 1979:193–195). Insofar as Kelley's thesis concerns commitment and participation, the present data support Kelley over his critics. For evidence that the criticism may not even apply to membership growth, see Kelley (1979:334–343).

12. Kelley (1986:95–96) did follow this assertion with the parenthetical provision that "there may be a point of diminishing returns beyond which increasing strictness does not produce significantly greater strength, and might in fact prove counterproductive." But his theoretical argument and real-world examples admit no such exceptions.

PART FOUR CATHOLICISM

1. For a much fuller development of these themes, see Greeley's *The Denominational Society* (1972) and *The American Catholic: A Social Portrait* (1977a).

2. All the following numbers are taken from "Numbers Don't Lie: A Priesthood in Irreversible Decline" in *Commonweal* 122 (April 7, 1995), pp. 11–14, in which Schoenherr summarizes the findings of the larger work.

Williams and Davidson, "Catholic Conceptions of Faith: A Generational Analysis"

1. Space constraints preclude a listing of all of the research citations. For a complete bibliography, see "Catholic Conceptions of Faith: A Generational Analysis," *Sociology of Religion* (Fall 1996).

PART FIVE JUDAISM

1. I draw heavily from the works of Davidman (1991) and Blau (1976) for the descriptions of these groups.

2. Sklare (1972) notes that a good portion of the Orthodox community is made up of the "nonobservant Orthodox" who maintain affiliation with an Orthodox synagogue because they prefer to follow Orthodox patterns but do not live by *halacha*.

PART SIX RELIGIOUS MOVEMENTS: LEFT, RIGHT, AND NONCONVENTIONAL

Moen, "From Revolution to Evolution"

1. Space constraints preclude a listing of all of the research citations. For a complete bibliography, see "From Revolution to Evolution: The Changing Nature of the Christian Right," *Sociology of Religion* 55 (Fall):345–357, 1994.

BIBLIOGRAPHY

AHLSTROM, S. 1972. *A Religious History of the American People.* New Haven, CT: Yale University Press.

AMMERMAN, N. 1987. *Bible Believers: Fundamentalists in the Modern World.* New Brunswick, NJ: Rutgers University Press.

ANDERSON, R. M. 1979. *Vision of the Disinherited: The Making of American Pentecostalism.* New York: Oxford University Press.

ANTHONY, D., T. ROBBINS, and P. SCHWARZ. 1983. "Contemporary religious movements and the secularization process." In J. Coleman and G. Baum (eds.), *New Religious Movements.* New York: Seabury Press.

ARIELI, Y. 1964. *Individualism and Nationalism in American Ideology.* Cambridge, MA: Harvard University Press.

ATKINS, G. G., and F. L. FAGLEY. 1942. *History of American Congregationalism.* Boston: Pilgrim Press.

BAINBRIDGE, W. S. 1978. *Satan's Power.* Berkeley: University of California Press.

———. 1985. "Cultural genetics." P. 159 in R. Stark (ed.), *Religious Movements: Genesis, Exodus, and Numbers.* New York: Paragon.

BAINBRIDGE, W. S., and R. STARK. 1981. "American-born sects: initial findings." *Journal for the Scientific Study of Religion* 20:130–149.

BALSWICK, J. O., and G. L. FAULKNER. 1970. "Identification of ministerial cliques: a sociometric approach." *Journal for the Scientific Study of Religion* 9:303–310.

BARGY, H. 1902. *La religion dans la Société aux Etats-Unis.* Paris: A. Colin.

BECK, S. H., B. S. COLE, and J. A. HAMMOND. 1991. "Religious heritage and premarital sex: evidence from a national sample of young adults." *Journal for the Scientific Study of Religion* 30(2):173–180.

BECKFORD, J. A. 1985. *Cult Controversies.* London: Tavistock.

BELLAH, R. N. 1970. "Civil religion in America." Pp 168–186 in R. Bellah (ed.), *Beyond Belief: Essays on Religion in a Post-Traditional World.* New York: Harper & Row.

———. 1975. *The Broken Covenant: American Civil Religion in a Time of Trial.* New York: Seabury.

BERGER, P. 1961. *The Precarious Vision.* Garden City, NY: Doubleday.

———. 1969. *The Sacred Canopy.* Garden City, NY: Doubleday.

———. 1974. "Some second thoughts on substantive versus functional definitions of religion." *Journal for the Scientific Study of Religion* 13:125–134.

———. 1981. *The Heretical Imperative.* Garden City, NY: Doubleday.

———. 1982. "From the crisis of religion to the crisis of secularity." Pp. 14–24 in M. Douglas and S. M. Tipton (eds.), *Religion and America: Spirituality in a Secular Age.* Boston: Beacon Press.

BLAU, J. L. 1976. *Judaism in America: From Curiosity to Third Faith.* Chicago: University of Chicago Press.

BOURG, C. 1976. "Symposium on Civil Religion." *Sociological Analysis* 37:141–149.

BROMLEY, D., and P. E. HAMMOND (eds.), 1987. *The Future of New Religious Movements.* Macon, GA: Mercer University Press.

BROMLEY, D., and A. SHUPE. 1981. *Strange Gods.* Boston: Beacon Press.

BRUCE, S. 1988. *The Rise and Fall of the New Christian Right.* New York: Oxford University Press.

BUDAPEST, Z. 1979. *The Holy Book of Women's Mysteries.* Oakland, CA: Z. E. Budapest.

CAPLOW, T., H. M. BAHR, and B. A. CHADWICK. 1983. *All Faithful People: Change and Continuity in Middletown's Religion.* Minneapolis: University of Minnesota Press.

CHRISTENSON, J. A. and R. C. WIMBERLY. 1978. "Who is civil religious?" *Sociological Analysis* 39(Spring):77–83.

COCHRAN, J., L. BEEGHLEY, and E. W. BOCK. 1988. "Religiosity and alcohol behavior: an exploration of reference group theory." *Sociological Forum* 3(2):256–276.

CORNWALL COLLECTIVE. 1980. *Your Daughters Shall Prophesy: Feminist Alternatives in Theological Education.* New York: Pilgrim Press.

DALY, M. 1968. *The Church and the Second Sex.* New York: Harper.

D'ANTONIO, M. 1990. "Fierce in the '80s, fallen in the '90s." *Los Angeles Times,* February 4, p. M3.

———. 1996. *American Catholic Laity: Transforming the Church.* Kansas City, MO: Sheed & Ward.

D'ANTONIO, W., and J. ALDOUS (eds.), 1983. *Families and Religions: Conflict and Change in Modern Society.* Beverly Hills, CA: Sage Publications.

D'ANTONIO, W., J. DAVIDSON, D. HOGE, and R. WALLACE. 1989. *American Catholic Laity in a Changing Church.* Kansas City, MO: Sheed & Ward.

DAVIDMAN, L. 1991. *Tradition in a Rootless World: Women Turn to Orthodox Judaism.* Berkeley: University of California Press.

DECKER, K., and A. McSWEEN. 1892. *Historic Arlington.* Washington, DC: Decker & McSween.

DEEDY, J. 1987. *American Catholicism: Now Where?* New York: Plenum.

DEMERATH, N. J. III. 1965. *Social Class in American Protestantism.* Chicago: Rand McNally.

DEMERATH, N. J. III, and P. HAMMOND. 1969. *Religion in Social Context.* New York: Random House.

DIAMOND, S. 1989. *Spiritual Warfare.* Boston: South End Press.

DITTES, J. E. 1971. "Typing the typologies: some parallels in the career of church-sect and extrinsic-intrinsic." *Journal for the Scientific Study of Religion* 10:375–383.

DOLAN, J. P. 1985. *The American Catholic Experience: A History from Colonial Times to the Present.* New York: Doubleday.

DONAHUE, M. J. 1991. "Prevalence of new age beliefs in six Protestant denominations." Paper presented at the meeting of the Society for the Scientific Study of Religion, Pittsburgh.

DURKHEIM, E. 1894. *Suicide.* New York: Free Press (reprinted 1951).

———. 1915. *The Elementary Forms of Religious Life.* Trans. by Karen E. Fields (1995). New York: Free Press.

DYNES, R. R. 1955. "Church-sect typology and socio-economic status." *American Sociological Review* 20:555–560.

EBAUGH, H. 1977. *Out of the Cloister: A Study of Organizational Dilemmas.* Austin: The University of Texas Press.

EDDY, S. 1941. *The Kingdom of God and the American Dream.* New York: Harper & Bros.

EISTER, A. W. 1967. "Toward a radical critique of church-sect typologizing: comment on 'Some critical observations on the church-sect dimension.'" *Journal for the Scientific Study of Religion* 6:85–90.

EVANS-PRITCHARD, E. 1937. *Witchcraft, Oracles and Magic among the Azande.* Oxford: Clarendon Press.

FALWELL, J. 1980. *Listen America!* Garden City, NY: Doubleday.

FEE, J., A. M. GREELEY, W. C. MCCREADY, and T. SULLIVAN. 1981. *Young Catholics.* New York: Sadlier.

FICHTER, J. H. 1951. *Southern Parish: Dynamics of a City Church.* Chicago: University of Chicago Press.

FINKE, R., and R. STARK. 1992. *The Churching of America, 1776–1990: Winners and Losers in America's Religious Economy.* New Brunswick, NJ: Rutgers University Press.

FURST, P. T. (ed.), 1972. *Flesh of the God: The Ritual Use of Hallucinogens.* New York: Praeger.

GALLUP, G., JR. 1984. *Religion in America.* Gallup Report No. 222. Princeton, NJ: Princeton Research Center, Inc.

GALLUP, G., and J. CASTELLI. 1987. *The American Catholic People: Their Beliefs, Practices, and Values.* Garden City, NY: Doubleday.

GEERTZ, C. 1973. *The Interpretation of Cultures.* New York: Basic Books.

GEHRIG, G. 1981. *American Civil Religion: An Assessment.* Storrs, CT: Society for the Scientific Study of Religion.

GERLACH, L. P., and V. H. HINE. 1968. "Five factors crucial to the growth and spread of a modern religious movement." *Journal for the Scientific Study of Religion* 7(Spring):23–40.

GLAZER, N. 1985. "On Jewish forebodings." *Commentary* 80:36.

———. 1989. "New perspectives in American Jewish sociology." In S. Bayme (ed.), *Facing the Future: Essays on Contemporary Jewish Life.* Hoboken, NJ: KTAV Press.

GLOCK, C. Y., and R. STARK. 1965. *Religion and Society in Tension.* Chicago: Rand McNally.

———. 1966. *Christian Beliefs and Anti-Semitism.* New York: Harper & Row.

GODWIN, R. K. 1988. *One Billion Dollars of Influence.* Chatham, NJ: Chatham House.

GOLDSCHEIDER, C., and A. ZUCKERMAN. 1984. *The Transformation of the Jews.* Chicago: University of Chicago Press.

GOLDSTEIN, S., and B. KOSMIN. 1991. "Religious and ethnic self-identification in the United States, 1989–90: a case study of the Jewish population." Paper presented at the annual meeting of the Population Association of America, Washington, DC.

GOODE, E. 1967. "Some critical observations on the church-sect dimension." *Journal for the Scientific Study of Religion* 6:69–77.

GORRIE, P. D. 1852. *Episcopal Methodism: As It Was and Is.* Auburn, NY: Derby and Miller.

GREELEY, A. 1972. *The Denominational Society.* Glenview, IL: Scott Foresman.

———. 1977a. *The American Catholic: A Social Portrait.* New York: Basic Books.

———. 1977b. *An Ugly Little Secret: Anti-Catholicism in North America.* Kansas City, MO: Sheed Andrews & McNeel.

———. 1979. *Crisis in the Church.* Chicago: Thomas More.

———. 1985. *American Catholics since the Council: An Unauthorized Report.* Chicago: Thomas More.

———. 1989. *Religious Change in America.* Cambridge, MA: Harvard University Press.

———. 1990. *The Catholic Myth.* New York: Macmillan.

GUSTAFSON, P. 1967. "UO-US-PS-PO: a restatement of Troeltsch's church-sect typology." *Journal for the Scientific Study of Religion* 6:64–68.

GUTMAN, R. 1966. "Demographic trends and the decline of anti-semitism." P. 354 in C. H. Stember (ed.), *Jews in the Mind of America*. New York: Basic Books.

HADAWAY, K. 1983. "Changing brands: denominational switching and membership change." Pp. 262–268 in C. H. Jacquet, Jr. (ed.), *Yearbook of American and Canadian Churches*. Nashville, TN: Abingdon Press.

HADDEN, J. K., and A. SHUPE. 1988. *Televangelism*. New York: Holt.

HADDEN, J. K., and C. E. SWANN. 1981. *Prime Time Preachers*. Reading, MA: Addison-Wesley.

HAMMOND, P. E. 1992. *Religion and Personal Autonomy*. Columbia: University of South Carolina Press.

HARRISON, P. M. 1959. *Authority and Power in the Free Church Tradition*. Princeton, NJ: Princeton University Press.

HARTZ, L. 1955. "The feudal dream of the South." Pp. 145–202 in L. Hartz (ed.), *The Liberal Tradition in America*. New York: Harcourt, Brace.

HASTEY, S. 1981. "Carter." *Baptist Press*, May 28, p. 1.

HATCH, N. O. 1983. "Christian conservatives are a major force on U.S. political scene." *Human Events* 43(July 9):10–12.

———. 1989. *The Democratization of American Christianity*. New Haven, CT: Yale University Press.

HEINZ, D. 1983. "The struggle to define America." Pp. 133–148 in R. C. Liebman and R. Wuthnow (eds.), *The New Christian Right*. New York: Aldine.

HERBERG, W. 1955. *Protestant-Catholic-Jew*. Garden City, NY: Doubleday.

HERTZKE, A. D. 1993. *Echoes of Discontent*. Washington, DC: CQ Press.

HOGE, D. R. 1979. "A test of denominational growth and decline." Pp. 179–197 in D. Hoge and D. Roozen (eds.), *Understanding Church Growth and Decline: 1950–1978*. New York: Pilgrim Press.

HOGE, D. R., and D. A. ROOZEN. 1979. *Technical Appendix to Understanding Church Growth and Decline: 1950–1978*. Hartford, CT: Hartford Seminary Foundation.

HUDSON, W. W. 1981. *Religion in America*. 3d ed. New York: Charles Scribner's Sons.

HUNTER, J. D. 1991. *Culture Wars*. New York: Basic Books.

IANNACCONE, L. R. 1988. "A formal model of church and sect." *American Journal of Sociology* 94:S241–S268.

———. 1992. "Religious markets and the economics of religion." *Social Compass* 39(1):123–131.

IANNACCONE, L., R. STARK, and D. OLSON. 1993. "Religious resources and church growth." Paper presented at the meetings of the Society for the Scientific Study of Religion, Raleigh, NC.

JACQUET, C. H., JR. (ed.). 1971. *Yearbook of American Churches*. New York: National Council of Churches.

———. 1981. *Yearbook of American and Canadian Churches*. Nashville, TN: Abingdon Press.

———. 1988. *Yearbook of American and Canadian Churches*. Nashville, TN: Abingdon Press.

JAMES, W. 1902. *The Varieties of Religious Experience*. London: Longmans.

JELEN, T. G. 1991. *The Political Mobilization of Religious Belief*. New York: Praeger.

JOHNSON, B. 1963. "On church and sect." *American Sociological Review* 28:539–549.

———. 1971. "Church and sect revisited." *Journal for the Scientific Study of Religion* 10:124–137.

———. 1985. "Liberal Protestantism: end of the road?" *Annals of the American Academy of Political and Social Science* 480:39–52.

JOHNSON, S. D., and R. BURTON. 1993. "Family values versus economy evaluation in the 1992 presidential election." Paper delivered at the annual meeting of the American Political Science Association, Washington, DC.

JOHNSON, S. D., and J. B. TAMNEY. 1982. "The Christian right and the 1980 presidential election." *Journal for the Scientific Study of Religion* 21:123–131.

JORSTAD, E. 1981. *The Politics of Moralism.* Minneapolis, MN: Augsburg.

KAUFMAN, D. 1985. "Women who return to Orthodox Judaism: a feminist analysis." *Journal of Marriage and the Family* 47(August):542–551.

———. 1987. "Coming home to Jewish Orthodoxy: reactionary or radical women?" *Tikkun* 2(3):60–63.

KEIM, A. N. (ed.). 1975. *Compulsory Education and the Amish.* Boston: Beacon Press.

KELLEY, D. 1972. *Why Conservative Churches Are Growing.* New York: Harper & Row.

———. 1979. "Is religion a dependent variable?" Pp. 334–343 in D. R. Hoge and D. A. Roozen (eds.), *Understanding Church Growth and Decline, 1950–1978.* New York: Pilgrim Press.

———. 1986. *Why Conservative Churches Are Growing: A Study in the Sociology of Religion.* Macon, GA: Mercer University Press.

KENNEDY, E. 1988. *Tomorrow's Catholics, Yesterday's Church.* New York: Harper & Row.

KLUCKHOHN, C., and D. LEIGHTON. 1946. *The Navaho.* Cambridge, MA: Harvard University Press.

KNUDSEN, D. D., J. R. EARLE, and D. W. SHRIVER, JR. 1978. "The conception of sectarian religion: an effort at clarification." *Review of Religious Research* 20:44–60.

LaBARRE, W. 1969. *They Shall Take Up Serpents.* New York: Schocken.

LANGER, S. 1953. *Feeling and Form.* New York: Scribner.

LARSON, R. F. 1964. "Clerical and psychiatric conceptions of the clergyman's role in the therapeutic setting." *Social Problems* 11:419–428.

———. 1968. "The clergyman's role in the therapeutic process: disagreement between clergymen and psychiatrists." *Psychiatry* 31:250–263.

LAWTON, K. 1988. "Unification church ties haunt new coalition." *Christianity Today,* February 5, p. 46.

LAZERWITZ, B., and M. HARRISON. 1979. "American Jewish denominations: a social and religious profile." *American Sociological Review* 44:656–666.

LEEGE, D. C. 1985. "Catholic parishes in the 1980s." *Church* 1(Summer):17–29.

———. 1993. "The decomposition of the religious vote." Paper delivered at the annual meeting of the American Political Science Association, Washington, DC.

LEVINE, S. 1984. *Radical Departures.* San Diego, CA: Harcourt, Brace, Jovanovich.

LIEBMAN, C. S., and S. M. COHEN. 1990. *Two Worlds of Judaism: The Israeli and American Experiences.* New Haven, CT: Yale University Press.

LIEBMAN, R. C. 1983. "Mobilizing the Moral Majority." Pp. 49–73 in R. C. Liebman and R. Wuthnow (eds.), *The New Christian Right.* New York: Aldine.

LIEBMAN, R. C., and R. WUTHNOW (eds.), 1983. *The New Christian Right.* New York: Aldine.

LINDER, R. 1982. "Militarism in Nazi thought and in the American religious right." *Journal of Church and State* 24:263–279.

LIPSET, S. M. 1964. *The First New Nation.* New York: Basic Books.

LYNN, R., and H. LYNN. 1937. *Middletown in Transition: A Study in Cultural Conflicts.* New York: Harcourt & Brace.

McLOUGHLIN, W. G. 1971. *New England Dissent, 1630–1833: The Baptists and the Separation of Church and State.* Cambridge, MA: Harvard University Press.

MALINOWSKI, B. 1925. "Magic, science and religion." In J. Needham (ed.), *Science, Religion, and Reality*. London: SPCK.

MANNHEIM, K. 1952. "The Problem of Generations." Pp. 276–320 in his collected *Essays on the Sociology of Knowledge*, ed. P. Kecskemeti. London: Routledge & Kegan Paul.

MARCUSE, H. 1964. *One-Dimensional Man*. Boston: Beacon Press.

MARKEY, J. J. 1994. "The making of a post-Vatican II theologian: reflections on twenty-five years of Catholic education." *America* 149(July):16–22.

MARTY, M. 1976. *A Nation of Behaviors*. Chicago: University of Chicago Press.

MARTZ, L., V. E. SMITH, D. PEDERSON, D. SHAPIRO, M. MILLER, and G. CARROLL. 1987. "God and money." *Newsweek*, April 6, pp. 16–22.

MEAD, S. 1963. *The Lively Experiment*. New York: Harper & Row.

MELTON, J. G. (ed.) 1989. *Encyclopedia of American Religions, and Supplement (1991)*. 3d ed. Detroit, MI: Gale Research.

———. 1992. *Encyclopedia of American Religions*. 4th ed. Detroit, MI: Gale Research.

MICHAELSEN, R. S., and W. C. ROOF (eds.), 1986. *Liberal Protestantism: Realities and Possibilities*. New York: Pilgrim Press.

MIYAKAWA, T. S. 1964. *Protestants and Pioneers*. Chicago: University of Chicago Press.

MOEN, M. C. 1988. "Status politics and the political agenda of the Christian right." *Sociological Quarterly* 29:429–437.

———. 1989. *The Christian Right and Congress*. Tuscaloosa: University of Alabama Press.

———. 1992. *The Transformation of the Christian Right*. Tuscaloosa: University of Alabama Press.

———. 1993. "The preacher versus the teacher." *Thought & Action* 9:124–143.

MORGAN, T. B. 1964. "The vanishing American Jew." *Look*, May 5, pp. 42–46.

NASH, D. 1968. "A little child shall lead them: a statistical test of the hypothesis that children were the source of the American 'religious revival.'" *Journal for the Scientific Study of Religion* 7:238–240.

NEITZ, M. J. 1987. *Charisma and Community: A Study of Religious Commitment within the Charismatic Renewal*. New Brunswick, NJ: Transaction Publishers.

NELSON, G. K. 1969. *Spiritualism and Society*. New York: Schocken Books.

NEVINS, A. (ed.). 1961. *Lincoln and the Gettysburg Address*. Urbana: University of Illinois Press.

NIEBUHR, R. 1961. "The religion of Abraham Lincoln." In A. Nevins (ed.), *Lincoln and the Gettysburg Address*. Urbana: University of Illinois Press.

NYHAN, D. 1980. "Attacks on religious right put its influence in doubt." *Boston Globe*, October 28, pp. 1–2.

OGINTZ, E. 1980. "Evangelists seek political clout." *Chicago Tribune*, January 13, p. 5.

OLDFIELD, D. 1990. "The Christian right and state Republican parties." Paper delivered at the annual meeting of the American Political Science Association, San Francisco.

OLSON, M. 1965. *The Logic of Collective Action: Public Goods and the Theory of Groups*. Cambridge, MA: Harvard University Press.

O'MALLEY, W. J. 1986. "Jesus, the warm fuzzy." *America* 154(March):204–206.

OSTLING, R. N. 1987. "TV's unholy row." *Time*, April 6, pp. 60–67.

PATRICK, T., and T. DULACK. 1976. *Let Our Children Go!* New York: Ballantine.

PICKERING, W. S. F. 1984. *Durkheim's Sociology of Religion: Themes and Theories*. London: Routledge & Kegan Paul.

POPE, L. 1942. *Millhands and Preachers*. New Haven, CT: Yale University Press.

POWELL, M. B. (ed.). 1967. *The Voluntary Church: Religious Life, 1740–1860, Seen through the Eyes of European Visitors*. New York: Macmillan.

PRESSMAN, S. 1984. "Religious right." *Congressional Quarterly Weekly Report* 38 (September 12):2315–2319.

PRINCETON RELIGIOUS RESEARCH CENTER. 1987. *Emerging Trends* 9(September):2.

QUINLEY, H. E. 1974. *The Prophetic Clergy.* New York: Wiley-Interscience.

RADCLIFFE-BROWN, A. R. 1952. *Structure and Function in Primitive Society.* Glencoe, IL: Free Press.

RAPHAEL, M. L. 1984. *Profiles in American Judaism.* San Francisco: Harper & Row.

REICHARD, C. 1950. *Navaho Religion.* New York: Praeger.

ROBBINS, T. 1988. *Cults, Converts, and Charisma.* London: Sage.

ROBERTS, K. A. 1984. *Religion in Sociological Perspective.* Homewood, IL: Dorsey.

ROCHFORD, E. B., JR. 1985. *Hare Krishna in America.* New Brunswick, NJ: Rutgers University Press.

ROOF, W. C. 1982. "America's voluntary establishment: mainline religion in transition." Pp. 130–149 in M. Douglas and S. M. Tipton (eds.), *Religion and America: Spirituality in a Secular Age.* Boston: Beacon Press.

ROOF, W. C., and W. MCKINNEY. 1987. *American Mainline Religion.* New Brunswick, NJ: Rutgers University Press.

ROOZEN, D. A., and C. K. HADAWAY. 1993. "Individuals and the church choice." Pp. 241–252 in D. A. Roozen and C. K. Hadaway (eds.), *Church and Denominational Growth.* Nashville, TN: Abingdon Press.

ROSE, S. 1987. "Women warriors: the negotiation of gender in a charismatic community." *Sociological Analysis* 48:245–258.

ROSENBERG, S. E. 1985. *New Jewish Identity in America.* New York: Hippocrene.

ROSTEN, L. 1975. *Religions of America: Ferment and Faith in an Age of Crisis.* New York: Simon & Schuster.

RUDAVSKY, D. 1967. *Emancipation and Judgment: Contemporary Jewish Religious Movements, Their History and Thought.* New York: Diplomatic Press.

RUETHER, R. R. (ed.). 1974. *Religion and Sexism: Images of Women in the Jewish and Christian Traditions.* New York: Simon & Schuster.

RUSSELL, G. W. 1975. "The view of religions from religious and nonreligious perspectives." *Journal for the Scientific Study of Religion* 14:129–138.

SCANZONI, J. 1975. *Sex Roles, Life Styles, and Childbearing: Changing Patterns in Marriage and the Family.* New York: Free Press.

SCHMELZ, U. O., and S. DELLAPERGOLA. 1989. "Basic trends in American Jewish demography." Pp. 75–76 in S. Bayme (ed.), *Facing the Future: Essays on Contemporary Jewish Life.* Hoboken, NJ: KTAV Press.

SCHOENHERR, R. 1995. "Numbers don't lie: a priesthood in irreversible decline." *Commonweal* 122: 11-14.

SCHOENHERR, R., and L. YOUNG. 1994. *Full Pews and Empty Altars: Demographics of the Priest Shortage in U. S. Catholic Dioceses.* Madison: University of Wisconsin Press.

SCHUMAN, H., and M. P. JOHNSON. 1976. "Attitudes and behavior." Pp. 161–208 in A. Inkeles, J. Coleman, and N. Smelser (eds.), *Annual Review of Sociology.* Vol. 2. Palo Alto, CA: Annual Reviews.

SCHUTZ, H. 1962. *The Problem of Social Reality.* The Hague: Nijhoff.

SHINN, L. D. 1987. "The future of an old man's vision: ISKCON in the twenty-first century." In D. Bromley and P. Hammond (eds.), *Future of New Religious Movements.* Macon, GA: Mercer University Press.

SHUPE, A. 1990. "Sun Myung Moon's American disappointment." *Christian Century* 107:764.

SHUPE, A., and W. STACEY. 1983. "The Moral Majority constituency." Pp. 103–116 in R. C. Liebman and R. Wuthnow (eds.), *The New Christian Right*. New York: Aldine.

SINGER, D. 1979. "Living with intermarriage." *Commentary* 68:48–57.

———. 1994. *American Jewish Year Book, 1994*. Vol. 94. New York: American Jewish Committee.

SINGER, M. 1955. "The cultural pattern of Indian civilization." *Far Eastern Quarterly* 15:23–26.

SINGH, K. 1953. *The Sikhs*. London: Allen & Unwin.

SKLARE, M. 1964. "Intermarriage and the Jewish future." *Commentary* 37:46–52.

———. 1970. "Intermarriage and Jewish survival." *Commentary* 49:51–58.

———. 1972. *Conservative Judaism: An American Religious Movement*. New York: Schocken Books.

SMITH, A. 1965. *An Inquiry into the Nature and Causes of the Wealth of Nations*. New York: Modern Library.

SPIRO, M. 1966. "The problem of definition in religion." In M. Banton (ed.), *Anthropological Approaches to the Study of Religion*. London: Tavistock.

STARHAWK. 1979. *The Spiral Dance: A Rebirth of the Ancient Religion of the Great Goddess*. New York: Harper & Row.

STARK, R. 1965. "The routinization of charisma: a consideration of Catholicism." *Sociological Analysis* 26(4):203–211.

STARK, R., and W. BAINBRIDGE. 1979. "Of churches, sects, and cults: preliminary concepts of a theory of religious movements." *Journal for the Scientific Study of Religion* 18:117–131.

———. 1985. *The Future of Religion*. Berkeley: University of California Press.

STARK, R., and C. GLOCK. 1968. *American Piety*. Berkeley: University of California Press.

STEINFELS, M. M. 1993. "The laity." *Commonweal* 120(September 10):8–20.

SWEET, W. W. 1950. *The Story of Religion in America*. New York: Harper & Row.

———. 1952. *Religion in the Development of American Culture, 1765–1840*. New York: Charles Scribner's Sons.

———. 1964. *Religion on the American Frontier, 1783–1840: The Presbyterians*. New York: Cooper Square Publishers.

SZAFRAN, R. 1976. "The distribution of influence in religious organizations." *Journal for the Scientific Study of Religion* 15:339–350.

TAMNEY, J. B., B. A. BUNCH, P. R. STIEBER, and D. L. ZIGLER-GEI. 1991. "The new age in Middletown: an exploratory study." Paper presented at the meeting of the Society for the Scientific Study of Religion, Pittsburgh.

TIPTON, S. M. 1982. *Getting Saved from the Sixties*. Berkeley: University of California Press.

TOCQUEVILLE, A. [1835] 1954. *Democracy in America*. New York: Vintage Books.

U.S. CONGRESS. 1965. House. *U. S. Congressional Record*, March 15, 1965.

WALD, K. D. 1987. *Religion and Politics in the United States*. New York: St. Martins.

WALD, K. D., D. OWEN, and S. HILL. 1989a. "Habits of the mind?" Pp. 93–108 in T. G. Jelen (ed.), *Religion and Political Behavior in the United States*. New York: Praeger.

———. 1989b. "Evangelical politics and status issues." *Journal for the Scientific Study of Religion* 28:1–16.

——. 1992. *Religion and Politics in the United States*. New York: St. Martin's Press.

WALKER, W. 1894. *A History of the Congregational Churches in the United States*. New York: Christian Literature Co.

WALLIS, R. 1977. *The Road to Total Freedom: A Sociological Analysis of Scientology*. New York: Columbia University Press.

————. 1984. *The Elementary Forms of the New Religious Life*. London: Routledge & Kegan Paul.

WALRATH, D. A. 1987. *Frameworks: Patterns for Living and Believing Today*. New York: Pilgrim Press.

WARNER, R. S. 1993. "Work in progress toward a new paradigm for the sociological study of religion in the United States." *American Journal of Sociology* 98:1044–1093.

WAXMAN, C. 1983. *America's Jews in Transition*. Philadelphia: Temple University Press.

WEBER, M. 1947. *The Theory of Social and Economic Organization*. New York: Free Press.

————. 1958. *The Protestant Ethic and the Spirit of Capitalism*. Trans. Talcott Parsons. New York: Free Press.

————. 1963. *The Sociology of Religion*. Trans. Ephraim Fischoff. Boston: Beacon Press.

————. 1971. "The three types of legitimate rule." pp. 169–179. In M. Truzzi (ed.), *Sociology: The Classic Statements*. New York: Random House.

WELCH, M. R. 1977. "Analyzing religious sects: an empirical examination of Wilson's sect typology." *Journal for the Scientific Study of Religion* 16:125–139.

WERTHEIMER, J. 1989. "Recent trends in American Judaism." In D. Singer (ed.), *American Jewish Year Book*. Vol. 89. Philadelphia: Jewish Publication Society of America.

WILLIAM PETSCHEK NATIONAL JEWISH FAMILY CENTER. 1987. *Newsletter* 6 (Spring):5.

WILLIAMS, R. H., and S. ALEXANDER. 1994. "Religious rhetoric in American populism: civil religion as movement and ideology." *Journal for the Scientific Study of Religion* 33:1–15.

WILSON, J. 1978. *Religion in American Society: The Effective Presence*. Englewood Cliffs, NJ: Prentice-Hall.

WIMBERLY, R., D. CLELLAND, T. HOOD, and C. M. LIPSET. 1976. "The civil religious dimension: is it there?" *Social Forces* 54:890–900.

WITTBERG, P. 1994. *The Rise and Fall of Catholic Religious Orders: A Social Movement Perspective*. Albany: SUNY Press.

WOOD, J., and M. ZALD. 1966. "Aspects of racial integration in the Methodist church: sources of resistance to organizational policy." *Social Forces* 45:255–265.

WUTHNOW, R. 1976a. *The Consciousness Reformation*. Berkeley: University of California Press.

————. 1976b. "Recent patterns of secularization: a problem of generations?" *American Sociological Review* 41:850–867.

————. 1978. *Experimentation in American Religion: The New Mysticisms and Their Implications for the Churches*. Berkeley: University of California Press.

————. 1986. "Religious movements and countermovements in North America." Pp. 1–28 in J. Beckford (ed.), *New Religious Movements and Rapid Social Change*. Beverly Hills, CA: Sage.

————. 1988. *The Restructuring of American Religion*. Princeton, NJ: Princeton University Press.

YINGER, J. M. 1957. *Religion, Society and the Individual*. New York: Macmillan.

ZABLOCKI, B. 1971. *The Joyful Community*. Baltimore: Penguin.

INDEX

CONTRIBUTORS

WILLIAM S. BAINBRIDGE is director of the sociology program at the National Science Foundation. He has coauthored *The Future of Religion*.

ROBERT N. BELLAH is Ford Professor of Sociology and Comparative Studies at the University of California at Berkeley. He is the author of *Habits of the Heart: Individualism and Commitment in American Life*.

PETER BERGER is professor of theology at Boston University. He is the author of *A Rumor of Angels* and *A Far Glory: The Quest for Faith in an Age of Credulity*.

LYNN DAVIDMAN is associate professor of sociology and Judaic studies at Brown University. She is coeditor of *Feminist Perspectives on Jewish Studies*.

JAMES D. DAVIDSON is professor of sociology at Purdue University. He has authored *Religion Among America's Elite: Persistence and Change in the Protestant Establishment*, a working paper by the Center for the Study of American Catholicism.

THOMAS E. DOWDY is associate professor of sociology at Oklahoma Baptist University. His research interests are individual belief systems, religious privatization, church and state issues, and patterns of academic mobility among social scientists.

EMILE DURKHEIM was one of the founders of modern sociology. He is the author of *Suicide*.

ROGER FINKE is professor of sociology at Purdue University. He is coauthor of *The Churching of America, 1776–1990: Winners and Losers in Our Religious Economy*.

CLIFFORD GEERTZ is a member of the faculty of social sciences at the Institute for Advanced Study, Princeton University. He is the author of *The Interpretation of Cultures*.

LAURENCE IANNACCONE is professor of economics at Santa Clara University. He is the author of *Sacrifice and Stigma: Reducing Free-Riding in Cults, Communes and Other Collectives.*

WILLIAM MCKINNEY is academic dean of Hartford Seminary. He is coauthor of *American Mainline Religion: Its Changing Shape and Future.*

PATRICK H. MCNAMARA is professor of sociology at the University of New Mexico. His most recent book is *Conscience First, Tradition Second: A Study of Young Catholics.*

J. GORDON MELTON is the director of the Institute for the Study of American Religion in Santa Barbara, California, and a research specialist with the Department of Religious Studies at the University of California at Santa Barbara. He is the author of a number of reference books on American religion, most notably the *Encyclopedia of American Religions.*

MATTHEW C. MOEN is professor of political science at the University of Maine at Orono. He has written *The Transformation of the Christian Right.*

MARGARET M. POLOMA is professor of sociology at the University of Akron, Akron, Ohio. She has authored *Assemblies of God at the Crossroads: Charisma and Institutional Dilemmas.*

WADE CLARK ROOF is professor in religious studies at the University of California, Santa Barbara. He has authored *A Generation of Seekers: The Spiritual Journeys of the Baby Boom Generation.*

ROSEMARY RADFORD RUETHER is Georgia Harkness Professor of Applied Theology, Garret Evangelical Theological Seminary. She is editor of *Women and Religion in America.*

EDWARD S. SHAPIRO is professor of history at Seton Hall University. He is the author of *A Time for Healing: American Jewry since World War II.*

RODNEY STARK is professor of sociology and of comparative religion at the University of Washington, Seattle. He is coauthor of *The Churching of America, 1776–1990: Winners and Losers in Our Religious Economy.*

ANDREA S. WILLIAMS is a doctoral student in sociology at Purdue University.